American Home Front in World War II
Almanac

American Home Front in World War II Almanac

**Richard C. Hanes
and
Sharon M. Hanes**

**Allison McNeill,
Project Editor**

U·X·L
An imprint of Thomson Gale, a part of The Thomson Corporation

Detroit • New York • San Francisco • San Diego • New Haven, Conn. • Waterville, Maine • London • Munich

THOMSON
★
GALE

American Home Front in World War II: Almanac
Richard C. and Sharon M. Hanes

Project Editor
Allison McNeill

Permissions
Emma Hull

Imaging and Multimedia
Robyn Young, Lezlie Light, Dan Newell

Product Design
Michelle Dimercurio, Pamela Galbreath

Composition
Evi Seoud

Manufacturing
Rita Wimberley

For permission to use material from this product, submit your request via Web at http://www.gale-edit.com/permissions, or you may download our Permissions Request form and submit your request by fax or mail to:

Permissions Department
Thomson Gale
27500 Drake Rd.
Farmington Hills, MI 48331-3535
Permissions Hotline:
248-699-8006 or 800-877-4253, ext. 8006
Fax: 248-699-8074 or 800-762-4058

Cover photographs reproduced by permission of © Corbis (Japanese American children) and courtesy of National Archives ("We Can Do It!" poster and "Buy War Bonds" poster).

While every effort has been made to ensure the reliability of the information presented in this publication,

Thomson Gale does not guarantee the accuracy of the data contained herein. Thomson Gale accepts no payment for listing; and inclusion in the publication of any organization, agency, institution, publication, service, or individual does not imply endorsement by the editors or publisher. Errors brought to the attention of the publisher and verified to the satisfaction of the publisher will be corrected in future editions.

078767608X

LIBRARY OF CONGRESS CATALOGING-IN-PUBLICATION DATA

Hanes, Richard Clay, 1946–
American home front in World War II. Almanac / Richard C. Hanes and Sharon M. Hanes ; Allison McNeill, project editor.
    p. cm. – (American home front in World War II reference library)
    Includes bibliographical references and index.
    ISBN 0-7876-7651-9 (hardcover)
1. World War, 1939-1945–United States–Juvenile literature. 2. World War, 1939-1945–Social aspects–United States–Juve-nile literature. 3. United States–History–1933-1945–Juvenile literature. 4. United States–Social conditions–1933-1945–Juve-nile literature. I. Hanes, Sharon M. II. McNeill, Allison. III. Title. IV. Title: Almanac. V. Series.
D769.1.H36 2005 940.53'73–dc22
                                                                                        2004008921

This title is also available as an e-book.
ISBN 0-7876-9385-5 (Set)
Contact your Gale sales representative for ordering information.

Printed in the United States of America
10 9 8 7 6 5 4 3 2 1

Contents

Introduction

Many people who lived on the American home front during World War II (1939–45; U.S. involvement 1941–45) proclaimed the period as "the best of times and worst of times." In the 1930s the United States and much of the rest of the world had been in the throes of the Great Depression. The Depression was marked by dramatically slowed business activity, high unemployment, and, for a significant portion of the population, much hunger. In the United States, society seemed, at times, to be falling apart as violent labor conflicts, food riots, and race riots punctuated the 1930s. Change came in 1940 as the United States began gearing up for a war that was already raging in Europe. As industries began receiving sizable government contracts to produce war materials, good-paying jobs once again became available for anyone who wanted to work. On December 7, 1941, the Japanese surprised and shocked the United States with a deadly attack on U.S. military bases at Pearl Harbor, Hawaii. Immediately an overwhelming spirit of patriotic fervor consumed America. A common cause and a common enemy became well-defined.

The war years were the "best of times" because the war effort united Americans as never before. The factories were humming, men and women were working and earning livable wages, even rationing of food and gasoline was viewed as necessary for the push to victory. At the same time, the "worst" aspect of the early 1940s involved separation from loved ones as millions joined the military and went overseas to fight for their country. Americans held their collective breath until their sons, husbands, brothers, and even daughters returned to the home front.

The United States was clearly a different nation in 1942 than the previous decade. Just about everything aspect of society was affected. Changes came in employment, living locations, and in driving and eating habits. Millions of new jobs caused personal income to rise dramatically and an improved standard of living. Taking advantage of new employment, individuals and whole families migrated to the war industry centers on each coast and the Great Lakes region. Millions of American men joined the military service and left for far off places. Change also came as everyone on the home front pitched in to do their part for the war effort. They volunteered for civil defense duties, complied with food and gasoline rationing, planted "victory gardens," and collected scrap metal and rubber tires that contained materials needed in producing war materials. Cities staged practice air raid drills with blackouts, as volunteer air raid wardens patrolled the streets and neighborhoods. Citizens, fearing spies and saboteurs, kept a vigilant watch, viewing anyone with an accent with suspicion. Housewives shopped with ration coupons and adapted recipes to find substitutes for sugar and meat, which were rationed items. Families readjusted transportation priorities to make do on four gallons of gasoline a week. Citizens on the home front also helped feed the nation and free up a portion of commercially grown fruits and vegetables for shipment overseas. Over twenty million home gardens, known as victory gardens, were planted. They provided one-third of all vegetables eaten in America. Youth joined the effort by rounding up scrap materials in the form of discarded pots and pans, bedsprings, tin cans, and rubber tires for use in manufacturing war materials.

The entertainment industry participated in the war effort as well. Hollywood directors produced war documentaries aimed at bolstering the wave of patriotism. New movie releases showed Japanese and German characters as villainous, while promoting traditional American cultural values and creating American heroes. Celebrities contributed to war bond drives, leading to the sales of millions of dollars of bonds. Others volunteered at canteens where servicemen could stop for food and entertainment before departing for overseas assignments. Still others enlisted in the regular armed services or volunteered in civilian defense roles.

Through the major government and private industry mobilization efforts and the patriotic fervor of the population, the American home front became the leading industrial and agricultural producer in the world. Existing factories were converted from production of civilian consumer goods, such as cars, toasters, alarm clocks, and refrigerators, to wartime materials such as warplanes, tanks, guns, ammunition, and military trucks. Major new factories were built, as well as massive new shipyards where thousands of freight transports, known as "Liberty" ships, were produced. U.S. industry produced almost three hundred thousand warplanes, over eighty-six thousand tanks, and almost twelve thousand ships between 1941 and 1945. Long workweeks became commonplace for war industry workers.

Corporations and farmers saw their investments grow. Corporate assets almost doubled as the government guaranteed profits on war production. Farmers also saw their prosperity rise to new heights by growing food for the armies of the Allied forces. Big business and military services formed a long lasting powerful alliance known as the military-industrial complex. The alliance would influence U.S. foreign policy and industrial production for decades following the war.

Despite the vastly improved economic outlook, for some Americans not all was rosy. Racial discrimination increased. With war quickly expanding in Europe in 1940, Congress passed the Smith Act requiring four million aliens, those not yet U.S. citizens, but living in America, to register with U.S. authorities. Following the bombing of Pearl Harbor, President Franklin D. Roosevelt signed an order labeling German, Italian, and Japanese immigrants as enemy aliens. Though restrictions on Germans and Italians would soon ease, Japanese aliens experienced harsh discrimination. In the spring of 1942 the U.S. government hastily rounded up some 112,000 Japanese aliens, as well as Japanese Americans with full U.S. citizenship, from their homes and businesses. They were transported to remote detention camps where they were held for the remainder of the war. Meanwhile their constitutionally protected rights were trampled.

Black Americans experienced much needed gains in the newly expanded job markets, but only after non-minorities were fully employed and labor shortages had become critical. Some new opportunities in the military services also opened for blacks. However the armed services remained racially segregated, as was civilian life in much of the home front. Triggered by job discrimination and severe housing shortages in the war industry centers, violent race riots broke out on the home front in 1943. The worst racial rioting occurred in Detroit, Michigan, where thirty-four were killed and seven hundred injured.

As with minorities, women found new opportunities in jobs never available before, such as factory assembly-line jobs. "Rosie the Riveter" became a mythical caricature symbolic of all women who took jobs in war industries. Millions of women entered the workforce during the war years. By late 1944 women made up some 40 percent of the workforce in aircraft factories and 12 percent in shipyards. Much of the wartime home front gains proved short-lived. Women were expected to leave their jobs at the war's end so that returning veterans could find work to support their families.

Though the home front worker had money to spend, fewer goods were available to purchase because factory production and raw materials were directed to military use. No new automobiles, radios, or appliances were produced during the war. The government introduced a rationing system to ensure fair distribution of limited goods. Rationed items and materials included sugar, coffee, meat, canned goods, leather shoes, and dairy products. Gasoline for automobiles was rationed in a complex system based on demonstrated need.

The most difficult home front shortage to overcome was the shortage of housing. Twenty million Americans relocated to industrial centers or military bases only to find little available housing. Because of war needs for war materials, few new houses were built.

With little to spend money on, savings grew and personal debt declined. The government encouraged citizens to invest their extra funds in war bonds to help finance the very expensive war effort. The war bond drives served to keep home front Americans involved in actively supporting the war. Congress also passed and instituted the modern federal income tax system. Forty million Americans were paying income tax by 1945, up from just five million in 1939.

By 1943 the war became a test of will and endurance. Most affected by war on the home front were those with loved ones in the military service, particularly those serving overseas. American casualties mounted as the war continued, with the most deaths occurring in the last twelve months. Ultimately fifteen million Americans served in the wartime military. Of those, three hundred thousand were killed and seven hundred thousand injured. As a reward to those who served in the military, the government introduced sweeping programs of financial assistance amounting to $100 billion in benefits for millions of war veterans and their families. The funds provided a significant boost to the U.S. postwar economy as veterans used the funds to buy homes and fund their education.

Early 1945 brought a rapid sequence of events. Germany surrendered on May 7. The following day became known as V-E Day for Victory in Europe. The Japanese surrendered on August 14, and the following day became known as V-J Day for Victory Over Japan. The war's end in mid-1945 brought wild jubilation on the American home front. As time passed and new generations grew up, the prominent place of World War II became fixed in U.S. history. Despite vast destruction of parts of Europe and Asia, the United States home front, with the exception of Pearl Harbor, was spared any physical harm. Many Americans later looked nostalgically back at World War II as a simpler time of patriotic unity and adventure.

Richard C. and Sharon M. Hanes

Reader's Guide

American Home Front in World War II: Almanac presents a comprehensive overview of events and everyday life that occurred within the United States while the nation was at war from 1941 to 1945. The volume concentrates on the actual events related to the World War II effort rather than simply relating all general happenings of the time period. The goal throughout is to provide a clear, accurate account of this challenging yet highly productive period in American history that changed the fabric of United States.

Features

American Home Front in World War II: Almanac is divided into thirteen chapters, each focusing on a particular topic such as mobilization of American industry and agriculture, the miracles of war production and economic growth, the experience of women and minorities on the home front, growth of civil defense and other organizations to assist the war effort, the changes to various home front communities, the effects of war on everyday life, and the preparations for a changed postwar world. The chapters contain sidebar boxes that highlight people and events of special interest, and each chapter offers a list of additional sources students can go to for more information. More than ninety black-and-white photographs illustrate the material. The volume begins with a timeline of important events in the history of home front America during World War II; a "Words to Know" section that introduces students to difficult or unfamiliar terms (terms are also defined within the text); and a "Research and Activity Ideas" section. The volume concludes with a general bibliography and a subject index so students can easily find the people, places, and events discussed throughout *American Home Front in World War II: Almanac*.

American Home Front in World War II Reference Library

American Home Front in World War II: Almanac is only one component of the three-part U•X•L American Home Front in World War II Reference Library. The other two titles in this set are:

- *American Home Front in World War II: Biographies* (one volume) presents the life stories of twenty-six individuals who played key roles on the American home front during the World War II years. Individuals from all walks of life are included. Some held prominent national roles in guiding America through the war, others were among the millions who eagerly did their share in contributing to the war effort. Profiled are well-known figures such as President Franklin D. Roosevelt, First Lady Eleanor Roosevelt, Secretary of War Henry Stimson, painter Norman Rockwell, social activist A. Philip Randolph, industrialists Donald Douglas and Henry Kaiser, entertainers Betty Grable and Dorothy Lamour, movie director Frank Capra, and journalist Elmer Davis, as well as lesser-known individuals such as industrial worker Peggy Terry, artist and author Mine Okubo, physicist Elda Anderson, and labor leader Luisa Moreno.

- *American Home Front in World War II: Primary Sources* (one volume) tells the story of the American home front in the words of the people who lived and shaped it. Approximately thirty excerpted documents provide a wide range of perspectives on this period of history. Included are excerpts from presidential addresses and proclamations;

government pamphlets; magazine articles; and reflections by individuals who lived through the tumultuous times.

A cumulative index of all three titles in the U•X•L American Home Front in World War II Reference Library is also available.

Dedication

The *American Home Front in World War II* volumes are dedicated to our new grandson Luke Clay Hanes. May he and his generation be spared the trauma and ravages of war.

Special Thanks

Kelly Rudd contributed importantly to the *Biographies* volume. Catherine Filip typed much of the manuscript for the *Primary Sources* volume. Constance Carter, head of the Library of Congress science research department, assisted in searching out primary source materials.

Comments and Suggestions

We welcome your comments on *American Home Front in World War II: Almanac* and suggestions for other topics to consider. Please write: Editors, *American Home Front in World War II: Almanac,* U•X•L, 27500 Drake Rd. Farmington Hills, Michigan 48331-3535; call toll free: 1-800-877-4253; fax to (248) 699-8097; or send e-mail via http://www.gale.com.

Timeline of Events

October 1929 The Great Depression arrives, leading to high unemployment rates and social unrest; over the next few years the Depression spreads worldwide, hitting Germany particularly hard.

September 18, 1931 Japan invades and occupies Manchuria to gain access to its natural resources, beginning Japan's military expansion in the Far East through the next decade.

January 30, 1933 Adolf Hitler becomes Germany's head of government.

March 4, 1933 Franklin D. Roosevelt is inaugurated as the thirty-second president.

1935 Germany introduces a military draft and begins mobilizing its industries to produce military materials, including tanks and war planes.

October 3, 1935 Italy invades Ethiopia and gains control by May 1936.

July 7, 1937   Japan invades China, capturing many of its major cities including its capital, Peking (Beijing).

March 12, 1938   Germany announces a union with Austria.

October 15, 1938   Germany gains control of part of Czechoslovakia, beginning its military expansion in Europe.

1939   Pocket Book Company introduces the paperback book, which will become highly popular through the war, selling 40 million in 1943 alone.

September 1, 1939   Germany invades Poland, thereby starting World War II. Several nations, including Britain and France, declare war on Germany two days later; President Roosevelt declares U.S. neutrality in the following days.

September 5, 1939   Congress revises the Neutrality Acts, ending the ban of sales of military supplies to foreign nations; the United States establishes a cash and carry program to sell war materials to Great Britain.

September 8, 1939   President Roosevelt issues a limited national emergency declaration and creates the War Resources Board (WRB) to begin planning for war.

1940   Roosevelt creates the Office of Emergency Management (OEM), located in the White House, to oversee war preparations.

March 16, 1940   Roosevelt, in a speech, asks for construction of 50,000 warplanes in preparation for war and sale to Britain.

April 9, 1940   Germany begins a military assault on Western Europe, first invading Denmark and Norway, eventually leading to the fall of France on June 22.

June 1940   Dr. Vannevar Bush meets with President Roosevelt, leading to the creation of the National Defense Research Committee (NRDC) to coordinate technological research benefiting advanced military equipment.

June 28, 1940   Congress passes the Alien Registration Act, more commonly known as the Smith Act, one week after the fall of France, making it illegal to advocate the overthrow of the U.S. government.

July 10, 1940   The German bombing of Britain begins; it lasts for eight months. Italy declares war on France and Great Britain.

September 15, 1940   Congress passes the first peacetime military draft in U.S. history.

September 27, 1940   Germany, Italy, and Japan form a military alliance.

November 5, 1940   With the public fearful of looming war, President Roosevelt is elected to an unprecedented third term in office.

December 29, 1940   In a Fireside Chat, Roosevelt delivers his "Arsenal of Democracy" speech calling for greater efforts in supporting the war against Germany.

January 1941   Roosevelt creates the Office of Production Management (OPM) to spur industrial war mobilization.

February 4, 1941   United Service Organizations (USO) is created to provide entertainment to American troops; it establishes Camp Shows, Inc., through which entertainers volunteer to perform for military servicemen, amounting to over 428,000 shows by 1947.

March 1941   The National Defense Mediation Board is formed to resolve labor disputes in industry and to ease the process of war mobilization.

March 6, 1941   The first houses in the Linda Vista housing development in San Diego, California, are completed for war industry workers; 16,000 residents are housed here by April 1943.

March 11, 1941   Congress passes the Lend-Lease Act, authorizing the United States to lend Britain and other nations fighting Germany money to purchase or lease military equipment and supplies from U.S. industry; the United States would spend $50 billion through the war, essentially ending the Great Depression.

April 11, 1941   Roosevelt creates the Office of Price Administration and Civilian Supply (OPACS) to control the prices of goods and corporate profits.

May 1941   Congress creates the Office of Scientific Research and Development (OSRD) to coordinate technological research.

May 20, 1941   Roosevelt creates the Office of Civilian Defense (OCD) to help communities prepare for war.

May 27, 1941   Roosevelt issues an unlimited national emergency declaration in response to continued Japanese expansion in Southeast Asia; the U.S. begins economic restrictions against Japan.

June 22, 1941   Germany invades the Soviet Union, drawing the Soviets into World War II; Roosevelt extends the Lend-Lease program to the Soviets.

June 25, 1941   Under pressure from A. Philip Randolph and other black American leaders, Roosevelt signs an executive order calling for an end to racial discrimination in hiring practices by war industries.

August 14, 1941   Roosevelt and British leader Winston Churchill sign the Atlantic Charter, spelling out their goals in the war.

August 28, 1941   Roosevelt creates the Supplies Priorities and Allocations Board (SPAB) to guide OPM in war mobilization.

December 1, 1941   The Civil Air Patrol is established to patrol the nation's borders and coastal areas by air.

December 7, 1941   Japan launches a surprise air attack on U.S. military installations at Pearl Harbor, Hawaii, drawing the United States into World War II; the United States declares war on Japan; the following day Germany and Italy declare war on the United States.

1942   Congress establishes the Emergency Farm Labor Program.

1942   The War Labor Board (WLB) is created to control wages.

January 1942   German submarines become more prevalent off the U.S. East Coast.

January 2, 1942   Japanese forces capture the capital city of the Philippines as American forces begin a retreat to the Bataan Peninsula.

January 16, 1942   Roosevelt creates the War Production Board (WPB), headed by Donald Nelson, to oversee mobilization and determine which consumer goods should be discontinued or limited in production and to set war production goals.

January 30, 1942   Congress passes the Emergency Price Control Act creating the Office of Price Administration (OPA), which has greater authority to control prices.

February 1942   A Japanese submarine briefly shells a coastal oil field near Santa Barbara, California; President Roosevelt establishes the Volunteer Port Security Force to protect ports and waterfront facilities.

February 7, 1942   The Pittsburgh *Courier,* a prominent black American newspaper, introduces the Double V campaign representing victory over the enemies abroad and victory over racial prejudice on the home front.

February 10, 1942   The WPB bans production of civilian automobiles, paving the way for conversion of the Michigan auto industry to production of warplanes, tanks, military trucks, and other military equipment.

February 19, 1942   Roosevelt signs Executive Order 9066 authorizing removal of Japanese aliens and Japanese Americans to detention centers.

March 21, 1942   The evacuation of Japanese Americans and Japanese aliens to internment camps begins.

April 1942   Roosevelt creates the War Manpower Commission (WMC) to direct workers to more critical industries and areas of workforce shortages.

April 6, 1942   By this date some six million citizens had planted victory gardens, leading to a major contribution to the nation's food supply.

April 28, 1942   OPA issues the General Maximum Price Regulation, known as General Max, setting price controls.

May 1942   Food rationing begins; War Ration Book One is issued, with sugar being the first table food rationed.

May 1942   The United States and Mexico reach agreement on the *bracero* program, which allows some one hundred thousand Mexican citizens to enter the United States to help solve the farm labor shortage.

May 8, 1942   In an early key military victory in the Pacific, the U.S. defeats a Japanese fleet in the Battle of the Coral Sea.

May 14, 1942   Congress creates the Women's Army Auxiliary Corp (WAAC); some 150,000 would serve.

June 7, 1942   In another major U.S. victory in the Pacific, the U.S. Navy defeats the Japanese fleet in the Battle of Midway.

June 13, 1942   Roosevelt creates the Office of War Information (OWI), with Elmer Davis as its head, to coordinate release of war information to the public.

July 16, 1942   The National War Labor Board (NWLB) establishes the "Little Steel Formula" to control wage increases.

July 30, 1942   Roosevelt signs a bill authorizing women to be accepted into the U.S. Navy, Coast Guard, and U.S. Marines, including the navy's Women Accepted for Volunteer Emergency Service (WAVES) in which 90,000 would serve.

August 7, 1942   U.S. forces begin the offensive in the Pacific with the invasion of Guadalcanal in the Solomon Islands.

September 1942   The first Hollywood World War II combat movie is released titled *Wake Island.*

September 9, 1942   A lone Japanese float plane, launched from a submarine, drops incendiary bombs in a remote forest area of southwest Oregon causing little damage.

September 10, 1942   The U.S. Army creates the Women's Auxiliary Ferry Squadron (WAFS) to fly planes to needed destinations.

October 3, 1942   Congress passes the Economic Stabilization Act creating the Office of Economic Stabilization (OES), headed by James F. Byrnes, to control the economy and guide the complex rationing program.

October 21, 1942   Congress passes the Revenue Act, restructuring the U.S. income tax system to help finance the war.

November 8, 1942   Allied forces launch a major military offensive in North Africa against German forces.

November 23, 1942   The Coast Guard creates their women's reserves, known as SPAR.

November 29, 1942   Coffee is rationed.

December 1, 1942   A complex system of gasoline rationing begins.

1943   Over 3.5 million American Red Cross volunteers repair military clothing, wrap bandages, and put together care packages for servicemen overseas.

January 12, 1943   Roosevelt declares this date Farm Mobilization Day, claiming food was also a weapon in the war.

January 15, 1943   The Pentagon building is dedicated in the Washington, D.C., area to house the War Department; construction had started in September 1941.

January 31, 1943   Russian troops defeat German forces at Stalingrad marking the first major defeat of Germany and a turning point in the war.

February 1943   Congress establishes a national farm policy for solving farm labor shortages with such programs as the Women's Land Army (WLA) and the Victory Farm Volunteers (VFV).

February 1943   Roosevelt signs an order expanding normal workweeks from 40 to 48 hours.

February 1943   War Ration Book Two is issued as canned goods, dried beans, and peas come under rationing; shoe rationing also begins to conserve the use of leather.

February 13, 1943   U.S. Marine Corps adds the Women's Reserve; 23,000 women joined.

March 29, 1943   The rationing of meat begins.

April 1943   Florence Hall is named head of the newly formed Women's Land Army (WLA).

May 28, 1943   Roosevelt creates the Office of War Mobilization (OWM) to resolve disputes over workforce and raw material shortages.

June 1943   Congress passes the Bolton Act establishing the Cadet Nurse Corps program to recruit and train nurses for wartime duty; 59,000 would serve in the Army Nurse Corps and 11,000 in the Navy Nurse Corps.

June 1943   A series of violent racial conflicts erupts in the United States, including one in Detroit, Michigan, and the "Zoot Suit Riot" in Los Angeles, California.

June 1943   Congress passes the Smith-Connolly War Labor Disputes Act that gives the government power to seize and operate plants where workers are on strike.

July 1943   War mobilization is complete, as industry is able to meet ongoing military needs through the remainder of the war.

July 3, 1943   The WAAC becomes the Women's Army Corp (WAC) to become a regular part of the army.

July 10, 1943   Following victory in North Africa, Allied forces invade Sicily, a large island south of Italy, and then Italy itself on September 3.

July 25, 1943   The Women's Aircraft Service Program (WASP) is formed from the WAFS and other organizations; it is ended December 20, 1944.

September 8, 1943   Italy surrenders to Allied forces.

November 28, 1943   Roosevelt, Churchill, and Joseph Stalin, premier of the Soviet Union, convene a three day meeting at Tehran, Iran, to discuss war strategies against Germany and Italy.

January 10, 1944   Congress passes the Servicemen's Readjustment Act, known as the GI Bill, that provides generous benefits in housing, education, and business loans to U.S. war veterans.

March 7, 1944   The United States reports that women constitute 42 percent of the workers in West Coast aircraft plants.

June 6, 1944   Allied forces launch the largest sea invasion in history, called Operation Overlord, on the shores of Normandy, France.

August-October 1944   An international conference held at Dumbarton Oaks in Washington, D.C., creates the beginning of the United Nations.

August 25, 1944   Paris, France, is liberated from German occupation by Allied forces.

September 13, 1944   Allied ground forces enter Germany.

October 26, 1944   In the largest naval battle in history, known as the Battle of Leyte Gulf, the U.S. Navy largely destroys the Japanese fleet.

November 1944   The WAVES and SPAR are opened to black American women; the WAC has been open to blacks since its beginning.

November 1944   Japanese begin launching balloon bombs, designed to float across the Pacific Ocean and explode in North America, from Japan; nine thousand are launched over the next several months.

November 7, 1944   Roosevelt wins reelection to a fourth term as U.S. president.

December 1944   Roosevelt revamps OWM to the Office of War Mobilization and Reconversion (OWMR) to coordinate change of war industries back to peacetime production.

December 16, 1944   German forces launch a major counterattack against advancing Allied forces, known as the Battle of the Bulge.

February 1, 1945   Soviet forces advance through Poland and into Germany to within one hundred miles of the German capital of Berlin.

February 4, 1945   The Yalta Conference, held in the Crimean region of the Soviet Union, begins and runs for seven days. The three key allied leaders, U.S. President Franklin D. Roosevelt, British Prime Minister Winston Churchill, and Soviet Premier Joseph Stalin, discuss German surrender terms, a Soviet attack against Japanese forces, and the future of Eastern Europe.

April 12, 1945   Roosevelt dies suddenly from a brain hemorrhage; he is replaced by Harry Truman.

April 18, 1945   Noted war correspondent Ernie Pyle is killed by enemy fire near Okinawa, Japan.

April 25, 1945   Fifty nations begin meeting in San Francisco, California, to write the United Nations (UN) charter.

April 28, 1945   Italian dictator Benito Mussolini is captured and executed by Italian resistance fighters.

April 30, 1945   German dictator Adolf Hitler commits suicide in a fortified bunker beneath Berlin.

May 1945   Six people are killed in southern Oregon by a Japanese balloon bomb.

May 7, 1945 Germany surrenders to allied forces leaving Germany and its capital of Berlin divided into four military occupation zones with American, British, French, and Soviet forces; Americans celebrate the following day, known as V-E Day (Victory in Europe Day).

June 21, 1945 Japanese forces are essentially defeated in major fighting for over two months on the island of Okinawa.

June 26, 1945 Fifty nations meeting in San Francisco, California, sign the United Nations charter.

July 16, 1945 First successful U.S. atomic bomb test occurs at Alamogardo, New Mexico.

July 26, 1945 U.S. president Harry S. Truman, Stalin, and Churchill meet at Potsdam to discuss postwar conditions of Germany.

August 6, 1945 The United States drops an atomic bomb on Hiroshima, Japan, followed by a second bomb on August 9 on Nagasaki.

August 14, 1945 Japan surrenders, ending World War II. Americans celebrate the following day, known as V-J Day (Victory over Japan Day).

September 2, 1945 Formal surrender papers are signed by Japan aboard a U.S. warship in Tokyo Bay.

June 12, 1948 Congress makes the Women's Army Corp (WAC) a permanent part of the U.S. Army.

1988 The U.S. government issues a formal apology to Japanese Americans for their treatment during World War II on the home front.

1997 The Franklin D. Roosevelt Memorial is dedicated in Washington, D.C., commemorating his leadership through the Great Depression and World War II.

June 29, 2001 A national monument is dedicated in Washington, D.C., in the memory of Japanese Americans in World War II.

May 2004 The World War II Memorial is dedicated in Washington, D.C. The memorial honors not only those who fought in the war, but commemorates the great efforts and sacrifices made by those on the American home front as well.

Words to Know

A

aliens: Immigrants who hold citizenship in a foreign country.

Allies: Over thirty nations, including the United States, Great Britain, and Soviet Union, who united in the fight against Germany, Italy, and Japan during World War II.

appeasement: Giving in to the demands of another nation in order to maintain peace.

atomic bomb: A bomb whose massive explosive force comes from the nuclear fission of uranium or plutonium.

Authoritarian: A political system in which authority is centered in a ruling party that demands complete obedience of its citizens and is not legally accountable to the people.

auxiliary: Volunteers who provide additional or supplementary assistance, or an organization that is supplemental to a larger one, such as the auxiliary police or firemen.

Axis powers: Nations who fought against the Allies in World War II including Germany, Italy, and Japan.

B

baby boomers: The population of 76 million children born after World War II, between 1946 and 1964.

barrage balloons: A network of balloons, steel cables, and nets placed over a town or city to protect against attacking enemy aircraft.

bereavement: Grieving over the death of a loved one.

black market: Illegally selling goods in violation of government regulations, such as selling rationed items at very high prices.

blackouts: Completely concealing or turning off all lights from outside view to guard against air raids.

Braceros: Mexican workers recruited by the United States to fill wartime labor shortages, particularly in the area of farm labor.

C

canteen: A place where food, rest, and entertainment are available, usually operated by volunteers.

capital: Money and property.

capitalism: An economic system in which private business and markets, largely free of government intervention, determine the prices, distribution, and production of goods.

cash and carry: The program established in late 1939 by the United States to sell war materials to Great Britain, but Britain had to transport them in their own ships.

civil defense: Non-military programs designed to protect U.S. citizens from enemy attack or disasters on the home front.

civil liberties: Protection of certain basic rights from government interference, such as freedom of speech and religion.

coalition: A temporary alliance of different groups.

Cold War: A prolonged conflict for world dominance from 1945 to 1991 between the two superpowers, the democratic, capitalist United States and the communist Soviet Union. The weapons of conflict were commonly words of propaganda and threats, not military conflicts.

commodity: An economic good produced by industry.

communism: A political and economic system where a single party controls all aspects of citizens' lives and private ownership of property is banned.

conservatism: Opposition to a large federal government and extensive social programs.

D

deficit spending: A government spending more money than the revenue coming in.

democracy: A system of government, such as that of the United States, that allows multiple political parties. Their members are elected to various government offices by popular vote of the people.

dictatorship: A form of government in which one person wields absolute power and control over the people.

dimouts: To turn out some lights, such as along a coastal shore area, particularly those lights pointed toward or easily seen from the ocean to guard against attacks from the sea.

draft: A legal requirement that young men serve in the military for their country for certain periods of time; also more formally known as selective service system.

E

espionage: Using spies to acquire information about the activities of a foreign nation.

F

fascism: A political system in which a strong central government, usually run by a dictator, controls the nation, gaining support through promotion of strong nationalism and often racism; promotes the good of the state above individual rights.

furlough: A brief leave of absence from duty granted to a soldier.

G

G.I.: Nickname for military servicemen derived from the term "government issue."

G.I. Bill: Formally known as the Servicemen's Readjustment Act of 1944; provided extensive economic benefits to World War II veterans, including school expenses and low interest loans for buying homes and starting businesses and farms.

Great Depression: A major economic crisis lasting from 1929 to 1941 leading to massive unemployment and widespread hunger in the U.S. and abroad.

Gross National Product (GNP): The total value of goods and services produced in a country for a particular period of time, such as annually.

I

incendiary bombs: Two- to ten-pound bombs designed to start fires.

incentives: Providing a reward to cause people to take specific actions, such as industries promised certain levels of profits to switch from production of consumer goods to war materials.

induction: A civilian enrolling into the military.

internment camps: A series of ten guarded camps mostly in the western United States where a total of 112,000 Japanese Americans and Japanese aliens were detained during the war for fear of sabotage or espionage. Also known as relocation camps.

isolationism: Opposition to foreign commitments or involvement in foreign disputes.

Issei: Japanese immigrants to the United States.

J

Jim Crow: Jim Crow laws enforced legal segregation, keeping races separated in every aspect of life from schools to restrooms and water fountains; particularly common in the South.

L

Lend-Lease: A U.S. program to supply war materials to foreign countries with payment to be delayed until after the war.

liberal: Those who look to social improvement through government action, such as providing financial security and healthcare not traditionally provided by the national government.

M

market: The world of commerce operating relatively free of government interventions, where demand and availability of goods and materials determines prices, distribution, and production levels.

mass production: To produce in large quantities in an assembly line fashion with the process broken down into many small steps.

mechanization: To replace human or animal labor with machines, such as tanks and trucks.

merchant marines: Officers and crews of U.S. vessels that engage in commerce.

migrant: A person who travels from place to place, often searching for work.

military-industrial complex: A politically powerful alliance of the military services and industry that provides materials to the military.

mobilization: To transform the national economy from peacetime production of goods and foods to wartime production.

munitions: Various types of ammunition such as guns, grenades, and bombs.

N

nationalism: Holding a strong loyalty to one's country and seeking or maintaining independence from other nations.

Nazi: A political party in Germany, more formally known as the National Socialist German Worker's Party, led by Adolf Hitler from 1920 to 1945.

New Deal: The 1930s programs designed by President Franklin D. Roosevelt to promote economic recovery from the Great Depression.

O

organized labor: A collective effort by workers and labor organizations to seek better working conditions.

P

patriotism: Love or devotion to one's country.

prefabricated: To build the parts in separate locations and assemble them at another site, such as a ship or a house.

propaganda: Information aimed at shaping opinions of people, usually by a government.

R

racism: To be prejudiced against people of another race.

rationing: A government system to limit the amount of certain foods and other items in short supply that could be sold to citizens to conserve materials.

riveter: One who fastens metal pieces together, such as airplane or ship parts, with flattened metal bolts.

Rosie the Riveter: A fictional female character appearing on posters and in advertisements recruiting women to work in the war industries.

S

sabotage: To destroy military or industrial facilities.

scrap drives: A public program of gathering discarded or unused items made of materials needed by the defense industry, such as rubber tires, metal pots and pans, and nylon hose.

segregation: To keep races separate, such as in public places and the U.S. military during World War II.

Social Security: A federal program that provides economic assistance for citizens including the aged, retired, unemployed, and disabled.

socialism: An economic and political system in which the government controls all means of production.

strike: A work stoppage to force an employer to meet worker demands.

subversive: People working secretly to overthrow a government.

T

theater of war: Specific regions of the world where World War II was fought, such as the European theater or the Pacific theater.

totalitarian states: Countries where every aspect of life is tightly controlled by a dictator and all citizens must conform.

V

V-E Day: The day victory in Europe was celebrated, May 8, 1945.

victory gardens: Small fruit and vegetable gardens grown by individuals or families, planted in their own yards and public places, such as parks, to supplement the commercial production of food.

V-J Day: The day victory over Japan was celebrated, August 15, 1945.

V-mail: Personal letters written to servicemen overseas on special forms that were photographed onto microfilm, transported to their destination, then printed on paper and delivered to the addressee; designed to conserve cargo space.

W

war bonds: Government certificates sold to individuals and corporations to raise money to finance the war, with the purchaser receiving their money back plus interest at a future time.

wildcat strikes: Worker strikes that do not have the support of organized labor unions.

Research and Activity Ideas

The following ideas and projects are intended to offer suggestions for complementing your classroom work on understanding various aspects of the American home front during World War II:

Wartime Government Posters: During the war years, colorful and informative posters printed by various U.S. government agencies appeared in home front work places, schools, recreation centers, and most all public areas of towns and cities across America. Messages on the posters shaped and directed the public's perception of the war effort and called Americans to action. Common themes included recruitment for the military, recruitment of men and women for war industries, volunteering, patriotism, war bonds, rationing for victory, doing your part for the war effort, and being careful not to let spies overhear your conversations.

Go to the Library of Congress' Prints and Photographs Online Catalogue at http://lcweb2.loc.gov/pp/pphome.html. Select "search ALL RECORDS in this catalogue." Type in the words "world war 1939-1945 posters." Go past the posters of foreign origin to find more than 450 U.S. government World War II posters. Carefully scan through the titles and images of the posters. Choose one of the interesting themes and create an original poster around that theme. Be sure your poster is clear, direct, forceful, and lists where to find more information if the reader chooses to do so.

Oral History Interviews: Make a list of people you know, such as your grandparents or great grandparents, that lived in the years of World War II, 1941 to 1945. Develop questions ahead of time. Tape record or video the interview if possible or take careful notes. Transcribe the tapes or rewrite the notes into a clearly written story retelling the interview. This process is known as taking or recording an oral history. Share the oral history with the class.

Local Communities in Wartime: With the help of a librarian at your public library, look into the wartime history of your own hometown. Was your community impacted by wartime activities? Were there military bases and war industries located nearby? Did the community change a great deal from 1940 to 1945? Perhaps you live in a rural area—what contributions did farmers, ranchers, and housewives make by diligently carrying out their everyday duties?

Aircraft Industry: By successfully building thousands and thousands of military aircraft on the home front between 1941 and 1945, the aircraft industry and its employees directly contributed to the Allied victory in World War II. Go to the website of the U.S. Centennial of Flight Commission at http://www.centennialof-flight.gov. From the home page choose the site map, next—history of flight, next—essays, and finally choose aerospace industry. Research the development of the various large aerospace companies, where they were located, how large they were, and the type of planes they built during wartime.

Rosie the Riveter: Visit the website of *Rosie the Riveter Trust* at http://www.rosietheriveter.org to learn about Rosie the Riveter World War II Home Front National Historic

Park located in Richmond, California, on the site of the former wartime Kaiser shipyards. Also check your favorite search engine using the words "Rosie the Riveter" to learn about employment of women in war industries during World War II.

World War II Advertising Campaigns: Advertisements placed in popular home front magazines between 1941 and 1945 provide a unique look at everyday American life during World War II. Not only did companies promote sales of their products in these advertisements, but they eagerly demonstrated their patriotism by urging Americans to do their part for the war effort. Magazines that had many full-page advertisements included *Life, Ladies Home Journal, Woman's Home Companion, Good Housekeeping, House & Garden, The Saturday Evening Post, McCall's,* and *Business Week.* At a public or college library request a few issues printed from 1941 through 1945 and look at the many advertisements.

See if you can detect a gradual transition in the ads that mirrored the progression of the war. For example, in 1942 Firestone Tire & Rubber Company or B.F. Goodrich might have advertised their use of synthetic rubber for products since the rubber imports to the United States had been cut off by the war. Bell Telephone touted its conservation of aluminum for planes by eliminating aluminum from the manufacture of telephone equipment. Philco Corporation bragged about their conversion from producing refrigerators, phonographs, and air conditioners to manufacturing war products to exhibit their patriotism and keep their name in front of the public for when the war was over. Likewise, Cody Cosmetics converted to camouflage makeup and made sure the public knew they were doing their part for the war. During the mid-war years, companies ran ads about how to keep items in good repair. For example, General Motors advertised free booklets to keep your automobile performing well. Near the end of the war companies such as Universal, makers of appliances and housewares, ran ads urging Americans to plan how they would spend their wartime savings after "Victory." Make copies of various advertisements and share with the class.

Women in Uniform: Study the chapter Women in Uniform. Divide the class into several groups. Each group choose one modern-day branch of the military service—army, navy, air force, marines, Coast Guard. Compare the participation of women in that service at the beginning of the twenty-first century with female participation in that branch in World War II.

Japanese American Internment Experience: At the beginning of the twenty-first century, many publications recounting the Japanese American internment experience became available in public and school libraries. Publication dates range from the mid-1940s to the 2000s. The recollections printed in the 1990s and early 2000s are written by Japanese Americans who were children or teens while in the camps. Examples include *The Children of Topaz: The Story of a Japanese-American Internment Camp* (1996) by Michael O. Tunnell and *Remembering Manzanar: Life in a Japanese Relocation Camp* (2002) by Michael L. Cooper.

Other books are collections of letters, diary entries, and the like that have surfaced through the years. One of these is *Only What I Could Carry* edited by Lawson Fusao Inada and published in 2000. Inada writes in the preface about her experiences gathering material for the book. Inada relates, "They [former detainees] pulled typed diaries from dark closets and dusty boxes tucked under beds; they slipped carefully preserved letters and memoirs into the mail; they let their stories unfold during long telephone conversations. . . . One astonishing voice after another emerged. . . ."

Locate and explore a book of recollections about Japanese internment during wartime. Read the peoples' stories closely. Report your findings to your class, friends, or family.

Wartime Music: Music, continuously played on the radio or jukebox, provided daily entertainment for Americans in wartime. Many songs were fun, fast, and uplifting. The Andrews Sisters—LaVerne, Maxene, and Patty—recorded one of the most popular songs of the 1940s, "Boogie Woogie Bugle Boy." Popular band leader Glenn Miller often performed with the Andrews Sisters and two of his favorite tunes were "Chattanooga Choo Choo" and "Jukebox Saturday Night." Louis Jordan had two lively hits, "G.I. Jive" and "Is You Is Or Is You Ain't (Ma' Baby)." A young Frank Sinatra sang "Saturday Night (Is the Loneliest Night of the Week)" bringing tears to the eyes of women whose "sweeties" were far away. Bing Crosby first performed "White Christmas" on Christmas Day 1941 and it became one of the most loved wartime songs. Locate a 1940s songbook. Have students play or sing some of these songs for the class. Discuss why the lyrics appealed to Americans caught up in the war effort. Compose your own song that would relate to Americans during the wartime.

Gas Rationing: Pretend your family has only four gallons of gas to use each week for a car that gets fifteen miles to the gallon. Calculate distances to essential weekly destinations. Decide where you would take the car and for what purposes. Would your family likely require additional alternative transportation? Which public services might you use?

Rationing and Recipes: To make sure families on the home front and servicemen at home and abroad all had access to adequate supplies of basic foods, the government began food rationing on May 5, 1942. Sugar was the first food rationed. Coffee was rationed by late November 1942, and, in early 1943, meat, including beef, veal, pork, and lamb, butter and oils, and cheese were all rationed. Remember, in the 1940s families ate a lot more meat than they tend to at the beginning of the twenty-first century and likewise used a lot more sugar for baking and desserts. Therefore eating habits and recipes had to be adjusted. For example, every family tried to observe meatless days so meatless recipes began to appear. Locate and cook a recipe or a whole meal that respected rationing realities. For a recipe source, try to locate a copy of Joanne Hayes' book *Grandma's Wartime Kitchen: World War II and the Way We Cooked* published in 2000 by St. Martin's press. Another source that is most likely available at a public library is *Good Housekeeping* magazine issues from 1943 and 1944.

Victory Garden: If your climate and space permit, research and choose vegetables, work the soil, then in the spring plant a victory garden. Choose a group of students to tend the garden through summer and write a report on the successes and failures. What would you do different the next spring to assure even better production?

Volunteering: Study the information in three chapters: Home Front Organizations and Services, Civil Defense, and Managing the Nation's Finances. Pretend your class is a wartime group of active and involved community residents. Have each resident choose an activity that they could volunteer for—perhaps a responsibility with Civilian Defense, the American Red Cross, United Services Organization (USO), or a war bond drive. Be sure your community has volunteers to cover various needs. Research the volunteer group you chose to join. Act out the contributions each of you will be making with props and dialogue.

Letters, Letters, Letters: "Be with him at every mail call" was a motto used by the U.S. government to encourage frequent letter writing to servicemen. The U.S. military considered letters a powerful morale booster. Writing to a son, brother, or husband or to an American woman serving in the military was frequently a nightly activity of family members. Guidelines appeared in popular magazines giving suggestions about how to write positive, cheery, newsy letters—just the kind of letters the government asked for. At your local library, locate books that contain collections of letters written by family members. *Since You Went Away: World War II Letters From American Women on the Home Front* (1991) edited by Judy Barrett Litoff and David C. Smith is an excellent source.

Scan the content of the letters. Put yourself in the shoes of an American student in the war years and write a letter from the home front to a family member in the military and far away from home. The letter can be no more than what fits on one standard (8 1/2 by 11 inch) sheet of paper. Be newsy, supportive, and do not forget a little humor.

Newspaper Search: Old issues of local newspapers are available at your public library, a nearby public university or college library, or from the local newspaper office itself. Locate and review newspapers for the days immediately following either the attack on Pearl Harbor on December 7, 1941, or for V-J Day (Victory over Japan) on August 15, 1945. Also compare articles from the same date in a large newspaper like the *New York Times, Washington Post,* or *Los Angeles Times* with your local paper. Choose interesting accounts to read to the class.

National World War II Memorial: Nearly sixty years after the end of World War II, the National World War II Memorial was completed in 2004. Located close to the Washington Monument on the Washington, D.C., mall, the memorial serves as a lasting visual legacy of the war. Research the issues surrounding the monument's development. Check your favorite internet search engine using the words "World War II Memorial." Do not miss the House Committee on Veterans' Affairs report at http://veterans.house.gov/issues/wwII.htm.

American Home Front in World War II
Almanac

Mobilization of the American Home Front

World War II officially began in Europe when Germany invaded Poland in 1939. By 1940 the war in Europe was in full swing, and the Allies, the nations fighting Germany and Italy, including Britain and France, needed U.S. support. At this time the United States was not involved in the war. However, it did agree to provide the Allies with weapons and other war materials. This agreement changed daily life in the United States as Americans began participating in a broad united effort to support the far-off military campaign. The biggest challenge involved industrial mobilization, the conversion of U.S. manufacturing from the production of civilian goods to the production of war materials. America had much to do to gear up for war production. It had to awaken from an economic lull brought on by the Great Depression. The Great Depression was the most severe economic crisis the United States ever experienced. It began in late 1929 and lasted throughout the 1930s. The Depression led to slowed business activity, high unemployment rates, and social unrest in many areas of the country.

To guide and coordinate the massive mobilization effort the U.S. government created numerous temporary federal agencies, including the War Resources Board, Office of Emergency Management, Office of Production Management, Supplies Priorities and Allocations Board, War Production Board, Office of Economic Stabilization, Defense Plant Corporation, and Office of War Mobilization. Under the guidance of these agencies, American businesses and workers brought about a giant increase in U.S. industrial productivity, and overall the mobilization effort created dramatic growth in large private corporations.

The World War I experience

Mobilizing the American home front for a worldwide war was not a new experience for the United States. U.S. war mobilization had occurred once before in the twentieth century—during World War I, which broke out in Europe in 1914. The United States did not enter that war until 1917, when the fighting had spread through much of Europe.

At that time the U.S. federal government was small and weak compared to what it would become by the end of the twentieth century. It had little influence over private business matters and played little role in the daily lives of Americans or in the national economy. Therefore, U.S. businesses took the lead in the mobilization effort. To organize this effort Congress created the National Defense Advisory Commission (NDAC), a group composed of corporate leaders. While

mobilizing U.S. industry, the NDAC sought to greatly limit any permanent growth of government. The commission did not want the government involved in what it regarded as private business matters. To avoid government intervention, the NDAC created various industry groups to assist in the award of government contracts for war materials These groups often directed contracts to their own industries. Public opposition to this arrangement grew quickly. People did not want privately owned businesses making decisions that affected the military and government spending, particularly if those businesses financially benefited from the decisions. The War Industries Board (WIB) was created in July 1917 in an attempt to decrease business influence in war-related decisions and spending. However, the board had little effect on the mobilization effort, and the World War I soon ended with the Allies defeating Germany in 1918. Later, in the 1930s, Congress investigated the role of private business in mobilizing for World War I and held numerous hearings to gather testimony from industry leaders and others. While no outright wrongdoing was uncovered, the public was angered by the high profits and inner dealings of certain private businesses exposed by the hearings.

A German power rises

The Allied victors imposed heavy economic penalties on Germany following World War I. The penalties caused great hardship for the German

Italian dictator Benito Mussolini (left) and German dictator Adolf Hitler in Munich, Germany, **1937.** © *Hulton-Deutsch Collection/Corbis.*

people, thrusting many into poverty. These difficult times gave rise to radical politics in Germany, because the German people were desperate and willing to follow leaders who promised to help. Adolf Hitler (1889–1945), leader of the National Socialist German Workers' Party (later known as the Nazi Party), rose to power by promising to bring Germany back to world prominence. He had established a dictatorship in Germany by 1933. Under Hitler's guidance Germany began military mobilization in 1935. Germany focused on military mechanization, relying more extensively on tanks and

warplanes to wage war, rather than the foot soldiers, horses, and much less armored vehicles it had relied on in the past. (In some of the last major battles of World War I, tanks and airplanes had played key roles.) Hitler also signed a cooperation pact with Italian dictator Benito Mussolini (1883–1945), thus posing a broader threat to European peace and existing governments of other nations. By 1939 Germany had the most modernized air force and tank divisions in the world, and these would soon play a critical role in hard-hitting attacks against other European nations. Germany also built modern submarines that would prove highly effective in sinking Allied ships in the early months of World War II (1939–45).

Other European nations and the United States had not produced so many new weapons since World War I. As late as 1939 Britain still had no armored divisions, and its warplanes were outdated. After the end of World War I in 1918, the U.S. military was significantly reduced to its prewar size. In addition the arrival of the Great Depression in late 1929 led to a major decline in U.S. industrial and agricultural production and caused substantial unemployment. Little money was available to spend on new military technology.

For the United States, war on the home front would begin much earlier than actual involvement on the battlefields. In 1936 and 1937, under the leadership of Adolf Hitler and Benito Mussolini, German and Italian troops began aggressively overtaking portions of Europe and North Africa. U.S. president Franklin D. Roosevelt (1882–1945; served 1933–45) and other world leaders took note: It was clear that massive industrial production programs on the U.S. home front would be needed to support the European nations locked in conflict with Hitler and Mussolini.

Asian military developments

Beyond Europe other threatening foreign events were unfolding. Japan, like Germany, was expanding its military. As the democratically elected Japanese government faltered during the early 1930s, the Japanese military gained greater power and strength.

Because the Japanese islands did not have many natural resources to support industrial growth, Japanese military leaders decided to establish a colonial empire to obtain the resources it needed, much as Great Britain had done in earlier centuries. In 1931 Japan invaded and seized the northeast Chinese province of Manchuria, a region rich in iron and coal. By 1937 Japanese forces began moving deeper into China, gaining control of other regions that would provide Japan with the resources it needed to establish a modern, powerful industrial nation. Though condemned by other nations for its aggressive actions, Japan remained largely unchallenged. The United States and other nations did not want to get involved in another war so soon after World War I.

An unprepared nation

President Roosevelt was very concerned about the lack of preparedness of the United States if it were drawn into another war. The effects of the Depression were still plaguing U.S. society in 1940. Nine million workers remained unemployed. Social unrest grew as the economy continued to languish. Many jobless Americans had packed up their families and taken to the road, looking for work and better times. However, they often found themselves unwelcome in new places because local job competition was fierce. Racial discrimination worsened as whites increasingly competed with black Americans for the precious few jobs traditionally held by blacks such as doormen and hotel elevator operators. Laborers struggled for greater recognition from management for their newly formed and expanded unions, labor organizations formed by workers to press management for improved working conditions and pay. A wave of labor strikes, incidences whereby workers refused to work until their demands for better pay or work conditions were met by management, occurred in 1937: Workers quit working but remained at their workstations, hoping to force management to recognize their concerns. These "sit-down" strikes involved some four hundred thousand workers. Some work stoppages turned into violent clashes with armed company guards. In one case, police fired into a crowd outside a Chicago steel mill, killing ten. Given all these events, Roosevelt knew that unifying the nation for possible involvement in another European war would be challenging. Besides rejuvenating the country's industrial productivity, he also needed to unite Americans to support a common cause.

The U.S. population was largely reluctant to get involved in another European war. U.S. involvement in World War I had been unpopular among many Americans. The great number of casualties and the use of chemical weapons horrified people on the home front. Many Americans preferred a policy of isolationism; that is, they wanted the United States to avoid any formal foreign commitments and involvement in foreign conflicts. This sentiment posed a major obstacle for Roosevelt as he prepared to mobilize the home front.

Adding to Roosevelt's obstacles, business leaders and an increasingly conservative Congress were unhappy with the government growth that had occurred during the Great Depression, particularly the growth of federal agencies designed to regulate the U.S. economy. By 1937 they had gathered enough strength to block any new government programs proposed under Roosevelt's New Deal. (The New Deal was the name given to a collection of programs initiated by the Roosevelt administration to help America recover from the Depression.) When Roosevelt began arguing for war preparedness, U.S. businessmen and Congress feared that the president's early mobilization efforts would involve more governmental controls over private business.

Plans to mobilize

The period from 1939 through 1941 was one of uncertainty for Americans. Tension grew in Europe and Asia, but Americans remained detached from international events. Germany's invasion of Poland in September 1939 officially started World War II. Honoring a defense agreement they had with Poland, France and Britain declared war on Germany. Although Roosevelt reasserted U.S. neutrality, he feared the United States would eventually be drawn into combat unless some U.S. financial aid was offered to France and

Britain. As the first step in home front activity, Roosevelt issued a "limited" national emergency proclamation on September 8, 1939. The proclamation set the stage to begin planning for home front mobilization. Under the proclamation the president created the War Resources Board (WRB) to develop a plan to mobilize U.S. industries. With isolationism still deeply rooted in the U.S. population, little resulted from the WRB plan. However, with strong pressure from Roosevelt, Congress reversed the existing neutrality laws so that U.S. arms could be sold to European democracies that were being attacked by Germany. In late 1939 the United States established a cash-and-carry plan to supply Britain, France, and other Allied countries with arms manufactured in America. Under this plan, these nations had to pay cash and transport the supplies in their own ships.

In early 1940 Germany invaded Western Europe. Denmark, Luxembourg, the Netherlands, Belgium, Norway, and France all fell to the relentless push of German troops. The German advances forced Roosevelt to take further action. He created the Office of Emergency Management (OEM) within the White House in an effort to personally guide mobilization. Following the fall of France in June, he requested and received $1 billion from Congress to manufacture fifty thousand planes. After capturing France, Hitler turned his aggression toward Britain. Germany launched massive air assaults against Britain in the summer of 1940; German bombers approached across the narrow English Channel, which separates Britain from the European mainland. Great Britain stepped up its orders for war materials from the United States, including planes. Also, with European agriculture disrupted by the fighting, U.S. farmers experienced a heavy demand for their crops to be exported to Britain.

With France under German occupation and Britain under attack, Roosevelt reestablished the National Defense Advisory Commission (NDAC), which had originally played a part in World War I. The advisory commission was composed of representatives from labor, industry, agriculture, and the general public. The purpose of the new NDAC was to advise Roosevelt and the OEM on mobilization issues and encourage industry to begin converting factories from the production of civilian consumer goods to the production of war materials. However, like the OEM, the NDAC had little authority to compel action because the conservative Congress, responding to business concerns, would not give the temporary war agencies power to regulate business activities. As a result, not much conversion occurred.

To spur military mobilization, Congress established the first-ever peacetime military draft, mandatory enrollment in the U.S. military for men meeting certain qualifications, in September 1940. Many American men who were still unemployed from the Depression entered military service and began receiving a paycheck once again. The U.S. Army had only 190,000 men in uniform when Germany invaded Poland in September 1939. It grew to

270,000 in 1940 and well over 1 million by 1941. However, despite the efforts of the NDAC and Congress, the home front remained largely quiet in the summer of 1940, as U.S. industry produced only limited amounts of wartime goods.

A reluctant nation

The German bombings of British cities increased in intensity during the winter of 1940–41. Following his reelection in November 1940, Roosevelt felt more politically secure and bold enough to take more aggressive action. For example, in an attempt to increase spur businesses' cooperation with increasing war production, he described the growing U.S. home front effort as "the Arsenal of Democracy" in a speech delivered on December 29, 1940. In January 1941 he replaced the NDAC with the Office of Production Management (OPM). Roosevelt appointed the former chairman of General Motors, William Knudsen (1879–1948), and Sidney Hillman (1887–1946) of Amalgamated Clothing Workers of America to jointly head OPM. They were charged with jump-starting industrial production of war materials and distributing necessary raw materials and manpower. However, like the previous mobilization agencies and commissions, OPM had no authority to *require* industry to place military needs over civilian needs. Most members of industry preferred making civilian goods, hoping that all the civilians who were newly employed in the war industry would be ready and willing to buy.

By late 1940 Britain was out of money to pay for the U.S.–produced war goods under the cash-and-carry plan. In response Congress established the Lend-Lease program in early 1941 to loan Britain the money to purchase U.S. goods. In return Britain granted the United States leases to place military bases on various British territories around the world. By May 1941 the British air defenses had prevailed. Hitler pulled back from the air assault and turned eastward, launching a massive surprise attack on the Soviet Union in June. Under the Lend-Lease program the United States began shipping war supplies to the Soviet Union. The U.S. supplies helped Britain and the Soviet Union survive until the United States entered the war in December 1941. The U.S. government contracted with industries to produce the war materials, creating much needed jobs for American workers. As a result, the orders for war materials helped the U.S. economy rebound from the Great Depression. The United States would ultimately spend $50 billion under the Lend-Lease program.

While Germany's air assault on Britain was beginning to wind down, Japanese forces pressed forward into Southeast Asia and took control of Vietnam, Laos, and Cambodia. The United States became concerned over the growing threat to the nearby U.S. territories of Guam and the Philippines. Roosevelt issued an "unlimited" national emergency declaration on May 27, 1941. He cut off trade with Japan, stopped much-needed oil shipments to Japan, and froze Japanese bank accounts and investments in the United States so that the Japanese could not withdraw the money to help finance its military expansion in Asia. Soon the United States and Japan were in a diplomatic standoff, neither side willing to back down. The emergency declaration gave Roosevelt sweeping powers to mobilize the home front. In late August 1941 Roosevelt created the Supplies Priorities and Allocations Board (SPAB) to establish policies that OPM would carry out, such as regulating what manufacturers could and could not produce and what raw materials were available to them. Still he proceeded cautiously to avoid confrontation with American industry leaders, knowing he would need their full cooperation in the near future.

Full mobilization

Full industry cooperation became a necessity in late 1941. The key event that finally spurred more aggressive home front preparation came on December 7. Shortly before December 7, Japanese leaders had traveled to the United States to resolve disputes related to Japanese military expansion. When the talks failed, the Japanese feared that the United States would stage a military intervention in Asia. In an effort to prevent U.S. military intervention in Japanese expansion, Japanese naval and air forces launched a major air attack on U.S. military installations at Pearl Harbor in Hawaii on December 7. The attack on Pearl Harbor completely surprised the American public and the entire U.S. government. Faced

with more than two thousand U.S. military casualties and major destruction of the U.S. Pacific Fleet, the U.S. home front was first shocked, then angered. Almost instantly, Americans became united in their resolve for action; the voices of isolationism quieted. Within the next few days the United States declared war against Japan, and Germany and Italy declared war against the United States. Japan, Germany, and Italy became known as the Axis powers. Their opponents, known as the Allied forces (or simply the Allies), included the United States, Great Britain, and other countries joining the fight against the Axis military expansion. With war formally declared, Roosevelt took immediate action to build the U.S. military and mobilize the home front.

In January 1942, one month after the attack on Pearl Harbor, Roosevelt established the War Production Board (WPB) to oversee war mobilization. He appointed Donald Nelson (1888–1959), former executive of Sears, Roebuck and Company, to head the WPB. The WPB consisted of corporate executives and military leaders. Unlike its predecessors, such as the NDAC and OEM, the WPB had the power to require industrial conversion. The WPB also had authority to limit or halt the production of civilian goods. It also controlled the distribution of much-needed raw materials, such as steel, rubber, and aluminum, to critical industries. Production goals set by President Roosevelt for 1942 included 60,000 warplanes, 45,000 tanks, and 20,000 antiaircraft guns. Through the

Battleships USS *West Virginia* and USS *Tennessee* burning after Japan's surprise attack at Pearl Harbor, December 7, 1941. © *Bettmann/Corbis.*

first half of 1942 the military services issued war contracts worth a total of $100 billion. However, industry was still slow in converting, and Nelson and others on the board were unwilling to wield their full power. As a result the WPB had difficulty matching industrial raw materials needs and supplies since businesses were slow in responding to its requests and struggled

The New Atomic Industry

The war mobilization effort included the creation of an industry to produce atomic bombs. To develop the atomic bomb many new facilities, including three new cities, were built. The cities, built for the purpose of testing the atomic bombs, were Oak Ridge, Tennessee; Hanford, Washington; and Los Alamos, New Mexico. Each was built in a remote location to maintain top secrecy and public safety. Congress provided $2 billion to the top-secret atomic development program called the Manhattan Project. Hundreds of scientists and more than 120,000 other workers were employed on this project. In July 1945 the first successful test of the atomic bomb occurred in the New Mexico desert at Alamogordo. The following month the United States dropped atomic bombs on two Japanese cities, Hiroshima and Nagasaki, ending the war with Japan.

to meet deadlines for military production. The year's production goals were reached, but for many businesses, private interests still took priority over national needs. That is, better money could still be made in the production of consumer goods rather than military goods.

To further spur mobilization Roosevelt decided to appoint specific individuals to oversee mobilization in

key industries, such as petroleum and rubber. For example, in late 1942 Roosevelt appointed William Jeffers (1876–1953) as director of rubber production. Rubber was a critically needed raw material. Japan had cut off more than 90 percent of the U.S. crude rubber supply when it seized the Dutch East Indies and Malaya as part of its expansion into Southeast Asia. In response, the United States began rubber drives, asking its citizens to gather up and turn in unused rubber that could be recycled for industrial production. Automobile tire rationing programs also began. Rationing refers to a government program of making certain foods or materials available to the general public and businesses in limited amounts. However, these efforts alone could not supply enough rubber for wartime needs. To fully meet the need for rubber, the federal government boosted the development and production of synthetic (man-made) rubber. As part of the boost, the government spent $70 million to construct fifty-one factories for lease to rubber companies. These measures worked: By 1944 the annual production of rubber equaled 800,000 tons. The giant United States Rubber Company plant in West Virginia produced 90,000 tons in one year. Synthetic rubber production provided 87 percent of the rubber used for the war.

To improve access to critically needed materials, Roosevelt created the Office of Economic Stabilization (OES) with Supreme Court justice James F. Byrnes (1879–1972) as the head. The OES adopted the Controlled

Materials Plan (CMP), which set a strict priorities system for the distribution of three vital materials: aluminum, copper, and steel. The CMP played an important role in finally putting order to U.S. war production.

Business holds the lead

From 1940 through 1942 business leaders controlled the progress of the nation's mobilization efforts. U.S. business leaders were hungry for profits after years of economic stagnation during the Great Depression. As employment began increasing in 1940 and 1941, many businesses wanted to keep producing civilian consumer goods, because greater employment meant more people would have money to buy things. Faced with the government's request to convert to war production, businesses wanted government assurances that they would make decent profits while producing war materials for the military. In seeking such assurances business leaders formed an increasingly strong relationship with U.S. military leaders, who desperately wanted to get war production going. Working together, business leaders and military leaders carried a great deal of political power, and could essentially force the president and Congress to rely on them for making key mobilization decisions.

The growing alliance of business and military leaders during the World War II mobilization effort had several consequences. The key result was that the alliance successfully blocked any efforts by President Roosevelt to create permanent bureaucracies to guide the conduct of the war and regulate home front activities. Instead of government administrators or even military servicemen, business advisers oversaw mobilization through small temporary agencies such as the WPB. This put a stop to the growth of new permanent agencies. Furthermore, in coordination with a conservative Congress, business leaders were able to roll back many New Deal programs that competed with private business.

Conceding to business demands so mobilization could proceed, Roosevelt appointed Republican Henry L. Stimson (1867–1950) as secretary of war. Stimson, a big business advocate, followed the guidance of industry leaders in preparing for war. War mobilization was essentially turned over to the nation's business leaders, who were quite willing to cooperate with the government as long as they were in charge. The majority of government military contracts went to corporations whose leaders and representatives were serving as government advisers. The larger industries in particular enjoyed handsome profits under this arrangement. In addition, thousands of businessmen were hired by federal agencies to guide relations between the government and business interests. Many were called "dollar-a-year" men, because they were paid a dollar by the government so that they would be officially on the payroll, but were able to keep their much higher-paying private incomes. Serving in various government departments and

Automobile Industry

As the American home front was converting industry to wartime production, numerous problems arose. The revived economy brought jobs and better income to the U.S population, and people were eager to spend their earnings on new consumer goods, including the latest automobiles. Busy meeting this demand, automobile manufacturers were slow to convert their assembly lines from car production to tank and warplane production. Although the automobile factories were crucial to government production plans, the manufacture of automobiles actually increased by almost one million from 1939 to 1941. However, in its first meeting in early 1942 the federal War Production Board (WPB) outlawed civilian car and truck production so that military production could proceed. Despite this move it still took several months for military production to improve as automobile manufacturers sought various exemptions and extensions for conversion. President Roosevelt, however, was patient with the automobile manufacturers, realizing that he needed their cooperation for the long term. In the end, Packard was contracted to build nine thousand airplane engines, Chrysler to build tanks, and Ford to produce bombers.

on government commissions, they greatly influenced home front activities during the war.

Incentives to mobilize

Private corporations received various financial incentives from the government to cooperate in the mobilization effort (an incentive is something used to influence or reward a desired action). The incentives included substantial tax breaks for building new manufacturing plants or expanding existing ones, subsidies (government money given directly to the business) for retooling to create war products, guaranteed profits for production of war materials, and looser antitrust laws so that companies could more freely cooperate with each other. (Antitrust laws were designed to increase competition between businesses by restricting cooperative relations or combining of businesses.) In addition, through the federal Defense Plant Corporation the government spent billions to build factories and lease them to companies on attractive terms. Companies were unwilling to build the needed war production plants without sufficient incentives, because they feared being stuck with empty, unneeded plants following the war. The government sold the federally built plants to private companies after the war at bargain prices.

To guarantee industry profits a cost-plus system was introduced.

The government promised to cover all development and production costs for wartime goods plus a certain percentage of profit. In addition, rules that required competition among businesses bidding for government contracts were suspended so that the government could more freely select whatever businesses it thought would be best suited for the particular job. With these additional government incentives, private business operated with little financial risk during the war.

Small companies overlooked

Many within Roosevelt's administration wanted the government war production contracts to be awarded to small companies, particularly to those located in areas hit hardest by the Great Depression. However, the military contracted primarily with larger companies that were located in established urban industrial centers. Between May and September 1942, for example, 80 percent of the contracts went to large companies. The military argued that they merely favored businesses that could build the most war products in the shortest time; the larger corporations won out because they already had established assembly lines, research staffs, and access to large labor pools.

Smaller firms did not get many government contracts. Even worse, they could not continue their usual production of civilian goods because of new wartime restrictions or because the raw materials they would use were

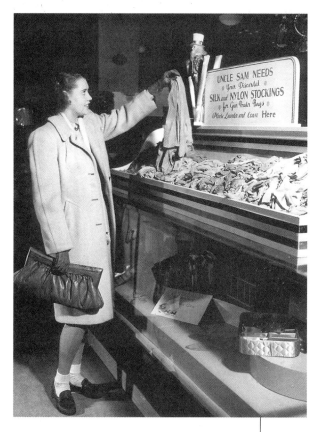

During World War II, American women were asked to donate their old pairs of silk hose to help further the war mobilization effort. The silk was used to produce war materials, such as parachutes. *Courtesy of the FDR Library.*

needed for war production. For example, until the Pearl Harbor attack in early December 1941, silk hose (stockings) were a staple of a U.S. woman's attire. By the end of 1941 silk, a Japanese product, was embargoed (prohibited by the government); because the U.S. government would not allow trade with Japan, silk became unavailable in the United States. The industry switched to using nylon, but soon nylon went into parachute making.

A War Production Board poster created during World War II to encourage the continued hard work of American laborers producing war supplies. *The Library of Congress.*

The American hose industry went into a rapid decline, as did the pairs of hose in women's dressers.

Migration for jobs

The war proved to be a time of opportunity for those who had been unemployed and underemployed (working less than full-time) during the Depression. The large industrial companies that received government contracts for war production in 1940 and 1941 employed all the local urban workforce, so by 1942 the stage was set for a major migration of job seekers. People living in areas of little job opportunity left their homes to find work with the major manufacturers. Approximately twenty million Americans—15 percent of the population—relocated. Rural families moved to industrial centers in cities. Americans from rural New England, the hills of West Virginia, the central farmlands from the Dakotas south to Texas, and the poverty-stricken Deep South began a mass migration. They ended up in steel mills in Indiana, immense aircraft factories on the West Coast, and shipyards along the East Coast. The population shift included many black Americans traveling from the rural South to industrial cities in the North.

Growth of big corporations

War production, government contracting, and the population shift had a significant effect on large companies and smaller businesses. Soon after the United States entered the war, some two hundred thousand smaller businesses closed. They could not function without government contracts or access to raw materials, and in many cases, the owners and employees were leaving for military service. By the end of 1942 three hundred thousand retailers had closed; manufacturers were producing fewer civilian goods, so retailers had less to sell. By the end of the war more than half a million small businesses had failed, far more than had failed during the Great Depression.

Meanwhile big business got bigger. In 1940 one hundred of the nation's largest companies produced 30 percent of U.S. output, and some 175,000 smaller companies produced 70 percent. By March 1943, however, the one hundred large companies were producing 70 percent of the nation's output. In a futile effort to counter this trend and promote small businesses, Congress had established the Smaller War Plants Corporation in mid-1942 to divert government military contracts to smaller businesses. Nevertheless, the growth of industrial giants, particularly in aircraft and electronics, was already well established. Between 1940 and 1944 over half of $175 billion in war contracts went to only thirty-three companies.

As home front mobilization progressed, disputes arose between industries and the WPB over access to manpower and raw materials. To help resolve these problems as they arose, Roosevelt created another small temporary agency, the Office of War Mobilization (OWM), in May 1943. James Byrnes, formerly head of the OES, was appointed as its head.

Mobilization is a success

War mobilization of industry and agriculture ended the Great Depression in the United States. The U.S. government paid billions of dollars to businesses that produced war goods and allowed farm prices to rise while farm costs were capped. In addition, millions of Americans joined the military and received regular paychecks. These factors led to full employment in the nation. Using funds raised through increased taxes, borrowing, and the sale of war bonds, the government increased its annual spending from $8.9 billion in 1939 to more than $95 billion in 1945. During that same period, as a result of government spending in industry, the gross national product (GNP) rose from $88.6 billion to $211.9 billion as worker productivity (a general measure of economic health based on how many hours a typical worker produces a certain good or performs a certain function) increased 25 percent. The GNP is the total value of goods and services produced by a nation in a particular time period. Total industrial production was staggering—almost 300,000 warplanes, 100,000 tanks and armored cars, 64,000 landing ships, 6,000 navy ships, 15 million guns, 41 billion bullets, 6 million tons of bombs (including two atomic bombs), and hundreds of thousands of trucks and jeeps. U.S. industry produced more than the three Axis countries (Germany, Italy, and Japan) combined. Historians credit this extraordinary production on the U.S. home front as one of the main reasons the Allies won the war. By July 1943 the conversion of U.S. industry to wartime production was essentially complete. Despite its difficult start and a series of ineffective government oversight agencies, industrial mobilization was an overwhelming success.

For More Information

Books

Adams, Henry H. *Years of Deadly Peril: The Coming of the War, 1939–1941.* New York: David McKay Co., 1969.

Eiler, Keith E. *Mobilizing America: Robert P. Patterson and the War Effort, 1940–1945.* Ithaca, NY: Cornell University Press, 1997.

Jeffries, John W. *Wartime America: The World War II Home Front.* Chicago: I. R. Dee, 1996.

Ketchum, Richard M. *The Borrowed Years, 1938–1941: America on the Way to War.* New York: Random House, 1989.

Wiltz, John E. *From Isolation to War, 1931–1941.* New York: Thomas Y. Crowell Co., 1968.

Winkler, Allan M. *Home Front U.S.A.: America during World War II.* Arlington Heights, IL: H. Davidson, 1986.

Production Miracles

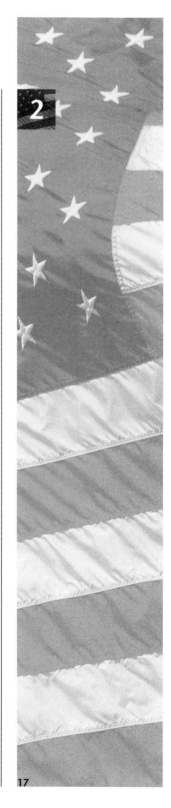

2

In the December 1942 *National Geographic Magazine,* Albert W. Atwood authored an article titled "The Miracle of War Production." Atwood penned the following words:

> This country which we love is producing all-out for war. At first there was only a trickle, then it became a mighty stream, and now it is a deluge [an overwhelming amount] of ships, planes, tanks, and guns roaring down the assembly lines of America.
>
> True, the war finally must be won on the battlefields, but it cannot be won without production, and it can be lost in the shops and factories. . . .
>
> This war has an incredibly voracious, an unbelievably stupendous appetite for materials, supplies, equipment, machines, munitions, and armaments. . . .
>
> By a sheer miracle of production America is now satisfying the yawning maw [mouth or jaws] of the war god. . . .
>
> Hence this country has become the most gigantic factory the world has ever seen, turning its plowshares into swords, transforming itself into an all-embracing, universal arsenal—all to meet the Axis challenge.

In his article Atwood relates the seemingly impossible requests for production that President Franklin D. Roosevelt (1882–1945; served 1933–45) made: 45,000 tanks in 1942 and 75,000 in 1943; 800 merchant (cargo) ships in 1942 and 1,500 in

Office of Scientific Research and Development

When World War II began in 1939, the United States was years behind Germany in technical military research. Foreign weaponry was clearly superior. The United States had to catch up and catch up fast. On June 12, 1940, Dr. Vannevar Bush (1890–1974), an electrical engineer and president of the Carnegie Institution, a prestigious research center, met with President Franklin Roosevelt. Bush, a brilliant, innovative scientist, urged Roosevelt to establish a group of American scientific, military, and business leaders who could coordinate technological research that would lead to the production of advanced military equipment. Roosevelt agreed and authorized formation of the National Defense Research Committee (NDRC); he put Bush in charge. Operating with presidential emergency funds alone, NDRC soon ran short of money. However, in mid-1941 the Office of Scientific Research and Development (OSRD) was established and funded by Congress. Bush became the OSRD director, and NDRC became the chief operating unit under OSRD. The visionary Dr. Bush brought together scientists from research universities such as Massachusetts Institute of Technology (MIT), California Institute of Technology, Harvard, and Columbia; he also brought in scientists from technological and industrial businesses such as Bell Laboratories, General Motors, Westinghouse, Philco, Sylvania, Standard Oil, and Dupont Chemical. These businesses sent their engineers to the university research labs to move new scientific breakthroughs into production.

Working with army and navy researchers and more than a billion dollars of government money, the cooperating scientists quickly created many technologically advanced innovations for the war effort. OSRD's many accomplishments included improved radar equipment; development of sonar (using sound waves to find objects underwater) by the Harvard Underwater Sound Lab for use on submarines; amphibious landing vehicles known as DUKWs, designed by General Motors; land warfare devices such as mine detectors, flamethrowers (a weapon that spews out fiery liquid), and bazookas (a hand-held rocket launcher); various rocket designs; medical advances such as the use of plasma in transfusions, and large-scale production and use of penicillin; invention of the pressurized cabin for aircraft and antigravity suits that kept pilots from blacking out in steep dives; and the tiny proximity fuse vacuum tubes. Made by Sylvania, the proximity fuse could be inserted in various projectile weapons; it used radar to detect a target. It was called the most significant scientific wartime achievement, next to the atomic bomb. Bush and OSRD were also involved in developing the atomic bomb.

1943 (only 4 had been built in America from 1922 to 1938); and in 1942 alone, 60,000 aircraft, more than triple the number built since the Wright brothers' first successful flights in the early twentieth century.

After the December 7, 1941, attack on Pearl Harbor by the Japanese, the U.S. government was able to initiate this miracle of production with three key strategies:

(1) Heavy financial support of industry. The federal government allocated roughly $240 billion over five years to finance war industry production.

(2) Production limits on nonessential goods, beginning in early 1942. Passenger cars, household electrical appliances, flashlights and batteries, metal signs, toys, and games were all considered nonessential goods.

(3) Allocation of (portioning out, or directing) key raw materials, specifically steel, copper, and aluminum, under the Controlled Materials Plan (CMP) of the War Production Board (WPB). The plan was put into effect by mid-1943 to match the raw material supplies with manufacturers' demand.

Keys to the miracles

To produce the massive quantities of war materials that President Roosevelt requested, manufacturers of locomotives, automobiles, farm implements, and heavy road-building equipment converted to the production of aircraft parts, tanks, jeeps, military trucks, machine guns, and shells. Small manufacturers also converted. For example, a maker of orange juice squeezers converted to bullet molds; a stove factory in Indiana converted to making lifeboats; and a merry-go-round manufacturer began making gun mounts, plane gears, and scaffolds for aircraft repair crews to stand on. Hundreds of thousands of these small businesses became subcontractors, supplying parts to the large corporations.

Assembly line mass production was one of the keys to success in industry's rapid conversion after Pearl Harbor. Most workers had never seen modern guns, not to mention complicated antiaircraft guns or tanks. Yet each person could be quickly trained to perform a task in a few simple steps and thereby carry out one small part in the overall production plan. For example, over one thousand mass-produced Garand rifles were completed each day at the Springfield Armory in Massachusetts. As the rifles moved along a conveyor belt, machine operators each made a small contribution to create the final product.

Another key to production success was the sharing of designs and methods among longtime competitors. The massive Willow Run operation, built by automotive giant Henry Ford (1863–1947) in 1941 outside of Detroit, Michigan, produced B-24 bombers. Ford's engineering staff learned the manufacturing process for B-24s by visiting and consulting with Consolidated

Women and men working together at what used to be an aluminum factory, now converted to the production of ammunition for the war effort. *The Library of Congress.*

Aircraft in San Diego, California. Ford put Buick engines into the planes—engines Buick had learned to build from Pratt and Whitney, aircraft engine experts in Connecticut.

As men enlisted or were drafted into the military, women kept production on track. By the tens of thousands they stepped up to do what had traditionally been considered men's work. They came from all levels of society and worked throughout production plants, from assembly lines to all phases of manufacturing, such as crane operators in shipyards and inspectors. Likewise, black American men and

women took the opportunity to fill production positions vacated by men joining the military. These war workers showed great dedication and pride in their work. War industry wages were high, which certainly helped the workers' morale, but the pride came from the workers' patriotic desire to do their part for the war effort. Factory owners rarely had to fire anyone for slacking off.

A national effort

The miracle of production spanned the entire United States. There were companies that built small arms in New England. Transport ships on Lake Erie awaited endless streams of open railroad cars carrying coal from West Virginia, Kentucky, Ohio, and Pennsylvania. The ships then traveled through the Great Lakes to deliver the coal at inland destinations, where it was used for steel production. Flashes of fire and the strongest of men and women, needed to pour large containers of molten iron while withstanding the heat from the blast furnaces, could be seen in the steel mills on the Monongahela River in Pennsylvania. Lumbering blimps built in Akron, Ohio, searched for German submarines along U.S. coastlines. In the Southwest, huge oil refineries produced gasoline. In the Midwest and interior Northwest, giant concrete grain storage facilities lined the horizons, holding vital food supplies for the Allied forces. Iron ore from Minnesota and Michigan was the basis for the war's two most important metals, iron and steel. Western mountains yielded ores—arsenic, bismuth, cadmium, copper, lead, manganese, and zinc—used in manufacturing tanks, planes, ships, and munitions. The towering chimneys of the ore-processing factories stood like exclamation points on the Western landscape.

Water was another valuable war resource. It was harnessed by the Grand Coulee Dam on the Columbia River in Washington to provide energy to run the war plants of the Northwest. These plants produced aluminum, plutonium (for atomic bomb development), and, most famously, the ships and aircraft used by Allied forces.

This team works on a bomber engine at the Douglas Aircraft factory in Long Beach, California. *The Library of Congress.*

U.S. aircraft industry

The history of the U.S. aircraft industry from 1939 to 1945 is a story of rapid expansion. In 1939 only about six thousand planes were built in the entire United States. Among all U.S. industries, the aircraft industry ranked forty-first. By early 1944 the U.S. aircraft industry had become the single largest industry, not only in the United States but in the world. Production doubled between 1939 and 1940 and doubled again in both 1941 and 1942. Between January 1, 1940, and the end of the war on August 14, 1945, 300,000 military aircraft rolled off production lines to supply both the U.S. military and its allies. Approximately 275,000 of those aircraft were built after the Pearl Harbor attack on December 7, 1941. The peak production month was March 1944, when 9,000 aircraft were completed. The dollar value of the aircraft produced by the aircraft industry increased over seventy times, from $225 million in 1939 to roughly $16 billion in 1944.

At the start of 1944 there were approximately eighty large production plants across the United States engaged in the manufacture of airplane bodies, engines, and propellers. More than two million workers were employed in these plants. Countless small companies employed millions more in the production of specific aircraft parts. The largest players in the industry included many companies that had evolved from the pioneer days of air flight in America: Boeing in Seattle, Washington, and Wichita, Kansas; Consolidated Vultee Aircraft, commonly known as Convair, in San Diego, California; Curtis-Wright Airplane, an aircraft engine and propeller manufacturer with several facilities in the Northeast and major plants in St. Louis, Missouri, and Buffalo, New York; Douglas Aircraft in southern California (three locations) and in leased space in St. Louis, Missouri; Glenn L. Martin Company in Maryland; Grumman Corporation at Bethpage, New York; Lockheed Aircraft in California; North American Aviation in Inglewood, California, Kansas City,

Kansas, and Dallas, Texas; Pratt and Whitney, an engine expert in Hartford, Connecticut; and Vought Aircraft in Long Island, New York.

Boeing, which had introduced its luxurious Stratoliner for passenger aviation in 1939, turned to bomber production in the 1940s, producing B-17s and B-29s. In 1942 the Boeing plants produced 60 planes a month, but by March 1944, 362 planes were completed each month. Participating in industrywide coordinated war production, Douglas Aircraft and Lockheed Aircraft also built Boeing B-17s, while the Glenn L. Martin Company helped produce Boeing B-29s. One assembly room at the Martin plant on the Atlantic seaboard could house four football fields. Further illustrating phenomenal growth patterns, Grumman Corporation started in a garage with 6 men in 1930. By fall of 1941 Grumman had 6,500 workers and grew at a rate of about 1,000 additional workers per month to reach 25,500 employees by September 1943. Lockheed had fewer than 2,000 employees in the late 1930s and had only produced a few hundred planes since 1913. By March 31, 1940, it employed 7,000; by 1941, 17,000; and by 1943, 90,000 workers. By 1945 Lockheed was completing 23 planes a day. Convair maintained an outstanding production record, too, with 28,000 aircraft completed and delivered between late 1941 and the end of the war. Doing its part, Vought produced over 5,000 Corsairs in 1944. The Corsair, with its Pratt and Whitney engine, was an exceptional fighting aircraft.

B-17 bombers being assembled at the Boeing aircraft factory in Seattle, Washington. *The Library of Congress.*

The construction of Douglas Aircraft's Long Beach, California, plant illustrates how government and private business worked together to meet production goals. The military was placing huge orders that included many new and different types of aircraft, and existing prewar plants were generally inadequate for such production. To encourage construction of new facilities, the government began the Emergency Plant Facilities program (followed quickly by the Defense Plant Corporation). The government asked manufacturers to pay for the construction of new facilities but promised to reimburse them over the next five years and then assume ownership of the plant. The Long Beach plant was constructed under this plan and began operation in November 1941. This arrangement allowed the U.S. government to avoid huge up-front expenditures and assured manufacturers that they would not be left with useless facilities at the end of the war. In many cases the companies were able to buy the plants from the government at very reasonable prices when the war ended.

By spring 1942 aircraft factories operated twenty-four hours a day, six or seven days a week. As effective assembly line strategies were created, increases in efficiency were dramatic. In 1941 it took fifty-five thousand man-hours to complete a B-17. (Man-hours is the measure of time spent producing goods, such as taking 55 workers a combined total of 1,000 hours to fully produce a plane, with the average worker spending fewer than 20 hours.) By 1944 it took an average of only nineteen thousand man-hours. With thousands of workers working on each aircraft, total production time could be measured in days. The outstanding achievements of the U.S. aircraft industry during the war helped ensure victory for the Allies.

A colossal task: Shipbuilding for the war

Ships for the U.S. Navy were built in government shipyards and in privately owned shipyards under contract to the navy. Oceangoing warships known as "large surface combatants" included battleships, cruisers, destroyers, and destroyer escorts. All were produced in yards full of lowering cranes, which lifted large parts of the ship into place for final assembly, and massive ways (ways are support structures on which ships are built and then launched). The navy also needed submarines, submarine chasers, minesweepers, patrol boats (PT boats), landing craft, naval auxiliaries, and large amphibious warfare ships. Naval auxiliaries included a wide range of craft, such as tugboats, net layers (which place large underwater netting to protect against enemy submarine intrusions into harbors), and small cargo ships, tankers, and transport ships. Large amphibious warfare ships transported troops, weapons, heavy equipment (such as tanks, trucks, jeeps, earthmovers, propellers), and various cargo to landing sites. They deposited troops and equipment directly onto beaches or transferred them to helicopters or smaller landing craft. Some amphibious ships had guns and short-range missiles for protection. Some served as command centers for complex operations, directing the ferrying of men and equipment to shore. The most famous amphibious ships in the war were LSTs, short for landing ship tanks, not a tank in the more popular notion of tank, rather a tankship or

Victory cargo ships lined up at a West Coast shipyard for final outfitting before they are loaded with supplies, 1944. *National Archives photo no. 208-YE-2B-7.*

Wartime Shipbuilding in America

Frederick Simpich wrote about America's shipbuilding effort in the May 1942 issue of *National Geographic Magazine*:

> Build ships faster than our enemies can sink them, that's America's job.
>
> We must get guns, planes, tanks, and food to our Allies and fighting men overseas to win this war. Everybody knows that . . . no nation in history ever faced so colossal a shipbuilding task in so short a time. . . . From Bath, Maine, clear around to Tacoma, Washington, old and new shipyards are busy building new ships and fixing old ones. . . . Day and night from these swarming yards rise the roar and racket of rivet guns, the creak and groan of giant cranes, the clang of forging shops, the thud of trip hammers, and the hiss of welding torches. . . . Whole armies of men [and women] are now at work building ships in the United States; this host [a large quantity of] will rise to 850,000 or more as production speeds up to two and three ships a day. Think what weekly payrolls—millions and millions!

tanker (large container/ capacity for hauling). LSTs could carry twenty tanks or several tons of cargo.

Equally vital to the U.S. war effort were the merchant or cargo ships known as Liberty ships and Victory ships, which were built for the U.S. Maritime Commission, the wartime government agency created to award contracts for ship construction Approximately fifty-six hundred were built during the war—more than enough to survive German U-boat (submarine) attacks in sufficient numbers. That is, the U.S. manufactured them at a faster rate than German submarines could sink them. These cargo ships were vital to the Allied war effort in transporting troops and supplies long distances across vast oceans and between continents to the war fronts.

Approximately twenty-nine states had large shipyards in operation between 1941 and 1945. Government shipyards included Boston NSY (naval shipyard), Charleston NSY (South Carolina), Mare Island NSY (Vallejo, California), New York NSY (Brooklyn, New York), Norfolk NSY (Portsmouth, Virginia), Philadelphia NSY, Portsmouth NSY (Kittery, Maine), and Puget Sound NSY (Bremerton, Washington), among others.

Some long-established, privately owned shipyards included Bath Iron Works Corporation in Bath, Maine; Bethlehem Steel Company in Quincy, Massachusetts, and San Francisco, California; Dravo Corporation in Wilmington, Delaware; New York Shipbuilding Company in Camden, New Jersey; Newport News Shipbuilding and Dry Dock Company in Newport News, Virginia; Todd Pacific Shipyards in Tacoma, Washington; Sun Shipbuilding and Dry Dock Company in Chester, Pennsylvania; and Alabama Dry Dock and Shipbuilding Company in Mobile, Alabama. Three submarine makers also had long histories building submarines and other vessels: Cramp Shipbuilding Company in Pittsburgh, Pennsylvania, began operation in 1830; Electric Boat Company in Groton, Connecticut, in

1899; and Manitowoc Shipbuilding Corporation in Manitowoc, Wisconsin, in 1902. The navy poured millions of dollars into these aging facilities for immediate submarine production.

The navy also invested millions in smaller yards to expand them for full shipbuilding. For example, the navy funded Lake Washington Shipyards in Houghton, Washington, for production of merchant marine and navy vessels, and repair of damaged ones. Willamette Iron and Steel Corporation in Portland, Oregon, received funding to build minesweepers, patrol craft, and submarine chasers. Missouri Valley Bridge and Iron Company in Evansville, Indiana, expanded for LST production.

Complementing the older, established yards were "emergency yards" that were built from scratch in 1940, 1941, and 1942 with government money from both the U.S. Navy and the Marine Corps. Most of these yards did not stay in business after the war. Examples include Bethlehem-Fairfield Shipyards in Baltimore, Maryland; Bethlehem Steel Company in Hingham, Massachusetts; and Kaiser Company in Vancouver, Washington.

Richmond Shipyards

The Richmond (California) Shipyards were perhaps the most famous of the emergency yards. Part of a wartime shipbuilding complex operated by industrialist Henry Kaiser (1882–1967), the Richmond Shipyards provide an excellent example of how

A skilled worker contributes to the construction of the Liberty ship SS *George Washington Carver,* being built at the Richmond Shipyards in 1943.
The Library of Congress.

shipyard activity affected the surrounding community. Shipyards often mushroomed into sprawling communities as new workers poured into an area for the well-paying jobs. Before the war Richmond was a quiet community with a population of twenty thousand. Its shoreline along the deep San Francisco Bay had not been developed. In early 1941 construction on the shipyards began, and soon these yards would become the largest and most productive of any in the world.

U.S. Maritime Service

In 1938 President Roosevelt established the U.S. Maritime Service (USMS) for the purpose of training merchant marines (officers and crews of U.S. vessels that engaged in commerce). Before World War II began, the United States had roughly fifty-five thousand experienced mariners, but just 1,375 ships by October 1940. After the United States officially entered the war in December 1941, U.S. production of cargo ships accelerated. By the end of the war, the U.S. and its Allies had 6,236 merchant ships. The USMS went all out to recruit men who could be trained to operate these ships, which carried essential supplies and U.S. troops to the battle zones overseas. USMS ads appeared in newspapers and were broadcast on the radio. Recruits as young as sixteen years of age poured in. Those who had been turned down by the army, navy, and Coast Guard (usually for medical reasons or because they were too old or too young) were welcomed into the USMS. Thirty-seven USMS recruiting stations were located across the country, often near the navy and Coast Guard recruiting offices. Navy and Coast Guard recruiters frequently sent men to the USMS office, telling them that was where they were most needed. Training schools for USMS officers, seamen, and radio operators were located in the Northeast, Florida, and California. Over two hundred thousand raw recruits were transformed into merchant marines.

Loaded with supplies, U.S. cargo ships were likely to come under attack as soon as they left their home ports. German submarines (U-boats) lurked off the eastern U.S. coast and in the Gulf of Mexico, and Japanese submarines patrolled the western coastline. Cargo ships were also vulnerable to mines planted in harbors. On the open seas they were subject to battleships, bombers, and kamikaze attacks (suicide airplane attacks). Between 1940 and 1942 German submarines sunk U.S. cargo ships faster than they could be built. By 1943,

Within the next two years Richmond grew to one hundred thousand residents. The Atchison Village, a 450-unit development, was hastily constructed to house workers, but housing remained in critically short supply. As men joined the military, tens of thousands of women replaced them in the yards. Schools were built, and the Maritime and Ruth C. Powers Child Development Centers opened to care for the children of the women workers. Henry Kaiser built Kaiser Permanente Hospital to provide health care for his workers.

Kaiser crisscrossed the country in search of more workers and found thousands of black Americans in the South eager to make the journey west.

however, the United States built more than could be sunk, and naval protection also improved.

To protect merchant marine cargo ships the U.S. Navy established the Armed Guard, which provided gun crews to defend the ships on the open seas. By the end of the war 144,900 navy personnel, trained at bases throughout the nation, had served on these gun crews. Approximately two thousand of them lost their lives defending the cargo ships. About one out of every twenty-six mariners was killed while serving in the USMS.

Unlike the U.S. Army, Navy, or Coast Guard, the USMS was racially integrated: Black and white crew members served on the same ships. The first black merchant officer in command of a ship was Captain Hugh Mulyac (1886–1992). At least seventeen ships were named in honor of well-known black Americans, including the *Frederick Douglass, Harriet Tubman, Booker T.* *Washington* (Mulyac's ship), and *George Washington Carver.*

Soldiers and supplies destined for the Pacific war zone embarked from San Francisco, California, and Seattle, Washington. New York ports sent cargo ships to Europe. Men and supplies headed for the Caribbean shipped out from New Orleans, Louisiana. The ports were scenes of frenzied activity throughout the war. Civilians had to be trained in transportation tasks such as loading and unloading ships, boat maintenance, and general shipyard repair. Military personnel continuously trained and kept account of soldiers who were preparing to ship out. By December 1944, U.S. embarkation ports had 62,646 military personnel and almost 78,000 civilian staff. New York and San Francisco were the largest operations. By the end of the war in August 1945, approximately 7.3 million people and 127 million tons of equipment had passed through U.S. embarkation ports.

They came to Richmond and were trained as welders, crane operators, shipfitters, and drillers; about half were women. A black community developed in Richmond, complete with a blues music scene and political organizations, such as a local chapter of the National Association for the Advancement of Colored People (NAACP) that promoted black American issues.

The Richmond Shipyards produced more ships faster than ever before. Kaiser applied a mass production system in which huge sections of ships were put in place by giant cranes and then welded together. Welding fused or melted the edges of two metal plates, a process much faster than the riveting that had previously been used. One Liberty ship was built in four days, fifteen hours, and twenty-six minutes. Kaiser's Richmond Shipyards produced 747 Liberty and Victory ships between 1941 and 1945.

When the war ended, the jobs ended—in Richmond and in other boom communities. Women and minorities immediately lost their jobs as men returned from the war. For those who stayed on to live and work in Richmond, the economic adjustment was very difficult as the city fell into an economic downturn that lasted decades.

Job market boom

Industrial mobilization improved job market prospects on the U.S. home front. The most important effect was the broad availability of jobs, which provided great economic hope after the high unemployment of the Great Depression (1929–41). Work could be had by nearly anyone who sought it. In 1939, just before home front mobilization began, approximately nine million workers were unemployed. Job opportunities began increasing through 1940 and greatly expanded after the Pearl Harbor attack in December 1941. Over fifteen million Americans entered the workforce or the military between 1940 and 1943. By early 1942 labor shortages began appearing; industry was continuing to expand, but many in the existing labor pool had joined the military. During the worst of the Great Depression, unemployment climbed to 25 percent; by late 1943 the unemployment rate had fallen to the incredibly low level of 1.3 percent.

With millions of men joining the military services, job opportunities rose for people who had never worked in industrial positions before. Black Americans traveled from the South for these jobs, and some 3.9 million women—both blacks and whites—joined the labor force for the first time. The new labor force also included youths, aged people, poor white Americans from the rural South, and small businessmen who had lost their businesses. Even teachers and white-collar workers were attracted by the fat war industry paychecks. Thanks to assembly line operations, which broke complicated processes into simple tasks, semiskilled workers could be quickly trained to do specific tasks.

Mobilization also created jobs in the federal government. Many new government agencies sprang up to aid the mobilization effort. Even though these were temporary agencies, combined with already established agencies such as the military services and U.S. Department of War, they led to a dramatic escalation in government employment. Federal employment had greatly expanded during the Great Depression as new government relief and recovery programs were established. During the war, federal employment expanded even more. The number of federal government jobs quadrupled from 950,000 in 1939 to 3.8 million in 1945.

Salaries on the rise

Overall, mobilization created seventeen million new jobs on the home front. Paychecks grew, partly because of a longer average workweek and large amounts of overtime (extra hours worked beyond the regularly scheduled number of hours, for which workers were paid). In February 1943 President Roosevelt signed an executive order expanding the normal workweek from 40 to 48 hours in munitions industries and in regions where labor shortages persisted. Overall, in war-related industries nationwide, the average workweek went to 45 hours. In the most critical industries, such as rubber production, shipbuilding, and aircraft manufacturers, the average workweek was 50 to 60 hours. Almost all laborers in the war industry worked at least a full six-day week, and many earned overtime pay for working on Sundays and holidays.

Salaries rose between 1939 and 1945—from $23.86 a week to $44.39 a week. Ironically, the conversion of industries to war material production left shortages in civilian consumer goods. So just when workers had money to spend, there were fewer goods available to buy. Many workers used their wages to pay off debts from the Depression. Some added to their personal savings, and some bought war bonds. (See Chapter 3: Managing the Nation's Finances.)

The dedication and output of America's workers was astounding. In 1944 the U.S. gross national product (GNP), the total value of goods produced and services provided that year, was $197.6 billion. War-related goods and services purchased by the government made up $90 billion of that total. The 1939 GNP had been $88.6 billion. Adjusted for inflation, that amount equals $138.32 billion in 1944 dollars.

Hence the GNP had risen 43 percent between 1939 and 1944.

Labor's role

Business leaders sought to limit the influence of labor unions, which had grown in prominence during the Great Depression. Labor unions are groups of workers who organize together to seek better pay and work conditions. Earlier in the twentieth century, labor unions were considered by many to be un-American as many union activists embraced radical politics in their confrontations with industry management. Violent conflicts arose and union workers were considered outside the mainstream of U.S. society. Rather than attempting to eliminate unions, which would not have been practical, business leaders decided to work with them. By war's end in 1945 labor unions were no longer seen as independent radical organizations; they were an accepted part of business. With plentiful jobs and rising wages, union leadership became less militant, and this broadened the appeal of union membership for many mainstream workers. From 1940 to 1945 labor union membership increased from approximately nine million to fifteen million, or about one-third of the U.S. labor force.

This change in labor-management relations was gradual and bumpy. At the beginning of the mobilization effort, radical behavior carried over from confrontations in the late 1930s. Forty-two hundred work stoppages (strikes) occurred in 1941 as industrial production began gearing up; the strikes involved 2.4 million union workers seeking improved wages and better working conditions. In response, the National Defense Mediation Board was formed in March to resolve the labor disputes. After the Japanese bombing of Pearl Harbor in December 1941, union leaders pledged that they would not conduct strikes during the war. They knew strikes would be very unpopular with the public during wartime, when all citizens were expected to sacrifice for the war effort. As a result, a cooperative working spirit between labor leaders and plant managers began to develop.

However, despite increased cooperation between labor and business management, some union workers still took action to seek improved working conditions. Even though the union leadership had pledged no strikes, numerous localized and brief wildcat strikes (worker strikes that are not supported by organized labor unions) did occur, generally in the coal, steel, and railroad industries. Public scorn for these strikers was severe, and Americans serving in the military felt great bitterness toward any grumbling home front worker.

In early 1942 the national War Labor Board (WLB) took over for the National Defense Mediation Board to resolve these worker conflicts. The WLB controlled wage increases during the war. Therefore, the key labor issues usually involved working conditions, such as safety in the workplace. As a result, the number of work stoppages dropped to two thousand in 1942.

The War Production Board (WPB) encouraged the formation of labor-management production committees. Approximately twenty-three hundred committees were operating by spring of 1943. The workers and management representatives serving on the committees made hundreds of thousands of suggestions to increase production, and the local WPB offices frequently called attention to and honored the best suggestions. The committees also resolved minor disputes and worked toward improving working conditions.

The WLB controlled wages by applying the so-called Little Steel Formula, which called for keeping wages within 15 percent of what wages were in January 1941. Many workers were dissatisfied with this control because wage increases did not keep up with the rising cost of goods. Primarily because of wage disputes, the number of wildcat strikes began to increase again, with 3,800 occurring in 1943 and almost 5,000 in 1944. By the end of the war in 1945 the WLB had been called on to settle approximately 20,000 worker disputes.

Secretary of Labor Frances Perkins (1880–1965) was quick to point out that most of the strikes that occurred during this intensive war production period were short, often lasting only one shift, and many involved only a few workers. She also pointed out that the damage caused by these strikes was blown out of proportion. The number of strike hours was generally less than one-half of 1 percent of total man-hours in any given month between 1942 and 1944.

The War Labor Board oversees testimony between management and striking coal miners at a hearing in January 1943. *The Library of Congress.*

Nearly double that number of man-hours had been lost to strikes between 1935 and 1941.

Though union-sponsored strikes were generally on a downward trend in the war industries, the hazardous coal industry was an exception. By May 1943, wartime coal production hit record high levels, but thousands of coal miners had been injured or killed in job-related incidents. In addition, miners' wages, unlike wages in other war industries, were subject to sizable deductions by the employer. In the company towns, in which the coal

company also owned the houses in which the workers lived, mine operators charged miners for rent, water, coal, and even for use of the miners' headlamps. A miner's paycheck could be $40 to $45 a week, but after the mine operator's deductions, the miner might take home only $20 to $25 a week. Flamboyant union leader John L. Lewis (1880–1969) led a controversial coal strike that lasted from 1943 to 1944. The strike brought considerable public scorn upon coal workers. However, the coal strike only slightly lowered total steel production (coal supplied energy to run the steel mills) in 1943, and steel production that year still broke all previous records.

In reaction to the wartime coal strike, Congress passed the Smith-Connolly War Labor Disputes Act, giving the federal government power to seize and operate industries if workers went on strike during wartime. Such federal action occurred on a number of occasions during World War II within various industries. However, overall, unions gained respect from industry leaders by handling wartime wage disputes with a minimum of disruption to production. As a result, labor union leaders became even more accepted in their negotiations with management in the postwar years.

Kinks in war production

Planes, ships, and tanks were being produced at record pace during the war years, but there were some kinks in the system. Strikes were generally small and of short duration, but absenteeism and labor turnover caused ongoing concern. In the month of December 1942, 16.7 million man-hours were lost to unexcused absences (other than illness) in U.S. shipyards. In all of 1942 only 430,000 man-hours were lost to shipyard labor strikes. Journalist Selden Menefee, who criss-crossed the country in early 1943 on assignment from Princeton University's Office of Public Opinion Research, reported that a Portland, Oregon, shipyard with 102,000 workers had an absentee rate between 3 and 17 percent in one month. In *Assignment: U.S.A.*, Menefee relates the findings of a Portland committee that studied the causes of absenteeism:

> Far too little attention had been paid to such important causes as unreported sickness, often due to inadequate housing and lack of community facilities; bad transportation, causing workers to be late on the job so that they are denied admittance; taking time off to shop, go to the bank, or conduct other personal business which could only be attended to during working hours; and finally, dissatisfaction with the job, the management and working conditions generally.

> 'It isn't all our fault,' said one of Henry Kaiser's Portland employees, who gets every eighth day off. 'Did you ever try cramming eight days of chores into one? We have to file our income tax, see the ration board [group of local officials who administered the distribution of limited foods and materials to private citizens and businesses], fix the car, clean the house, plant our victory gardens [private gardens planted by individual families to add to the nation's wartime food supply], all on one day. Shipyards are crowded and hard to get home from. We don't have long evenings like on our old jobs. We try hard to stay on the job, and most of us do, but it isn't easy.'

> Then there is the increasing age of workers. One construction foreman said: 'I had six men in their 60's in key jobs who worked themselves into sick-beds trying not to be absent during the winter. Flu caught up with them.'

The Portland study clearly indicated that the war production "miracle" took a serious toll on workers. The long work hours, crowded housing conditions, and exposure to toxic substances during manufacturing led to health and morale problems at times.

Labor turnover was another kink in production. When well-trained workers left their jobs, managers had to hire new, usually less experienced workers, who could not immediately match the production of the workers who had left. Reasons for quitting varied from location to location, but the most common included worker dissatisfaction with inexperienced managers who created inefficient production plans that left laborers idle for hours; insufficient housing, transportation, and recreational facilities; poor allocation of needed materials, which caused downtime; and wages that did not keep pace with the prices of everyday consumer essentials. Insufficient food for workers also led to discontent. The Department of Labor found that many factories offered no eating facilities and that laborers frequently had inadequate food intakes. It was not until mid-1943 that food rations increased for those doing heavy labor.

For More Information

Books

Bilstein, Roger E. *The American Aerospace Industry: From Workshop to Global Enterprise*. New York: Twayne Publishers, 1996.

Cott, Nancy F., ed. *No Small Courage: A History of Women in the United States*. New York: Oxford University Press, 2000.

Lingeman, Richard R. *Don't You Know There's a War On? The American Home Front, 1941–1945*. New York: G. P. Putnam's Sons, 1970.

Menefee, Selden. *Assignment: U.S.A.* New York: Reynal & Hitchcock, 1943.

Periodicals

Atwood, Albert W. "The Miracle of War Production." *National Geographic Magazine* (December 1942): 693–715.

Simpich, Frederick. "As Two Thousand Ships Are Born." *National Geographic Magazine* (May 1942): 551–588.

Web Sites

"The American Aerospace Industry During World War II." *U.S. Centennial of Flight Commission*. http://centennialofflight.gov/essay/Aerospace/WWII_Industry/Aero7.htm (accessed on June 21, 2004).

Boeing Aircraft. http://www.boeing.com (accessed on June 21, 2004).

Rosie the Riveter Trust: A History of the Richmond Shipyards. http://www.rosietheriveter.org/shiphist.htm (accessed on June 21, 2004).

World War II Shipbuilding. http://www.coltoncompany.com/shipbldg/ussbldrs/wwii/merchantsbldg.htm (accessed on June 21, 2004).

Managing the Nation's Finances

U.S. president Franklin D. Roosevelt (1882–1945; served 1933–45) had two major home front financial concerns during World War II (1939–45): how to finance the very expensive war effort and how to control the greatly altered home front economy. Solutions for both problems were intertwined. During World War I (1914–18) prices of goods and services in the United States had risen 62 percent, causing much economic hardship on the U.S. home front. Roosevelt was determined to avoid such dramatic inflation (prices of goods rising faster than wages) during World War II. This meant making major changes to the U.S. economy during the war years. Under Roosevelt's direction, the economy changed from a peacetime free market economy—an economic system with very limited government control over business activities, whereby the price of goods is primarily determined by the public demand and availability— driven by consumer spending to what is called a "command" economy. A command economy is driven largely by government funding and controls, under command of various temporary agencies that are directed by private business leaders. In fact, many of the wealthy and prestigious business leaders who greatly influenced the market economy prior to the war continued to strongly influence the wartime command economy and prospered greatly from it.

The "Good War"

The wartime economy led to a new period of national prosperity, ending the economic crisis called the Great Depression. The Depression began in the United States in late 1929 and spread throughout the world during the 1930s. During the Depression, U.S. unemployment hit 25 percent, and those who kept their jobs had to accept, on average, a 40 percent decrease in their salaries. During World War II the unemployment rate dipped below 2 percent; almost everyone who wanted a job could easily find one. The nation's gross national product (GNP)—the total value of goods and services produced by a nation in a particular time period—more than doubled, going from $88.6 billion in 1939 to $211.9 billion in 1945. Worker productivity, a general measure of economic health based on how many hours a typical worker produces a certain good or performs a certain manufacturing task, increased 25 percent. Farm output increased more than 30 percent.

The strong wartime economy inspired good spirits among the general public on the home front. As they contributed to the war effort, Americans felt a sense of pride in their work, and the entire population was unified by a desire to help win the war. These sentiments caused people to label World War II as "the Good War." However, the prosperity World War II brought was different from good economic times such as the 1920s, when business activity boomed. During the 1940s civilian consumer goods were scarce, the quality of available goods declined, shoppers wrestled with a complex system of rationing (a government program of making certain foods or materials available to the general public and businesses in limited amounts), housing was inadequate in many areas, workers spent long hours on the job, and families or family members were dislocated to far reaches of the country or overseas. It was not prosperity in a normal sense. Nonetheless, it was a definite economic improvement from the 1930s. Wartime jobs provided Americans with much better incomes. As a result, U.S. consumer spending rose 12 percent between 1939 and 1943. Savings accounts grew, and people were able to pay off their Depression-era debts.

Financing the war

Fighting World War II was very expensive. The U.S. government spent well over $300 billion for battlefield expenses and home front mobilization. That amount was almost twice as much as the United States had spent in its entire history up until the war. The annual federal budget grew from about $9 billion in 1939 to over $98 billion in 1945. The government spent an average of $75 billion a year during the war. This unprecedented spending called for a new approach to raising public funds. Two key avenues for fund-raising included raising taxes and selling war bonds.

A New Tax System

President Roosevelt strongly preferred paying for the war primarily through increased taxes. He wanted the highest tax increases to be paid by the wealthy, by corporations, and by the war industries, whose large profits came directly from the war effort. Taxing would serve two important purposes: The money raised by taxes would pay for the war, and paying higher taxes would reduce the disposable income (money left after paying for basic necessities, such as food and rent) of American consumers. Taking this money out of circulation would guard against another wartime inflation spiral. Economic inflation means the prices of goods and services rise faster than peoples' incomes, and the supply of money being printed by the U.S. Treasury increases, causing the value of money to decline and thus the price of goods to rise.

The public, business, and Congress opposed relying so heavily on taxes to pay the war costs. Congress did not want to lay the full burden of higher taxes on the wealthy and corporations, who were the main taxpayers under the existing system. In 1942 Congress passed the Revenue Act, which was formulated using the ideas of private financier Beardsley Ruml (1894–1960). Ruml was head of the Committee for Economic Development, a group of businessmen appointed to revise the federal tax structure. A key goal of Ruml and the rest of the committee was to increase the number of people who had to pay personal income tax in the United States. Ruml's committee recommended increasing the amount of personal income subject to taxes by taxing a person's income over $624 a year, a substantially lower figure than before. This new system lowered the minimum income threshold, so that even lower-income people had to pay some tax. As a result, this change would dramatically increase the number of taxpayers in America. Signed into law, the Revenue Act brought major change to the nation's tax system. For the first time, more taxes would be paid by individuals than by corporations. Only 4 million workers paid income tax in 1939. In 1942, 28 million Americans would pay taxes, and by 1945, 43 million were paying taxes. The amount of national income paid to income taxes rose from 7 percent in 1940 to 24 percent in 1945. Despite the increase, taxes paid for less than half of the war costs.

In the past all personal income taxes were paid at the end of a year. Because the new tax system created more taxpayers, it required a more effective collection process. To answer this need, the federal government introduced payroll tax deductions for the first time; taxes would be taken directly out of workers' paychecks on a regular basis. (This was another of Ruml's ideas.) Withholding taxes through the payroll system helped guard against inflation by reducing the disposable income consumers had each month.

Under the old collection system citizens would have paid their 1942 taxes in early 1943. To avoid having workers pay income taxes twice in one year, Congress chose to not collect most personal income taxes for the year 1942 and begin payroll withholding at the beginning of 1943 for 1943 taxes.

Even though more people had to pay taxes and all citizens paid a higher tax rate, the revised tax system received very little opposition. Wartime patriotism brought a quiet acceptance of the new system, and regular payroll deductions turned out to be more popular than the old, end-of-the-year tax collection. A public poll in January 1943 showed a 90 percent approval rating for the new system. The importance of the personal income tax in the U.S. economy significantly increased during World War II and remained the key source of government operating funds afterward.

Other Tax Proposals

The 1942 Revenue Act raised much less money than President Roosevelt needed, so he introduced another tax bill in 1943. His chief economic adviser, Leon Henderson (1895–1986) of the Office of Price Administration (OPA), pressed for higher tax rates to slow inflation. Roosevelt sought a $10.5 billion tax bill. Congress responded with only a $2 billion bill. Roosevelt angrily vetoed the tax bill in February 1944, but Congress overrode his veto.

A national sales tax was also considered for raising money. Under this proposal, citizens would have paid a tax whenever they bought certain consumer goods at the store. However, Secretary of the Treasury Henry Morgenthau Jr. (1891–1967) opposed the idea because it would burden the poor. The Victory tax was another means of raising funds and fighting inflation. Passed as part of the tax legislation in 1942, the Victory tax took another 5 percent from workers' income in addition to the regular income tax. However, the Victory tax proved so unpopular that Congress repealed it in 1944.

War Bonds

Even with the new tax increases, the government did not raise nearly enough money to finance the war. Other means of fund-raising had to be found. One way was to sell government war bonds. Selling war bonds was a form of borrowing: The government asked citizens to buy war bonds and promised to buy back the bonds later, with interest. War bonds were available in denominations (values) ranging from $25 to $10,000. War bonds had the potential to take money out of circulation; that is, if individuals bought war bonds, they would have less disposable income to spend elsewhere. So, like taxes, war bonds helped fight inflation. However, unlike taxes, war bonds were a form of personal investment for Americans. The government had to eventually pay them back the original value of the bonds plus interest. This arrangement increased the national debt and raised the possibility of postwar inflation (money might flood back into circulation when the bonds were

BUY WAR BONDS

A 1942 poster encouraging Americans to support the war effort by buying war bonds.
National Archives.

American Home Front in World War II: Almanac

redeemed). By selling bonds and pursuing other forms of borrowing, the federal government increased the national debt from $49 billion in 1941 to $259 billion in 1945.

The U.S. Treasury Department conducted seven major bond drives during the war. Morgenthau and Roosevelt hoped war bond sales would spur greater home front participation in the war and maintain patriotic unity. Therefore, the drives were aimed at the general public rather than the wealthy and corporations.

To attract public interest in bonds Hollywood stars pitched in. Seven tours were conducted in some three hundred communities. Actress Dorothy Lamour (1914–1996) was credited with selling $350 million in bonds. Singer Kate Smith (1909–1986) raised $39 million during a one-day radio drive. Another star, actress Carole Lombard (1908–1942), was killed in an airplane crash while returning from a bond drive. Bonds were available in relatively low denominations, and most Americans who were financially able purchased bonds. Despite the focus on general public sales, the overall highest dollar amounts of bonds were purchased by banks, large corporations, and insurance companies, who recognized war bonds as safe investments. In all, the United States raised $135 billion from the bond drives, including $39 billion raised from individuals.

Defense Stamps were another item that raised money for the war. The stamps, available at schools, sold for only pennies but provided a way for children to contribute directly to the war. However, unlike war bonds, the stamps were not meant to be redeemed at the end of the war.

Economic controls

The disposable income of Americans rose through 1941 as wages in the war industries increased. Economists and government leaders were concerned that this excess of spending money could cause high rates of inflation and cripple the nation's economy. Furthermore, with manufacturers concentrating on war materials, shortages of certain consumer goods could cause the prices of those goods to skyrocket. It would take time to introduce the new tax system to help guard against inflation. In the meantime, a system was needed to balance the increasing supply of spending money with the decreasing availability of goods. The government also needed to manage the shortages of various goods in a way that was fair to all citizens. To address all these needs the government established a system of controls on how much money workers could make, what they could spend it on, what would be available to purchase, and how much it would cost (wage and price controls and rationing).

Controlling Prices

Efforts to control the economy began in April 1941. President Roosevelt established the Office of Price Administration and Civilian Supply (OPACS).

Movie stars helped bring attention to home front activities. Here, actress Rita Hayworth sacrifices her car's metal bumpers to the war's scrap collection effort. *National Archives.*

Leon Henderson, Roosevelt's chief economic adviser at the time, was appointed head of the small agency. OPACS was charged with ensuring that prices of goods did not rise too sharply and that retailers did not make excessive profits. However, like the small temporary agencies created to mobilize industry (see Chapter 1: Mobilization), OPACS lacked any real power to force companies to comply with its recommendations.

Responding to the wartime industry boom and workers' rising wages, companies began to raise the prices of consumer goods in 1941. Between March and September, prices rose at the high rate of 13 percent. Alarmed by the growing inflation rate, President Roosevelt revamped OPACS into the Office of Price Administration (OPA), still headed by Henderson. Roosevelt also went to Congress and asked that OPA be given greater authority than OPACS had wielded. In response, Congress passed the Emergency Price Control Act in late January 1942. It gave OPA the authority to set maximum prices for a wide range of consumer goods and to freeze rents in war industry areas where housing shortages were occurring.

Using its newly granted authority, OPA issued the General Maximum Price Regulation, known popularly as General Max, in April 1942. Affecting about 60 percent of consumer goods, General Max froze prices at the highest levels they had reached during March. General Max was not very effective in keeping prices down. To get around the price freeze on their regular products, businesses found creative ways of altering or repackaging the goods and then charged higher prices for these "new" products. As a result, prices on consumer goods rose 18 percent between 1941 and 1943.

Controlling Wages

On April 27, 1942, as General Max was going into effect, President Roosevelt gave a public address on managing the nation's economy. He spelled out a seven-point program that called for higher taxes, price controls, and wage controls. In July 1942 the National War Labor Board (NWLB) established a limit on further wage increases by ruling that wages could increase no more than 15 percent above their level back in January 1941. This rule became known as the "Little Steel formula" when the NWLB applied it in a labor dispute involving small steel producers. The wage control was designed to stop the surge in prices of consumer goods. However, workers could still earn more income by working overtime (working more than their prescribed weekly hours) or obtaining promotions.

The wage controls proved more effective than price controls in curbing inflation because companies were clever to avoid price controls by producing new items not covered by the limitations. The average industrial wage rose from 66 cents an hour in January 1941 to 85 cents an hour by January 1943, an increase of about 29 percent. (The 15 percent wage control measure was not totally successful but helped slow down increases.) Consumer prices rose

Women wait in line at the local grocery store to receive their weekly ration of sugar during World War II. *National Archives photo no. 208-AA-322I-2.*

18 percent during that period. To maintain an effective control on any further inflation, Roosevelt issued an order in April 1943 to hold wages and prices where they were.

Controlling Purchases

In addition to controlling prices and wages, the government had to deal with growing shortages of consumer goods and critically needed resources for war industries. Common foods such as sugar, coffee, and meat were diverted for military use, causing home front shortages. To ensure a fair distribution of limited goods, especially essential items, the government established a rationing program. Rationing means limiting how much of a product a person can buy within a certain period of time.

Working together with the War Production Board (WPB), created in January 1942 to control the production of consumer goods, OPA established a civilian rationing program. Locally established ration boards were set up in every county to operate the program. Some thirty thousand local citizens staffed the boards as volunteers. The system for rationing included a series of

Sugar and Coffee

Sugar was the first table food rationed during World War II; sugar rationing began in the spring of 1942. Sugar shortages had occurred in World War I (1914–18). Remembering this, Americans rushed to stockpile sugar when the United States entered World War II in December 1941. So many shoppers were purchasing hundred-pound bags that stores soon set a limit of ten pounds for each purchaser. The U.S. government issued War Ration Book One in early May 1942 to ration sugar and coffee. This first book contained coupons to present at each purchase. The sugar ration was eight ounces for each person per week. The amount was later increased to twelve ounces. Office of Price Administration (OPA) inspectors enforced the rationing restrictions as best they could. Later in 1942, the sugar shortage worsened when sugar shipments from the Philippines and Latin America declined. Sugar would be rationed throughout the war—and even afterward through 1946—before the supply was once again sufficient to meet the demand.

The sugar shortage meant putting less sugar in drinks and foods and finding substitutes such as saccharin and corn syrup. Honey was another popular sugar substitute; beehives were reportedly stolen in California for their honey. Coconut kisses sweetened with honey and molasses replaced chocolate kisses. Restaurants put less sugar in their sugar bowls and asked customers to limit their use. People bought more goods from bakeries to avoid depleting their own sugar supplies at home.

The rationing of coffee started in November 1942. The threat of looming coffee shortages and rationing led to much hoarding, which only caused shortages to occur sooner than expected. To combat hoarding, the government froze all sales of coffee in late October 1942. Citizens were allowed one pound of coffee per adult every five weeks. Coffee drinkers who wanted more than their rationed amount had to resort to the black market or rebrew their used coffee grounds. Many who were not coffee drinkers began drinking coffee to make use of their coupons; others gave coffee ration coupons as wedding presents. Rationing of coffee stopped in July 1943.

ration books containing coupons and colored stamps. The books were issued to every man, woman, and child. For convenience, rationing books were made available at local schools. The rationing system grew to include 90 percent of the items found in six hundred thousand retail stores. Important items that were rationed included sugar, coffee, meat, fish, dairy products such as butter, canned goods, tires, and gasoline. Fresh fruits and vegetables were never rationed. To purchase the rationed items shoppers had to present cash and the proper coupon or number of stamps. Americans became accustomed to standing in lines with their ration books of coupons and stamps. Over fifteen million housewives signed pledges promising to follow the ration system and price controls without breaking the guidelines implementing them.

Although Americans grumbled about rationing, it was generally accepted as necessary for the war effort. Nevertheless, a black market (an illegal system of trade that violates government regulations) sprang up for certain restricted items as well as counterfeit ration coupons. For example, restaurants had their own ration allotments, including a ration of meat; this made it difficult for them to obtain as much meat as they wanted to sell. To get around this problem, restaurants began purchasing meat in a different, nonrationed form: cattle. Cattle, which were then butchered for their beef, became a popular item on the black market. However, black market prices were quite steep. Those who chose to sell their cattle on the black market profited greatly.

Rationing Point Systems

The OPA issued War Ration Book Two in February 1943. Beginning in March newly rationed items included canned goods, dried beans, and peas. Sales of canned meats and fish had been frozen the first of February to save existing supplies for rationing. Book Two had a different look than Book One. The first book contained coupons for specific items, for example sugar, or for a certain quantity of something. The new ration books contained rows of tiny blue and red stamps marked A, B, C, and so forth. Blue stamps were for processed goods, and red stamps were for meats, cheeses, and fats. Each stamp and each rationed item was worth a certain number of points. To purchase rationed goods, shoppers had to turn in the corresponding colored stamps with the correct point total. For example, every man, woman, and child had forty-eight blue points to spend each month. In 1943 a one-pound can of beans cost eight points, and a pound can of fish was seven points. Baby foods cost few points and, as a result, were regularly eaten by adults.

The number of points required to purchase certain items changed frequently. When an item became scarce, OPA would increase its point value to restrict sales. Similarly it would lower point values for goods that had become more plentiful. The flexible but confusing point system required families to recalculate their ration points every week or even daily. Shoppers had to budget both money and points and keep track of when particular stamps were valid. In addition, decisions made by local ration boards often led to different points being assigned to specific items in one city than they were in another. Local newspapers published the ever-changing point values of rationed food items. Point values were also posted in small red numbers on the shelves below rationed items.

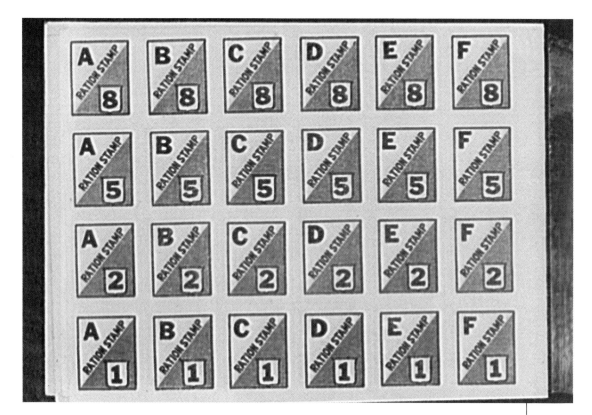

An example of War Ration Book Two. The letter on each stamp stands for a type of food, such as canned goods, meats, or cheeses, and the number is the amount of points assigned to a stamp. Shoppers needed the correct stamp and corresponding number of points to purchase certain food items. *The Library of Congress.*

To help guide the complex rationing program Congress passed the Economic Stabilization Act in October 1942. The act created the Office of Economic Stabilization (OES). Roosevelt appointed U.S. Supreme Court justice James F. Byrnes (1879–1972) to head OES. Byrnes left the Court to take the new post. Two more ration books containing more stamps would be issued by the fall of 1943.

Meat shortages began occurring during the winter of 1942–43. First steak and then hamburger meat ran out. The lucrative black market, as well as the legitimate shipment of meat overseas to feed the troops, was draining the beef supply away from the U.S. retail market. Meat rationing began on March 29, 1943. Each person was allowed twenty-eight ounces of meat a week and four ounces of cheese. To ensure fairness among the shoppers, OPA issued detailed instructions to butchers, describing how to make certain cuts of meat so there would be minimum variation in the common cuts of meat available.

goods. However, as fighting overseas increased through 1944, shortages developed again. Rationing was restarted at the beginning of 1945. Congress reluctantly extended the life of OPA to June 1946.

Rubber and Gasoline

Aside from foods, rubber was the first material to be restricted in public availability. Japan's military expansion into Southeast Asia through 1941 cut off 90 percent of the rubber used by the United States. Japan wanted the rubber for its own use; that was the purpose of its military expansion, to gain control of much-needed raw materials for their growing industries. Rubber quickly became scarce when the U.S. went to war. To conserve the remaining rubber supply, President Roosevelt froze the sale of tires and then banned recapping (adding a new strip of molded rubber to a worn tire). Car owners could possess no more than five tires. Any extra tires had to be turned in at gas stations for industrial reuse. Other little-used rubber items were gathered in scrap drives. To further conserve rubber, Roosevelt reduced the national maximum speed limit to 35 miles per hour (rubber is worn from a tire more quickly when a car travels at a higher rate of speed over time).

To limit the use of rubber by civilians, the government decided to ration gasoline. Rationing gas would reduce the use of automobiles and thus reduce wear on rubber tires. Gas itself was not especially scarce except in the eastern part of the United States. Gas

A boy tosses a rubber ball onto a rubber collection pile at a Washington, D.C., gas station. From tires to dolls, Americans contributed whatever rubber products they could to the effort. *The Library of Congress.*

By early 1944 OPA ended rationing of canned goods and some meats, while maintaining rationing of other

Gas Rationing

The Office of Price Administration (OPA) developed a nationwide gas rationing system that went into effect on December 1, 1942. The oil industry and its assigned wartime government coordinator, Secretary of the Interior Harold Ickes (1874–1952), immediately protested the rationing of gas, because it was not in short supply anywhere except on the East Coast. Nevertheless, gas rationing proceeded. Five windshield stickers identified priority levels: A, B, and C stickers for automobiles, E stickers for emergency vehicles, and T stickers for trucks. Category A stickers entitled drivers to the smallest amount of gas, only 4 gallons a week. (For the average car at that time, 4 gallons would last approximately 60 miles.) Later the allotment was reduced to 3 gallons a week. Category B stickers were for drivers who had more-essential driving to do, such as war industry workers who drove car pools to the factory and back. They received the A-sticker allowance (3 or 4 gallons) plus a certain supplementary amount. Category C stickers provided even greater allowances for people who used their cars for work, such as doctors making house calls and driving to hospitals. E stickers were reserved for emergency use by police, doctors, and clergy and provided essentially all the gas these workers needed. T stickers

Gas rationing stickers. *AP/Wide World Photos. Reproduced by permission.*

ensured truckers whatever amount of gas they needed to complete their routes. The local OPA ration boards issued the stickers and determined the allowances. Hoping to get as much gasoline as possible, many drivers argued that they needed a B or C sticker. More than half the driving population, or about fifteen million drivers, received the B or C classification.

shortages in the Northeast first appeared in May 1942. They were primarily the result of German U-boats (submarines) sinking oil tankers in the Atlantic Ocean.

The East Coast received 95 percent of its oil, which could be refined into gasoline, from the tanker shipments. Leon Henderson of OPA began gas

When you ride ALONE you ride with Hitler!

Join a Car-Sharing Club TODAY!

A World War II poster encourages Americans to carpool on the way to and from work to make the most of gas rationing restrictions. *National Archives.*

for leather led to a hide shortage, and shoe rationing began in February 1943. Each person was limited to three new pair of shoes a year. In 1944 the limit was reduced to two pair, still not very demanding compared to Great Britain's limit of one pair per year.

Gas rationing and the reduced availability of tires forced department stores to cut back on home deliveries, and residential milk delivery was also cut back. America's streets became much less congested, and the incidence of automobile fatalities dropped. Unfortunately for state budgets, state revenues from gas taxes also dropped, because less gas was being sold.

By January 1943 OPA further tightened driving restrictions by banning all pleasure driving. This meant that even if a person had plenty of gas in his or her tank, driving was limited to work, church services, funerals, medical needs, and emergencies. These restrictions were difficult to consistently enforce, but many citizens tried to help by writing down license plate numbers of cars parked in front of nightclubs, restaurants, or ball games. Violators of the pleasure driving ban could lose their gasoline ration sticker.

Because of its "watchdog" role in controlling the economy, OPA was not very popular. By the end of 1942 Henderson, who was not skilled at public relations, left his post. Chester Bowles (1901–1986) replaced him. Bowles was a millionaire advertising man who managed to improve OPA's public relations while implementing the unpopular measures. After 1942

rationing on the East Coast that same month. Henderson announced that each driver would receive 2.5 gallons of gas for each week. Still, by summer the East Coast was largely out of gas. When drivers spotted a gasoline tank truck going through town, they would follow the truck to the service station. Lines of cars, sometimes several blocks long, would form at the service station as drivers anxiously waited to fill their tanks (see sidebar on page 49).

Those who chose to walk faced shoe rationing. The military demand any anger over rationing gradually diminished. Rationing helped wage and price controls work more effectively. Under the rationing system, scarce goods were generally distributed fairly, and inflation was largely held in check. From mid-1943 to the end of the war in August 1945, consumer prices rose only 2 percent.

A changed economy

Americans were not accustomed to government so closely controlling day-to-day economic matters. They believed that they should be able to spend as much as they wanted on whatever they chose. During the war years they could no longer spend so freely. As a result the new economic measures were sometimes not well received. Nonetheless, taxes, wage and price controls, and rationing largely accomplished their purpose: maintaining a stable economy on the home front. These economic measures distributed the sacrifice of war among all citizens. In general, the actual financial demands on American civilians were relatively small compared to the economic hardships suffered on the home fronts of other nations involved in the war.

A public poll taken in February 1945 indicated only 36 percent of the American public felt that they had made serious sacrifices for the war. (The people who stated that they had made real sacrifices were people who had a loved one in the armed forces.) The home front was relatively comfortable for most Americans, much more so than during the Great Depression of the 1930s. Unlike other Allied nations, the United States lost no major comforts during the war.

For More Information

Books

Bentley, Amy. *Eating for Victory: Food Rationing and the Politics of Domesticity*. Urbana: University of Illinois Press, 1998.

Goodwin, Doris Kearns. *No Ordinary Time: Franklin and Eleanor Roosevelt, the Home Front in World War II*. New York: Simon & Schuster, 1994.

Lingeman, Richard R. *Don't You Know There's a War On? The American Home Front, 1941–1945*. New York: G. P. Putnam's Sons, 1970.

Polenberg, Richard. *America at War: The Home Front, 1941–1945*. Englewood Cliffs, NJ: Prentice-Hall, 1968.

Spinney, Robert G. *World War II in Nashville: Transformation of the Homefront*. Knoxville: University of Tennessee Press, 1998.

Warren, James R. *The War Years: A Chronicle of Washington State in World War II*. Seattle: University of Washington Press, 2000.

Agricultural Mobilization

In an April 1943 *National Geographic Magazine* article titled "Farmers Keep Them Eating," Frederick Simpich writes:

> In the fields. *That's where American farmers, including women, girls, and school children are fighting now—fighting frost, heat, dust, drought, mud, flood, and insect pests, growing our biggest crops in history.*
>
> *Food is as much a munition as TNT. Farm tractors and milk wagons, like tanks and cannon, are war machines.*
>
> *Farmers don't get killed and wounded on battlefields, get decorated with medals, or have to sleep in mud and snow. Yet without this 'soldier of the soil' all armies would soon have to quit, for it is still true that an army travels on its stomach.*

During World War II (1939–45) the American farming community gained more from the wartime economy than any other segment of the U.S. population. The more acreage a farmer owned and cultivated, the more he profited. Prior to World War II American agriculture had suffered through twenty years of depressed farm prices. The decline began after World War I (1914–18), when the demand for U.S. farm produce worldwide decreased, and lasted through the 1920s, a period of prosperity for the rest of America. During the 1930s farmers were severely affected by the economic hardships of the Great Depression. Although World War II ultimately raised the income and social status of America's farmers, the early 1940s were still difficult. During that period about five million small farmers who were barely making a living left their farms and sought work in the newly expanding war industries.

Poverty-stricken tenant farmers (a farmer who rents farmland from another and often pays with part of his yield) and field laborers (blacks and whites alike) migrated from the rural South to the urban war industry centers. There they enjoyed higher incomes and a better standard of living (the level of comfort maintained in everyday life). The farm population in the South decreased 20.4 percent from 1940 to 1945. Those on marginal farming lands—rocky New England, the hills of West Virginia and Kentucky, and the drought-ravaged Midwest—joined the migration. They ended up on both coasts, where giant aircraft factories and shipyards were in need of an ever-increasing number of workers. Ex-farmers also moved to the large industrial centers of the Great Lakes region. One and a half million joined the military.

Sharp rise in demand

By 1941, as Europe's agricultural production became increasingly disrupted by the war, the demand for U.S. agricultural products began to rise sharply. On March 11, 1941, the Lend-Lease Act became law. The act authorized President Franklin D. Roosevelt (1882–1945; served 1933–45) to lend money and send weapons, equipment, and food to the Allies, the nations combating the so-called Axis powers of Germany, Italy, and Japan. Under the Lend-Lease program, U.S. goods worth billions of dollars flowed to Great Britain, the Soviet Union, and China. Suddenly the American agricultural industry had to scramble to keep up with the food demands of the Allied countries.

With the commencement of the Lend-Lease program and the formal entrance of the United States into the war in late 1941, American farmers were expected to produce enough food for U.S. civilians, the U.S. Army and Navy, and Allied civilians and military forces overseas. Just as U.S. industry had mobilized to produce war products, farmers had to mobilize for massive increases in food production. However, agricultural mobilization presented farmers with a set of challenges very different from those faced by industry leaders. Farmers dealt with living, growing commodities. Grain took a certain number of months to grow and mature; cattle and hogs took time to fatten up. Agricultural production had to proceed on nature's schedule, not the war's schedule.

Like the mobilization of industry for production of guns, warplanes, and ships, agricultural mobilization required immense effort and a complex set of strategies. Millions of acres of new fields had to be plowed and irrigated. Huge increases in the demand for fertilizers had to be met. Farm machinery had to be kept in excellent working condition, and new machinery

FOOD COMES FIRST

Once the United States entered World War II in late 1941, American farmers were expected to produce enough food for U.S. civilians, the U.S. military, and Allied civilians and military forces overseas. *National Archives photo no. 44-PA-785.*

for new crops often had to be procured. Nearly 690,000 new tractors put two million horses and mules out of work. Greater numbers of cattle, hogs, and sheep meant grazing land had to be expanded; production of feed grains and corn had to increase, too. Transportation presented more challenges. To transport their goods to railroad shipping yards farmers needed trucks, gas, and tires—all items that were hard to obtain during wartime.

Despite the challenges, most farmers were caught up in the patriotic fervor of wartime and vowed to "keep them eating," a common catchphrase during the war. To meet production goals farmers worked from sunup to sundown every day, often calling on the entire family to help in the effort. For average, hardworking "dirt" farmers, as they liked to call themselves, 1942 was a very good year. Most were inclined to go on with this effort, as the Department of Agriculture requested, "for the duration," meaning at least until the war ended.

Farmers also had to grow many nonfood crops. Before the war approximately 600 million pounds of wool were used for clothing each year. In 1942 about one billion pounds were used for military uniforms, jackets, heavy fleece-lined coats, and pants. Hemp for cordage had previously been imported from such countries as the Philippines, but those imports were halted during the war. Therefore, U.S. farmers needed to produce 150,000 tons of hemp, which required the planting of 300,000 additional acres.

Wartime products

Certain products were emphasized to meet the demand of the military and home front. These included fats and oils, hogs, cattle, chickens, corn, wheat, and sugar.

Fats and Oils

Unlike Americans in the twenty-first century, the U.S. population in the 1940s had no concerns about eating too much fat. On the contrary, they ate large quantities of high-calorie fats and oils. High-fat foods such as bacon and pork were staples of the U.S. diet and favored by U.S. troops. In 1942 U.S. farmers produced twelve billion pounds of fats, but Lend-Lease exports quickly consumed these record amounts. There was real concern over shortages of fat. To prevent such shortages the U.S. Department of Agriculture (USDA) demanded that farmers plant more acres of peanuts, soybeans, and flax, all to be used for oil production. The USDA also required farmers to raise more hogs for lard and pork. In 1942, four million acres of

peanuts were harvested, twice as much as in 1941. Soybean production nearly doubled, from about six million acres to eleven million acres. Processed soybeans provided cooking fats, oils, and margarine. Milled into soy flour and added to cereal, they provided significant nutritional value. Because a large percentage of pork was shipped overseas, soy sausage, a new product, became a popular substitute. Noting the high nutritional value of soybeans, the Allies also ordered more and more soybean products through the Lend-Lease program.

Hogs were raised in record numbers in 1942 and fed record amounts of corn. These hogs provided both pork meat and lard. Lard was used extensively in cooking (for frying and baking) for civilians and troops. The Soviets spread it right on their bread, the way Americans would spread butter and jam. Tons of lard were sent overseas, and it was difficult for U.S. farmers to fill all orders.

Hogs, Cattle, and Chickens

Hogs were the finest fat makers known. In 1942 U.S. farmers raised approximately 105 million hogs, and even more hogs would be needed in 1943 and 1944. To increase the number of hogs, various agricultural scientists at the USDA Regional Swine Breeding Laboratory in Ames, Iowa, focused on cutting the infant mortality of young pigs.

Although a bit leaner than pork, beef also hit all-time production highs in 1942. The USDA asked for even larger amounts of beef for 1943

A Georgia farmer and his wife harvest peanuts to be used for wartime oil production.
The Library of Congress.

and 1944. Before the war, cattle were transferred into feeding pens to fatten for market for ninety to one hundred eighty days. By 1942 and 1943 the fattening period lasted only thirty to ninety days. Americans resigned themselves to less choice cuts of steak (cuts with less fat). Nutritionists suggested that, with less fat available, the war years would be an opportune time for Americans to lose weight, not a popular opinion among the public.

Dairy farmers were asked to produce more milk, cheese, and butter from their dairy cows. By the end of 1942, half of U.S. cheese production was being shipped overseas to Allied forces (including American soldiers) and civilians. For shipment, milk was generally dried and sent in boxes or evaporated and sent in cans. Up to 90 percent of dried milk, 40 percent of evaporated milk, and 20 percent of butter went overseas. Dairy farming was extremely labor-intensive. Dairy cows had to be milked twice a day, every day. Whole families plus hired hands worked the farms without days off. Some workers left for jobs in the war industries, gaining better pay and better hours; others joined the military.

These departures caused a labor shortage in the dairy industry, making production goals even more difficult to reach.

By the early 1940s poultry farmers had introduced better breeding, feeding, and care of chickens. The average American hen laid 111 eggs a year, up from 86 in World War I (1914–18). Chickens had become such efficient egg producers that eggs never had to be rationed during the war.

Corn and Wheat

During World War II American farmers planted nine million more acres of corn than they had before the war. They produced three billion bushels (a bushel is 2.2 cubic meters of dry harvested corn or wheat) of corn in 1943. Europeans did not like corn very much, so little was sent through the Lend-Lease program. Most of the record corn crops were used on the home front. What the people didn't eat, U.S. hogs, cattle, and poultry did. Corn was also put to industrial uses, producing fuel and explosives.

Farmers planted two million extra acres of wheat to meet wartime demands. Flour, breads, macaroni, and spaghetti were produced from wheat. Europeans needed huge quantities of U.S. wheat products. Hundreds of thousands of flour sacks were shipped out. In late 1942 the United States had more than a billion bushels of wheat on hand. Grain storage facilities were full. Growers then stored the grain in old garages, abandoned farmhouses, and even airplane hangars. In addition to being ground into flour, wheat was

Oregon's branch of the Women's Land Army (WLA) included a Dairy Maids Training School. After undergoing training, many women contributed to the war effort by working in the dairy industry. *Oregon State University Archives, [425]. Reproduced by permission.*

used like corn for feed and for production of industrial alcohol.

In Omaha, Nebraska, a new grain alcohol plant built by the Farm Crops Processing Corporation processed 20,000 bushels of wheat, corn, and barley each day and produced 17.5 million gallons of ethyl alcohol per year. The alcohol was used to manufacture synthetic rubber and explosives. (Rubber was a vital resource during wartime.

However, natural rubber was unavailable because the United States had stopped importing it from Southeast Asia, a region that was controlled by Japan during the war.)

Sugar

Americans in the 1940s, on average, ate 104 pounds of sugar a year—in cookies, cakes, candies, and ice cream, as well as in their coffee. Before the war the United States imported about 70 percent of its sugar from Puerto Rico, Cuba, Hawaii, and the Philippines. The 15 percent that came from the Philippines was completely cut off by the war. (Similar to rubber, the United States had stopped importing sugar from Southeast Asia, a region that was controlled by Japan during the war.) Ships to transport sugar from Puerto Rico and Cuba were scarce. To strengthen domestic production of sugar, the U.S. government paid American beet and cane growers to plant 25 percent more land.

Processing and transporting foods

New problems arose with the increased production of foods—notably, how to preserve this produce for shipment over long distances, and how to safely and economically get the produce to its destination.

Dehydration processing plants were a significant war industry. At the plants, heat was used to remove all water content from food items. Foods were dehydrated for two reasons: to prevent spoilage and to reduce the size of food items so that more could be packed into each shipment. Eggs, meat, vegetables, and fruits all underwent dehydration. Three dozen eggs, susceptible to spoiling and breakage in transit, would reduce to one pound of easily transportable egg powder. Scrambled eggs from dehydrated egg powder tasted almost exactly like scrambled eggs from whole fresh eggs. Through dehydration a 700-pound steer could be reduced to a relatively small portion of dried beef, about enough to fill a medium-size suitcase. Dehydrated vegetables—including beans, tomatoes, potatoes, and cabbage—could be stored in boxes. They were favored over non-dehydrated, canned vegetables, which took up more space and wasted tin, a scarce material during wartime.

Getting food products to market during the war was a challenge for U.S. farmers. Normally, trucks were used, but in 1942-43, trucks were in short supply. Gasoline and tires were tightly rationed. As a result railroads hauled twice as much food as they had before the war. In 1942 over four million railcars transported livestock and produce across the country. Rail stopping points were combined in central locations to make transportation more efficient. The U.S. government urged farmers to share their truck space with neighbors and completely fill each truck before driving to a rail stopping point to deliver their products. Railroads also carried goods that would have traveled by cargo ship during peacetime. Via railroads, these shipments evaded the enemy submarines that

What Is a Shipload of Food?

According to author Frederick Simpich in "Farmers Keep Them Eating," a *National Geographic* magazine article, the average U.S. freighter could carry the following amounts of goods:

- 6,000 barrels of dried eggs, equal to a year's work for 229,137 hens.

- 6,000 barrels of dried milk, a year's work for 2,783 cows.

- 16,522 cases of evaporated milk, a year's work for 304 cows

- 20,000 boxes of cheese, a year's work for 3,037 cows.

- 14,500 big cans of pork, the meat from 5,021 hogs.

- 16,800 boxes of lard, the fat of 27,632 hogs.

- 6,061 sacks of flour, the wheat from 838 acres.

- 26,111 cases of canned vegetables, equal to 40 acres of tomatoes, 100 acres of snap beans, and 102 acres of peas.

To fill this ship took the products from 3,824 average farms.

prowled the coastal waters. Railroad companies provided huge food storage facilities that were located up and down both coasts. There, goods ordered through the Lend-Lease program awaited ships that would carry them to China, Europe, and the Soviet Union.

Farm bloc

During the war farming became a big business, called agribusiness, with increased political power in Washington, D.C. In 1943 the U.S. farm population was between 25 million and 27 million. Historically, most American farmers did not belong to organized labor groups (groups of workers in a particular industry who band together to seek better work conditions, or better prices for the goods they produce or crops they grow), and they did not belong, as a whole, to any large political organization. A small percentage of the farm population, about 600,000, belonged to the American Farm Bureau Federation. The members of this group were mostly big farm operators and packing companies. They were the center of the so-called farm bloc, which was highly influential in Washington, D.C., in shaping government policy toward the farming industry. Local farm bureau branches controlled county agricultural agents, who were in charge of implementing government policies. At times the goals of the national farm bloc were not the same as those of the local farm

Put your muscle
on a war basis!

SIGN UP FOR A FARM JOB
...at your local U.S. Employment Office

This poster was issued in 1943 to encourage all available men and women to sign up for a farm job to help slow the shortage of farm labor. *The Library of Congress.*

organizations. For example, the average "dirt" farmer was pleased with wartime profits and eager to cooperate with the federal government's plans and requests, at least for the duration of the war. In contrast, the Farm Bureau Federation adamantly opposed government intervention in the business of farming because it reduced or controlled profits.

The farm bloc's overall goals were inexpensive labor, low operating costs, and increasing prices for bloc members' produce, all of which would bring higher profits. Members were especially dedicated to preserving cheap farm labor, even though this goal often hurt small farmers. For example, in late 1942 the Farm Security Administration (FSA) received authorization to move fifty thousand farmworkers from poor farming regions to areas in need of labor. The FSA also tried to establish a corps of several hundred seasonal workers. (Established during the Great Depression, the FSA was an agency designed to aid small farmers.) Fearing it might have to pay those workers higher wages, the Farm Bureau Federation effectively blocked both programs through congressional lobbying.

The farm bloc resisted any government price controls on farm products, even though such controls were designed to halt inflation, or a continuing rise in the price of goods. (Inflation would have eventually led to increased prices for farm equipment, as well as supplies and laborer wages, thus hurting the farmer, particularly small farmers.) Members also tried to block government attempts to influence farmers' choice of crops. For example, the government wanted farmers to switch from two nonessential crops, cotton and tobacco, to essential wartime crops such as soybeans and peanuts. One-fourth of U.S. farms were cotton and tobacco farms, and at least two years' supply of cotton and tobacco was available. It took only one-half acre of land and 6.5 man-hours of work to obtain the same amount of oil from soybeans as one and a third acres and

132 man-hours of work for cottonseed oil. The big farmers opposed the shift to soybeans for two reasons: They opposed any type of government intervention in their industry and they believed they would lose money by switching crops. Their machinery was already geared toward the traditional crops on large blocks of land and continuing with cotton and tobacco would still be more profitable, even if they were in less demand. They did not want small farmers to switch, because they might become more profitable and create more competition.

Farm labor shortage

By the end of 1942 farmers' major concern was the shortage of farmworkers. When the war began, many farmers' sons and hired farmhands enlisted in the military or migrated to war industry jobs in urban areas. During the course of the war, six million left farms. A policy of military deferment (exemption from military service) for men who worked on farms began in November 1942 as the government tried to head off the farm labor crisis. By mid-1943 over a million farmers and farmworkers had been deferred by the military draft system known as selective service, and by the end of 1943 three million deferments were expected to be in effect. Nevertheless, approximately 75 percent of farmers expected labor shortages in 1943. Of those farming more than 100 acres, at least half believed the shortage would be severe enough to affect production.

After the robust agricultural production of 1942, several million people had migrated back into some farming areas, hoping to get in on the profits. However, workers filling in for the farmers were not available in many areas between 1941 and 1943. To ease the labor shortage and get the crops in at harvest, many farmers began to recruit women, students, Mexican workers, and even prisoners of war.

In 1941 several state government agencies also began recruiting nontraditional farmworkers. By 1942 a few states, including Oregon, Vermont, New York, and California, had the U.S. Employment Service, a temporary agency assisting industries in finding workers as labor shortages increased, actively recruiting women from urban areas for critically needed farm work. Oregon and Vermont set up model cooperative recruitment programs.

In Oregon, the Oregon State College Extension Service, an agency providing educational assistance on the latest farming methods, teamed up with the U.S. Employment Service to organize farm labor committees in every county. These committees worked to assess needs and get workers to the farmers. Civil defense organizations, churches, and local chambers of commerce all worked together to send their members as volunteers into the fields. Radio stations and newspapers publicized the patriotic call to aid American farmers. In the spring of 1942 Oregon's Department of Education offered agricultural classes to schoolchildren from fifth grade through high school. That fall Portland schools sent eleven

Women took to the fields by the thousands to help lessen the labor shortages on farms and contribute to the war effort. *Oregon State University Archives, [P120:2396]. Reproduced by permission.*

thousand youths into the field with their teachers. Likewise, women took their families into the fields. Journalists, office workers, and other professionals also headed out to harvest crops. By the end of the 1942 harvest season Oregon's entire vegetable and fruit crop had been saved, harvested on time by nontraditional workers and volunteers.

The same year in Vermont well-known journalist Dorothy Thompson (1894–1961) founded the Volunteer Land Corps (VLC). VLC recruited men over sixteen years old and women over eighteen. Many college students in the Northeast participated in the various organizations. Then, working in cooperation, the VLC, the U.S. Employment Service, and Vermont state agencies, including the extension service, placed the young recruits in farm jobs in both Vermont and New Hampshire. In Maine Katherine L. Potter, a home economist, established the Women's Emergency Farm Service. Eleanor Roosevelt (1884–1962), long a proponent for increased work opportunities for women in U.S. society, gave the

Mexican workers arriving in California by train in 1942 as part of the Bracero program. Workers brought in from Mexico helped to bridge the farm labor shortages in California and states in the Southwest. © *The Dorothea Lange Collection, Oakland Museum of California, City of Oakland. Gift of Paul S. Taylor.*

project her support. Her home state, New York, had a similar program, known as "Farm For Freedom." This program was run by a large private organization. Other programs included the "Volunteer Land Army" of Hunter College and New York City's "Land Army."

Women's groups often established their own drives to recruit female farmworkers. In California, where crop and harvest seasons ran year-round, these groups recruited as many women as they could find to work in the fields. One California group, American Women's Voluntary Services, organized the Agricultural Committee. Working with state and local government agencies, this committee recruited women over the age of eighteen for the 1942 crop harvest; many of them continued working on a year-round basis. Other women's groups that joined in the effort included the Young Women's Christian Association (YWCA) and the National Federation of Business and Professional Women's

Clubs. The Federation urged its members to spend their vacation time on the farms.

Congress established the Emergency Farm Labor Program in 1942, allowing thousands of Mexican workers to come to the United States and relieve the labor shortage in California and the Southwest. In May 1942 the United States and Mexico negotiated an agreement to bring the Mexican workers into the United States. The program was known as the Bracero program. (In Spanish, *bracero* means "day laborer" or "people who work with their arms.") The U.S. War Food Administration served as contractor for the Mexican workers, whose contract promised minimum wage—either subsistence payments or employment for 75 percent of their time in the United States—as well as living expenses while traveling, and transportation to and from work sites. More than one hundred thousand Mexican workers came to the United States during the war years under the Bracero program. Despite the contract rules, these workers experienced substandard living conditions and working conditions. In reality the program enabled U.S. growers to contract for an unlimited supply of Mexican workers and pay them very low wages.

Farmers in the West and Southwest accepted any reliable source of labor to harvest crops, but farmers in the Midwestern and Southern states tended to prefer using their own families. They resisted hiring women laborers from outside the farm. By 1942, 50 percent of women in farm families were in the fields planting, cultivating, and harvesting, and caring for livestock.

Movement to a national farm labor program

From mid-1941 to 1943 the federal government debated whether a national farm labor program should be created. Many looked at the success of a few state programs and decided states could handle the farm labor shortage by themselves. Others, including Secretary of Agriculture Claude R. Wickard (1893–1967), were reluctant to use nontraditional labor and considered women not physically capable of relieving the farm labor shortage. However, during the same period farmers clearly demonstrated the ability to increase production and bring in the harvests with nontraditional labor. The idea of city women standing in as farm laborers gained a great deal of support from local government agencies, in agricultural publications, and in popular magazines such as *McCall's, Time, Saturday Evening Post,* and *Country Gentleman.* The *Farm Journal* in April 1942 urged farm women throughout the nation to be ready to train thousands of small town and city women. Likewise the National Federation's magazine *Independent Woman* urged the formation of a new woman's land army.

President Franklin Roosevelt declared January 12, 1943, as Farm Mobilization Day. In a statement that day he called food a "weapon in total war."

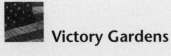

Victory Gardens

During World War I (1914–18), when food was in short supply on the American home front, people planted vegetable gardens for their own personal use; these gardens were called "victory gardens." When the United States entered World War II in December 1941, Americans needed no encouragement from the government to get started on their victory gardens. They began planting in the spring of 1942, and soon small garden plots were everywhere—backyards, vacant lots, public parks, and even in front of city halls, schools, and prisons. By April 1942, six million gardens had been planted.

In 1943 twenty million victory gardens yielded eight million tons of produce. Once harvested, the vegetables had to be canned for preservation, a job that Americans took on in their own kitchens. The victory gardens produced more than one-third of all vegetables grown in the United States and provided 70 percent of the vegetables consumed by Americans on the home front. Victory gardens became a key symbol of the will of the American people on the home front to pitch in to win the war.

The U.S. government finally established a national farm labor program in early 1943. Several factors influenced Congress to act on this issue: In 1918, during World War I, fifteen thousand women from all across the United States had joined the Women's Land Army of America (WLAA) to aid farmers; during World War II, various states had employed women and youths for farm work, with successful results; women family members, especially in the Midwest and South, were already maintaining farms; and several international women's land army programs (including the British Land Girls and similar programs in Australia, New Zealand, and Canada) had been successful in their efforts. Looking at the evidence,

Congress saw that the United States could benefit from adopting similar programs nationwide.

In February 1943 Congress passed Public Law 45, which established a national farmworker policy. The USDA put the Emergency Farm Labor Program, passed in 1942, under the jurisdiction of the agricultural extension service, an agency that provided educational services covering all aspects of farming. The national extension service cooperated with state and county extension services, so women and high school students across the nation could be utilized to relieve the farm labor crisis. The women's group was called the Women's Land Army (WLA), and the youth program was

Women of all backgrounds and ages participated in the Women's Land Army (WLA), doing everything from harvesting fruit to working on cattle farms. *The Library of Congress.*

known as the Victory Farm Volunteers (VFV).

Women's Land Army

The Women's Land Army (WLA) was officially launched in April 1943. Many farm and nonfarm women had worked as wartime farm laborers before that time, and then continued their work as part of the WLA through 1945. The WLA focused on cities to recruit thousands more. The women cultivated crops—hoeing, weeding,

thinning—and harvested them. Some picked fruit from orchards, and others worked in canneries. They worked on sheep, poultry, and cattle farms. Women of all backgrounds and ages participated in WLA. Homemakers, college students and faculty, and working women on vacation time all worked in the fields. Pay was supposed to be at least 30 cents per hour or equivalent piecework rates (pay based on the amount harvested). Instead, rates were usually determined by locality and worker scarcity. Rates were higher in the West than in the East. Rates in the Pacific Northwest were 60 to 95 cents an hour, but in the Southeast they were only 20 cents an hour. The Southern and Midwestern states, which originally opposed the creation of WLA, ended up using several hundred thousand women farm laborers by the end of the war.

Heading the WLA was Florence L. Hall (1888–1952), an experienced home economist with the U.S. Extension Service who had grown up on a Michigan farm. She coordinated state and local supervisors overseeing the placement of thousands of women. At the end of WLA's first year of operation, forty-three states had full- or part-time supervisors. County supervisors assisted state supervisors in the larger programs. Supervisors recruited women, managed public relations, provided training, organized worker camps (in locations where commuting to the fields each day was not practical), and opened childcare centers. Nearby hotels, Girl Scout camps, and tourist cabins offered their rooms to the women farmworkers during harvest season.

Farmers came to the camps each day to hire and transport workers. The camps were popular with women because they offered nutritious meals, group companionship, and recreation.

The Woman's Bureau of the USDA reported that, by 1945, 22.4 percent of all agricultural workers were women. That figure was up from 8 percent in 1940. Between mid-1943 and the end of 1945, 1.5 million women worked with WLA. An equal number found work on farms on their own. Although often overlooked in historical accounts of working women in World War II, these women enabled U.S. farmers to meet wartime production goals set by the federal government. They were the largest group of wartime farm laborers under the Emergency Farm Labor Program.

Victory Farm Volunteers

The second largest group in the Emergency Farm Labor Program was the Victory Farm Volunteers (VFV). By the end of 1945 two and a half million youths between the ages of eleven and seventeen participated in VFV. These young people cultivated and harvested crops just as WLA women did. Each young person had to pass a physical fitness test and have parental consent. Six-hour days were generally the limit.

Growers and youth leaders formed youth committees to organize plans in each county. In the spring, schools offered classes and training in agriculture to prepare students to work in the summer. Students would sign

A 1943 poster advertising for Victory Farm Volunteers. Posters such as these were hung in schools, where children between the ages of eleven and seventeen would be likely to see them. *The Library of Congress.*

up for VFV at their schools. Often WLA members oversaw the youth laborers in the fields. In the fall, in certain localities, schools closed during part of the day or for a short period when seasonal work, such as harvesting or planting, needed to be accomplished, so students could work in the fields

Teenaged Victory Farm Volunteers (VFV) picking strawberries on a farm in Yamhill County, Oregon, 1946. *Oregon State University Archives, [P120:2718]. Reproduced by permission.*

at harvest time. Workers were generally paid by the piece; for example, strawberry pickers were paid 42 cents per carrier full of strawberries. Generally workers could pick between fourteen and eighteen carriers in a six-hour day.

Foreign workers and prisoners of war

In addition to workers from Mexico, farm workers were also brought to the United States from the Bahamas, Barbados, Jamaica, and Canada. In all, approximately 230,000 foreign workers came to the United States to relieve the farm labor shortage during World War II.

Approximately 265,000 prisoners of war (POWs) also helped relieve the farm labor shortage. In California, south of the San Francisco Bay area, Italian prisoners of war aided at harvest times. From 1944 to 1946 thirty-five hundred German and other prisoners of war from six POW camps in Oregon worked to harvest potatoes, onions, lettuce, and pears in that state.

Prosperity comes to American farms

Farmers experienced a peak of prosperity during the World War II years. Through the course of the war, the U.S. farm population fell by 17 percent. The remaining farmers prospered greatly. The number of farms decreased, but the size of farms increased. Major scientific and technological advances, such as commercial fertilizers, substantially improved crop yields. Increased mechanization helped make up for the loss of workers who were enlisting in the military or taking factory jobs in the war industry. Farmers invested in new and improved tractors, trucks, and combines (a machine for cutting and threshing grains; threshing means separating out the seeds) that improved farm productivity. The federal government made a significant contribution to farmers' prosperity. While tightly controlling the prices of many American products (including products used by farmers, such as tractors), the government allowed prices for farm products to rise freely throughout 1942. Therefore, farmers' incomes rose faster than their costs. According to the Office of War Information, between 1939 and 1942 farm prices on average rose 92 percent, but the cost of supplies and equipment rose only 25 percent. Farm income rose from $8.7 billion in 1939 to $16.1 billion in 1942. As their profits soared, farmers built new farm buildings and homes, erased their debts, and enjoyed higher social status in their local communities.

For More Information

Books

Carpenter, Stephanie A. *On the Farm Front: The Women's Land Army in World War II.* De Kalb: Northern Illinois University Press, 2003.

Hurt, R. Douglas. *American Agriculture: A Brief History.* Ames: Iowa State University Press, 1994.

Lingeman, Richard R. *Don't You Know There's a War On?* New York: G. P. Putnam's Sons, 1970.

Menefee, Selden. *Assignment: U.S.A.* New York: Reynal & Hitchcock, 1943.

Periodicals

Borah, Leo A. "Nebraska, the Cornhusker State." *National Geographic Magazine* (May 1945): p. 513.

Simpich, Frederick. "Farmers Keep Them Eating." *National Geographic Magazine* (April 1943): p. 435.

Web Sites

United States Department of Agriculture (USDA). http://www.usda.gov (accessed on June 26, 2004).

Wartime Politics

Before World War II, during the Great Depression of the 1930s, the main political concerns in the United States involved social and economic issues. During the war, which lasted from 1939 to 1945, the key issues driving U.S. political debates and election campaigns were foreign policy and national defense. The two main political parties in the United States, the Republicans and the Democrats, held to their traditional ideas of how the nation should be governed. The Republicans favored the idea of a relatively small and limited federal government, whereas the Democrats preferred the federal government to take a leading role in providing services and protections for the nation's citizens. During World War II Americans reelected President Franklin D. Roosevelt (1882–1945; served 1933–45), a Democrat, to an unprecedented third term and fourth term. Franklin Roosevelt is the only American president who served more than two terms, and he greatly influenced U.S. politics during the war.

Politics before the war

During the mid-1930s, as Germany and Japan were busy building large militaries, the United States concentrated on domestic issues. The nation was in the depths of the Great Depression, an economic crisis that began in the United States in late 1929 and spread throughout the world during the 1930s. By the late 1930s the Republican Party and the Democratic Party had each developed a distinct ideology (a set of beliefs or ideas) strongly influenced by the Great Depression experience. President Roosevelt, a Democrat, first took office in March 1933. Roosevelt introduced a set of programs designed to combat the suffering caused by the economic crisis; the new programs were collectively known as the New Deal. To administer these programs the federal government greatly expanded in size and power. From that point on, the Democratic Party, led by Roosevelt, stood for a big, central government that would support social services and provide economic assistance for the aged, disabled, and poor. People referred to members of the Democratic Party as liberals because they looked to the government to improve their financial security and healthcare, things not traditionally supported by the government prior to the 1930s.

The Republican Party, whose members were called conservatives, opposed having a large federal government and extensive social programs. Republicans favored a much smaller national government and greater local rule. They were the dominant political power throughout the 1920s, as the nation's economy boomed and unemployment was low. However, by 1933, at the depths of the Great Depression,

many people began to see the benefits of large government—namely, assistance during times of great crisis—and gave their votes to the Democrats.

In 1936 Roosevelt won a sweeping victory in his bid for a second presidential term, receiving almost 61 percent of the public vote. The Democrats held the majority of seats in both the U.S. Senate and the U.S. House of Representatives, and, as a result, had much control over legislative activities in Congress. Political support for the Democrats in 1936 came from a diverse group of voters, including white Southerners, large-city urban dwellers, Catholic immigrants, Jews, black Americans, and lower-income voters. In contrast, the Republicans were generally supported by white Protestants and higher-income voters.

Although Roosevelt and the Democratic Party held great political power after the 1936 elections, major problems soon arose for Roosevelt. Because the U.S. Supreme Court had ruled that some of his new federal programs in the 1930s were unconstitutional, Roosevelt introduced a proposal to reorganize the Court. This proposal proved highly unpopular with Congress and the public. They feared Roosevelt's presidency was becoming too powerful. Then the economy, which had gradually been improving, took another downturn in 1937. Many of the Democrats elected to Congress were Southerners with conservative views. They worried about the growth of government and feared Roosevelt would increasingly support greater rights for women and minorities. With Roosevelt's public support somewhat weakened after the attempt to reorganize the Supreme Court, the Southern Democrats began to join forces with Republicans to form a conservative coalition (a temporary alliance of different groups). They blocked further growth of government and new domestic social measures that Roosevelt had hoped to initiate.

In the 1930s the American public favored a foreign policy of isolationism (the policy of avoiding formal foreign commitments and involvement in foreign conflicts). Congress shared the public's attitude: When German troops, under the dictatorship of Adolf Hitler (1889–1945), began to march through Europe in 1937, both Democrats and Republicans believed the United States had no business getting involved in the unfolding European events. The horrifying experiences of chemical warfare in World War I (1914–18) had made Americans deeply reluctant to enter another war. A public poll taken several years after World War I showed that a majority of Americans believed U.S. entrance into the war had been a mistake. Charles Lindbergh (1902–1974) was a key spokesman for isolationism. As the first person to make a solo nonstop flight across the Atlantic Ocean (in 1927), Lindbergh was an American hero. With U.S. government assistance, he made three trips to Germany between 1936 and 1938. Greatly impressed by the massive level of Nazi (the ruling political party of Germany, more formally known as the National Socialist German Worker's Party, led by dictator Adolf Hitler from 1920 to 1945) militarization, Lindbergh became convinced that the United States should not try to militarily oppose Hitler's actions in Europe if they did not directly threaten the United States. When Germany invaded Poland in September 1939, setting off World War II (1939–45), Lindbergh became even more vocal for U.S. isolationism. He gave five national radio talks during a fifteen-month period after the Polish invasion. By April 1941 he was a top spokesman for the America First Committee, the leading organization opposed to war with Germany. Lindbergh lost influence after he made anti-Semitic statements (statements that express hostility toward Jews) in a speech. However, the majority of Americans would continue opposing war with Germany until late 1941.

In 1938, with his domestic agenda effectively blocked and war appearing imminent in Europe, Roosevelt quietly turned to foreign policy issues. He considered the possibility that the United States could be drawn into the European conflict. Despite the public's isolationist mood, Roosevelt and Congress worked together to pass a bill creating the Selective Service System in 1940. This bill called for the first peacetime military draft (a legal requirement that young men serve their country in the military for a certain period of time) in U.S. history. Congress expanded the draft in 1941; the bill passed by only one vote in the U.S. House of Representatives.

Presidential Term Limits

Franklin Roosevelt's reelection to an unprecedented third and fourth term as U.S. president during World War II had a permanent impact on American politics: It inspired the Twenty-Second Amendment to the U.S. Constitution, the amendment that limits presidents to two terms in office.

In his first term as president, during the Great Depression, Roosevelt demonstrated an impressive ability to relate to the common person. He instilled confidence and hope during hard times, and in 1936, though the Depression dragged on, the American public reelected him for a second term. In 1940 Americans were uneasy about the prospect of entering the worldwide war; again they chose Roosevelt—a familiar and comforting leader—as their president. Four years later, when victory appeared certain, new worries arose: When war production

ceased, the U.S. economy might go back into a depression. Trusting that Roosevelt could prevent this, the public made him president for a fourth time.

Many Americans, though perhaps highly supportive of Roosevelt, generally believed a person should not hold the presidential office for so long. Their increased powers and influence would likely be unhealthy for the U.S. governmental system that relies on a balance between the executive, judicial, and legislative branches. Therefore, in 1951, the Twenty-Second Amendment to the U.S. Constitution was adopted. The brief amendment begins simply, "No person shall be elected to the office of President more than twice. . . ." Because of this amendment, Roosevelt's political legacy will likely remain unique in U.S. history.

Politics on the eve of war

In the history of the United States before 1940, no one had ever been elected to three terms as president. In the later part of Roosevelt's second term, the public seemed well opposed to his running again. However, during the presidential election year of 1940, the powerful German military made major advances. In early 1940 the Germans gained control of much of Western Europe, and France surrendered to Germany in June. Then, as U.S. political

parties were preparing to nominate their candidates in the summer of 1940, the Germans began bombing Britain. The possibility of Britain falling to Hitler caused a good deal of public concern, and the political debate grew between interventionists (those who favor involvement in foreign affairs) and isolationists.

Roosevelt decidedly fell on the side of intervention but cautiously avoided getting involved in any discussion of the issue. However, public debate over U.S. foreign policy would greatly influence which candidates were nominated for president. Gradually, public opinion shifted toward Roosevelt; one poll showed that 60 percent of voters said they would support Roosevelt for a third term. Roosevelt had provided leadership and comfort through one major crisis, the Great Depression. Now people were hoping he could help them through another potential crisis, a worldwide war. Roosevelt easily won the Democratic nomination.

On the Republican side, Ohio senator Robert A. Taft (1889–1953) and New York district attorney Thomas E. Dewey (1902–1971) were initially the main candidates vying for the party's nomination. Taft was a staunch isolationist. This position caused concern among the public, because the rapidly deteriorating situation in Europe seemed to demand some response from the United States. On the other hand, Dewey seemed too young to be president. A third candidate, Wendell L. Wilkie (1892–1944), came to the forefront. The head of a major Midwest utility company, Wilkie was attractive to Republican voters because he opposed big government, including Roosevelt's New Deal programs. On foreign policy Wilkie was an interventionist, differing little from Roosevelt, and supported U.S. aid to Britain. Wilkie won the Republican nomination.

As election day drew near and Germany's bombing of Britain continued, Roosevelt held a firm lead in the polls. Wilkie began challenging Roosevelt more on the war issue. He accused Roosevelt of being a warmonger

(one who readily threatens war) who would readily thrust the United States into another costly war. Roosevelt responded with a famous pledge: In a Boston speech he stated that he would not send America's youth into a foreign war. (However, when Japan later attacked the United States at Pearl Harbor on December 7, 1941, he broke that pledge with strong public support.) Desperately trying to gain an advantage in the campaign, the Republicans began saying that Roosevelt's possible third term could be the beginning of an American dictatorship, similar to the dictatorships that had recently been established in Germany and Italy.

On election day Roosevelt received almost 55 percent of the vote, and the Democrats retained control of both houses of Congress (the House of Representatives and the Senate). The Democratic coalition that had formed in the 1936 election held together. It included diverse segments of society, from white Southerners to urban black Americans, from Catholic immigrants to Jews. Concern over the war played a major role in the outcome of the election: A growing number of people were becoming more interventionist as the threat of German military expansion grew. Polish Americans also favored a tough stance against Germany, because German troops had invaded and taken over Poland. These voters chose Roosevelt over Wilkie. If America was forced to enter the war, Americans felt safer with Roosevelt's pro-British position and his experience in managing crisis. People hoped that the domestic security he represented could

Gene Tunney (left), Robert M. Rownd, and Wendell Wilkie (right) during Wilkie's election campaign, November 5, 1940. © *Bettmann/Corbis. Reproduced by permission.*

be translated to home front security in the event of a war. Congress remained cautious, however, in supporting Roosevelt's calls for war mobilization in U.S. industry. Nonetheless, isolationism was weakening, and in 1941 Congress passed the Lend-Lease Act, approving a program that would supply Great Britain with war materials produced in the United States.

Politics during the war

After the Japanese attacked U.S. military bases at Pearl Harbor, Hawaii, on December 7, 1941, the United States made its official entrance into World War II: The United States declared war on Japan, and Germany and Italy declared war on the United States. Sensing that the shocked and enraged public would no longer accept political bickering between the Democratic and Republican Parties, leaders of the two parties suggested that they work together for the sake of winning the war. After all, Britain had gone so far as suspending public elections throughout the war and formed a special coalition government made up of representatives from all the British political parties. Congress decided to give Roosevelt a free hand in foreign policy and home front defense. However, the political truce over home front issues proved impossible to sustain. Before long, traditional partisan politics (taking positions on political issues primarily based on party allegiance rather than the general good of the nation) would return on the home front.

The first public elections after the Pearl Harbor attack came in November 1942. The war played a much greater role in these congressional midterm elections than it had in the 1940 presidential election. At this point, the war was not going well on the battlefield, and on the home front industrial mobilization (converting from production of civilian consumer goods to war materials) seemed chaotic. Critical industries lacked key resources, such as rubber, aluminum, and steel, because of scarcity and distribution problems, and shortages of consumer goods occurred more frequently. An unpopular and complex rationing program (a system to make foods and other items of short supply available in limited amounts to ensure citizens receive a fair share) was growing, wage and price controls had begun, and labor shortages were frustrating America's effort to meet production goals. Bickering between Republicans and Democrats in Congress grew; they accused each other of hampering U.S. war efforts by either allowing the government to intervene in industrial activities too much or not enough. Republicans claimed they could bring greater efficiency to war mobilization. Democrats called for continuity in leadership and support for the wartime president. The war had become the number one political issue.

The Republicans made substantial gains on election day, winning new seats in both houses of Congress. Though the Democrats still held majorities in both houses, the coalition of conservative Republicans and Southern Democrats was strengthened. Not only were there more Republicans, but some conservative Democrats replaced those who had supported Roosevelt's social programs of the 1930s. The strengthened coalition would seriously restrict Roosevelt's home front war policies by limiting government control over industrial mobilization and blocking any newly proposed social service programs. In explaining the Republican success, some political analysts pointed to the low voter turnout as a key factor.

Only twenty-eight million voters turned out, whereas fifty million had voted in 1940. Some political analysts thought the ongoing movement of young servicemen and workers seeking war production jobs hurt the Democratic vote since that segment of society was considered strong supporters of Roosevelt and the Democrats. However, most analysts thought it more likely that the public was dissatisfied with management of the home front economy, particularly the complex rationing system and the unpopular Office of Price Administration (OPA) that administered it. This dissatisfaction may have caused a mild withdrawal of support for the Democrats. Perhaps the biggest factor in the loss of Democratic seats in Congress was simply that Roosevelt was not running. It was a midterm election, not a presidential one, and the Democratic supporters of Roosevelt's policies could not generate as much enthusiasm to counter the rising conservative coalition.

A conservative Congress

Through 1942 and 1943 America was becoming increasingly politically conservative on the home front. In times of war and faced with uncertainty, people are often less open to accepting new political or social ideas. The focus is on winning the war and protecting closely held traditional social beliefs. Opposed to federal planning, spending, and social programs, the conservative Congress went to work cutting back the smaller and more vulnerable New Deal programs

that still existed from the previous decade. In 1942 Congress cut funding for the Civilian Conservation Corps (CCC) and the Works Progress Administration (WPA). The CCC had been one of Roosevelt's favorite New Deal programs. Originally it trained enrollees in outdoor conservation programs such as wildfire fighting, tree planting, and trail construction. As America edged closer to entering the war, the CCC began teaching skills that would be useful in the military. Roosevelt unsuccessfully argued that the CCC could teach boys under draft age to look after public parks and forests. The WPA had provided much-needed work during the Depression, assisting with large public projects such as building schools and dams. However, as better-paying jobs became available in the war industries, fewer people took advantage of the WPA work program.

During 1943 Congress exerted its control over Roosevelt's home front agenda. It shut down the National Youth Administration (NYA), an agency that helped unemployed youths, especially black Americans, by teaching them vocational skills for war industries. Congress also reduced funding for the Farm Security Administration (FSA) and the Rural Electrification Administration (REA). The FSA helped small, marginal farmers buy land and machinery. The REA provided electricity to sparsely populated rural areas. Congress did not tackle more-popular New Deal efforts such as Social Security (a federal program that provided economic assistance for citizens including the aged, retired, unemployed, and

Franklin D. Roosevelt signing the GI Bill in 1944. The bill offered many benefits to veterans returning to the home front from the battlefield. © *Bettmann/Corbis. Reproduced by permission.*

disabled), banking regulation, farm price supports, and labor laws.

Congress also terminated the National Resources Planning Board (NRPB), a group in charge of planning a postwar home front economy. The NRPB was considering an expansion of Social Security and other social services. It also planned to restart public works projects, government-funded construction projects to build schools, highways, and ports for public use, to maintain full employment after the war. Opponents, including business

leaders, claimed that the plan represented socialism (a political and economic system in which the government owns and controls most means of production). In socialism, the government controls all means of economic production and sets prices of goods. In capitalism, upon which the U.S. economy is based, private business and markets largely free of government intervention determine the prices of goods. Through its House Un-American Activities Committee, Congress opened investigations of supposed political radicals in the Roosevelt administration. HUAC was driven by the conservative members of Congress who adamantly opposed those in the Roosevelt administration who advocated social service programs and industry regulation; they were considered political radicals by the conservatives. The investigation was another way to put Roosevelt on the defensive regarding home front politics.

Roosevelt realized that Congress was unwilling to consider any new social reform legislation. In a press conference in late 1943 he declared that "Dr. Win-the-War" had replaced "Dr. New Deal." These were nicknames he had been given in editorial cartoons. However, Congress was still uncooperative and rejected some of Roosevelt's war-related proposals as well. Among the rejected ideas was a new tax proposal to help fund war expenses. Congress proposed a far smaller tax bill, which the president angrily vetoed. Undeterred, Congress passed the bill despite the veto.

Looking to the future

In January 1944 Congress passed a notable piece of legislation that pleased President Roosevelt. It was the Servicemen's Readjustment Act, more popularly known as the GI Bill. The bill offered many benefits to veterans returning to the home front from the battlefield; it would also serve as a major social reform program. The bill pumped millions of dollars of government funds into the home front

economy as the war came to a close. It provided veterans $20 a week for up to one year to help them make the transition back to civilian life. It also provided educational benefits, low-interest loans for the purchase of homes, and loans to run farms and start businesses. The GI Bill greatly contributed to the nation's postwar prosperity. By 1950 U.S. war veterans had purchased 4.3 million homes with the GI loans. Housing construction increased to meet the demand, providing jobs and ending a long-standing housing shortage. Almost eight million veterans went to school under the bill, enrolling in high schools, trade schools, and colleges. In all, sixteen million veterans and their families—one-third of the U.S. population—benefited from the GI Bill. They passed the benefit along to millions of nonveterans by spending the government funds in all sectors of the economy.

Despite the conservative political climate in Congress, Roosevelt kept some of the NRPB's postwar economic plans alive. In his State of the Union address in January 1944, Roosevelt called for an expanded postwar economy with the government providing work programs for those not able to find employment elsewhere and social service programs to help the disadvantaged. He proposed a "second Bill of Rights" that addressed home front economic prosperity and security. It would ensure jobs, food, medical care, housing, and social insurance, such as Social Security, to provide economic safety nets for those unable or unfit to find work, for all Americans. There was

A group of military veterans lines up to purchase school books using funds provided by the GI Bill. © *Bettmann/Corbis. Reproduced by permission.*

no chance that Congress would act on such an idea, but Roosevelt wanted to at least express the future hopes of the Democratic Party.

The 1944 presidential election

With the presidential election looming in November 1944, a political battle erupted over how the eleven million people serving in the armed forces would be able to vote. More than half of them were stationed overseas. Polls showed that those in the military were strongly Democratic. Consequently, the Democratic Party wanted to make it as easy as possible for them to vote. The Republicans, hoping to make the voting more difficult, raised concerns about states' rights. (Normally the states determine voting eligibility requirements and the federal government plays little role except to guard against discrimination.) After months of debate, an absentee ballot system was devised as a compromise. Ballots were made available to those serving in the military, and four million soldiers made use of the system to vote.

The Republicans needed to find a new candidate to challenge Roosevelt. The 1940 candidate, Wendell Wilkie, had lost favor with the party for his increasingly liberal views. The party returned to Thomas Dewey, who had been elected as governor of New York in 1942. In Republican tradition, Dewey promoted limited government and a postwar economy led by private enterprise with little federal involvement through regulation or social service programs.

The Democrats were considering who Roosevelt's running mate should be. Roosevelt's health was declining; his running mate could very likely become president (that is, Roosevelt might not live through the entire four-year term). Henry A. Wallace (1888–1965) had been Roosevelt's vice president since 1941. However, Wallace held unconventional and liberal views— he was in favor of establishing strong economic ties with the Soviet Union and avoiding military escalation; he was also known as a strong supporter of government social and research programs—on both domestic and foreign policy issues, and he was not well liked by many Democrats. To replace Wallace on the ticket, the party considered former senator and U.S. Supreme Court justice James F. Byrnes (1879–1972). Byrnes was known as Roosevelt's "assistant president" on home front economic issues. However, Byrnes, a strongly conservative South Carolinian, supported racial segregation programs and opposition to labor organizations and, therefore, was unacceptable to liberals, labor union members, and black Americans, all of whom were traditionally Democratic voters. The Democrats instead turned to Harry S. Truman (1884–1972), a senator from Missouri. Truman had become well known to the public when he headed a Senate committee investigating the performance of big business (a group of large, profit-making industries that exert a major influence over national politics) in the war mobilization effort. Truman was considered a political moderate (not tending to favor extreme views on political issues and favoring a conservative viewpoint on some issues and a liberal perspective on others), and he had supported Roosevelt's New Deal programs during the Depression. He was known as an excellent political campaigner who appealed to the common person.

Campaign issues

By the fall of 1944, with the election approaching, both Germany and Japan were in retreat. Battlefield victories for the Allies (the nations fighting alongside the U.S., including Great Britain, France, and others) were mounting, and it was becoming obvious that they would win the war. With nearly twelve years of experience as the leader of the United States, Roosevelt firmly believed that he was the candidate best suited to deal with other world leaders in shaping the postwar world. Few were willing to argue that point.

1944 presidential election poster supporting Franklin D. Roosevelt. © *Corbis. Reproduced by permission.*

Besides winning the war and establishing peace, the key election issue was postwar prosperity on the home front. American business was still booming, but postwar employment was a major concern. For example, in Connecticut nine out of ten workers were in war production industries, and it was uncertain whether they could find new jobs after the war. With Roosevelt showing strong support of labor during the 1930s before the war, he continued to enjoy a large labor following through the early 1940s. Almost 70 percent of labor union members considered themselves Democrats, so unions launched a sweeping voter registration drive. They registered thirty-six thousand voters in a single day in St. Louis, Missouri. The Congress of Industrial Organizations (CIO), an important labor group, established a political organization to support pro-labor Democratic candidates.

For their campaign the Democrats pointed out that continuity in leadership would be crucial during the last, critical stages of the war. Roosevelt promoted his economic bill of rights to ensure economic security following the war. He promised to sustain full employment in the postwar period. Republicans took aim at Roosevelt on personal issues, claiming that he was too old and tired to tackle a fourth term, that he might be dying. Roosevelt had been paralyzed below the waist by polio since the early 1920s and had suffered a bad bout of influenza in late 1943; the latter seriously damaged his health. In February 1944 doctors discovered that Roosevelt was also suffering from hypertension (a heart condition causing abnormally high blood pressure) and heart disease. However, much of the information on Roosevelt's health was not released to the public. Indeed, even close friends of the president did not know the extent of his health problems.

Republican attempts to cast doubt about Roosevelt did not do much good. The Republican candidate, Thomas Dewey, was unable to connect with the common citizen; his cool and aloof manner worked against him. In desperation, Republicans charged that Communists were infiltrating the Roosevelt administration. (Communism is a political and economic system calling for the elimination of private property so that goods are owned in common and, in theory, available to all. A single political party controls all aspects of society, as was the case in the Soviet Union from 1917 until 1991.) They also attacked Roosevelt's pro-labor union positions. Many believed labor unions were un-American, infiltrated by political radicals eager to change the U.S. capitalistic system.

Election results

Despite Republican efforts to unseat him, Roosevelt won a fourth term of office, earning more than 53 percent of the vote. He attracted the same diverse voter support as before: urban dwellers, lower-income voters, blue-collar workers, Jews, Catholic immigrants, and black Americans.

Roosevelt had been successful as commander in chief during the war, and the public felt comfortable with him leading the nation into the unknown of the postwar period. Polls showed that the public had great faith in Roosevelt's ability to achieve home front economic security. Though the Democrats gained a stronger hold in the House of Representatives, the Republicans made some gains in the Senate with the support of higher-income, white Protestant, and Midwestern voters.

Politics as usual

The Democratic coalition of diverse voters, forged during the Great Depression, stayed intact throughout the war years. The conservative coalition of Republicans and Southern Democrats remained strong and increasingly influenced home front politics. In the 1944 election, the last public election held during the war, the home front remained politically much the same as before the war. The war had brought little political change, though debate over domestic issues grew more heated.

The 1944 election was the last time Southerners would vote so strongly for the Democratic presidential candidate. The war had intensified racial conflict in the South as blacks moved into already overcrowded towns to work in war industry jobs. Racial concerns began to dominate Southern politics, and white Southerners turned away from the Democratic Party because it supported increased civil liberties (protection of certain basic rights from government interference, such as freedom of speech and religion) for racial minorities.

End of a political era

For most Americans Roosevelt remained the top political figure in the United States through 1944—a symbol of home front security and a champion of the common man. Roosevelt's presidency ended on April 12, 1945, when he died suddenly of a brain hemorrhage (bleeding in the brain) while vacationing at his Georgia retreat. His vice president, Harry Truman, took over as president and led America to war's end. Truman soon faced major decisions: how to handle Germany's surrender in May and whether to use atomic bombs (a bomb whose massive explosive force comes from a nuclear reaction involving uranium or plutonium) to end the war with Japan. Truman also continued Roosevelt's home front agenda, promising a strong government role in the postwar economy.

For More Information

Books

Fleming, Thomas J. *The New Dealers' War: F.D.R. and the War within World War II.* New York: Basic Books, 2001.

Foner, Eric. *The Story of American Freedom.* New York: W. W. Norton, 1998.

Freidel, Frank. *Franklin D. Roosevelt: A Rendezvous with Destiny.* New York: Little, Brown & Co., 1990.

Goodwin, Doris Kearns. *No Ordinary Time: Franklin and Eleanor Roosevelt, the Home Front in World War II.* New York: Simon & Schuster, 1994.

Morgan, Ted. *FDR: A Biography.* New York: Simon & Schuster, 1985.

Web Sites

Franklin D. Roosevelt Library and Museum. http://www.fdrlibrary.marist.edu (accessed on June 30, 2004).

Minorities on the Home Front

Historian Allan M. Winkler, in his 1986 book *Home Front U.S.A.: America During World War II*, provides the following saying, which was familiar among black Americans during World War II (1939–45), "Here lies a black man killed fighting a yellow man for the protection of a white man." This saying reflected the wartime frustrations of many minorities in the United States. Americans on the home front generally supported the Allies' fight against the Axis powers of Germany, Italy, and Japan during World War II. The country was united in its patriotic desire to win the war. However, American minorities felt a contradiction in the wartime experience. While they were fighting overseas to save democracy, freedoms at home were still limited for people of color. Strong racial prejudices, centuries old, still existed in the United States, and racial conflicts on the home front escalated during the war years. Throughout the war, black Americans fought hard for new opportunities on the home front, with limited success; Japanese Americans had their rights as U.S. citizens ignored; and Mexican Americans, though welcomed into the job market, faced the same prejudices as they had in the past.

Black Americans

When the United States entered World War II in late 1941, the largest racial minority group in the United States was black Americans. They made up about 10 percent of the general population. After being freed from slavery only a few generations earlier, blacks still faced daily racial discrimination. In the South, where 75 percent of black Americans lived, racism was particularly bad. In many Southern states the so-called Jim Crow laws enforced legalized segregation (the separation of blacks and whites) in public places such as schools, theaters, and restaurants. In the North, urban ghettos (a section of a city where minorities live, often with overcrowding and poverty) and slums were growing as blacks migrated from the rural South to seek jobs. The National Association for the Advancement of Colored People (NAACP) and other organizations fought discrimination and segregation, but progress was slow. Blacks continued to be denied access to better education and higher-paying jobs, and life expectancy (the average lifespan of a group of population of people) for black Americans was considerably shorter than for white Americans. Discrimination continued throughout World War II, both in the military and in the civilian workforce.

Black Americans in military service

Like other minorities in America, black Americans hoped that the nation's war needs might improve

General Benjamin O. Davis (left) and Lieutenant Lee Rayford in 1945. *The Library of Congress.*

race relations on the home front. The United States needed people to help fight the war, and blacks hoped that serving in the military would bring them fair treatment, both in the service and at home. However, a great deal of racial prejudice was ingrained in the military, from top officers to lower ranks. As a result, at the beginning of the war the military draft favored whites over blacks. Blacks who enlisted in the military were assigned to service positions on the home front rather than to overseas combat units.

Keep us flying!

BUY WAR BONDS

A World War II poster advertising war bonds and featuring a member of the Tuskegee Airmen. *National Archives.*

The army, the air force, and the marines excluded blacks totally at the beginning of the war. In the navy, blacks served only as waiters. Faced with pressure on the home front to change its policy, the army formed several all-black combat units and promoted a black officer, Colonel Benjamin O. Davis (1877–1970), to the rank of brigadier general in October 1940. He was previously a colonel, but President Franklin D. Roosevelt (1882–1945; served 1933–45) was under pressure during the 1940 election campaign from black voters because of the continued racially segregated military. However, the black units could only be led by white officers; Secretary of War Henry Stimson (1867–1950) believed blacks were mentally unfit to be battlefield officers. Many of the white officers assigned to lead black units also had strong racial prejudices and, thus, did not believe blacks could acquire sufficient technical skills for certain tasks or provide leadership. Proposals to integrate combat units drew a negative response from these officers. General George C. Marshall (1880–1959), for example, said that integration would be bad for morale. Even blood donated for medical needs was segregated. Following the guidance of the American Red Cross, the army also kept the blood plasma of blacks and whites separate.

Most black servicemen were assigned to home front service units, where they unloaded supplies, maintained vehicles and equipment, and built barracks and other facilities. Discrimination on the home front against black soldiers was common and widespread. In Kansas a restaurant served German prisoners of war being transported to prisoner camps but not their accompanying black American soldiers.

Progress was made despite these major social hurdles. Black representation in the army rose from less than 98,000 in November 1941 to almost

468,000 in December 1942. The navy began recruiting blacks in 1942, and by late 1944 there were five hundred black sailors. The U.S. Marine Corps also began recruiting blacks. Among the 504,000 U.S. troops serving overseas in the spring of 1943, 79,000 were black. The only black army division to see combat was the Ninety-Second Infantry. In the air force the all-black Ninety-Ninth Pursuit Squadron out of Tuskegee, Alabama, known as the Tuskegee Airmen, excelled in providing protection to bomber squadrons. Bomber squadrons were eager to have the Ninety-Ninth assigned to protect them. Overall, more than a million black Americans would serve in the armed forces throughout the war. Blacks who served abroad returned to the home front with an expanded view of the world and a better appreciation of their abilities. Black Americans were treated more fairly in foreign countries than in the United States and in the military they were given opportunities to develop skills and show their abilities; these opportunities were generally not provided on the home front.

Jobs on the home front

As mobilization of war industries began in 1940, black Americans were still suffering from a 20 percent unemployment rate; the unemployment rate of white Americans at the time was about 10 percent. Black Americans' family income was one-third of what white families made. Blacks worked mostly in unskilled positions, and only 5 percent of black males held professional, white-collar jobs, mostly with black-owned businesses in black communities. Blacks were at first denied access to the new, high-paying war industry jobs. Many companies had "whites only" hiring policies. In 1940, 100,000 workers were employed in the aircraft industry, but only 240 of them were black. These black employees were commonly assigned to low-paying, unskilled positions, serving as janitors and garage attendants, for example. Black women worked primarily as domestic servants or on farms.

Seeing such open discrimination by defense contractors motivated A. Philip Randolph (1889–1979) to take action. Randolph was a black union leader and president of the Brotherhood of Sleeping Car Porters, the only all-black union. In January 1941 he called for blacks to march on Washington, D.C., to protest job discrimination. The march was set for July 1. Randolph expected between fifty thousand and a hundred thousand people to join the march. President Roosevelt feared that the event could cause violence in the nation's capital. He also thought it could set back his efforts to unite Americans for the war effort. On June 19, less than two weeks before the scheduled march, Roosevelt met with Randolph and other black leaders to search for a compromise. Randolph and the other black leaders bargained hard for a ban on racial discrimination in private industry and federal employment; they also asked for an end to segregation in the military. When Roosevelt agreed to most of these terms, Randolph called off the march.

To make his agreement with Randolph official, President Roosevelt issued an executive order, Executive Order 8802. It was the first official action Roosevelt had taken on civil rights (rights of personal liberty granted by the U.S. Constitution, such as the right to vote and freedom of speech, assembly, and religion) since he entered office in 1933. In fact, it was the first civil rights action taken by any U.S. president since the 1870s, following the Civil War (1861–65). Roosevelt's executive order banned discrimination in defense industries and government but did not end segregation in the military. The order also established the Fair Employment Practices Commission (FEPC), which was put in charge of investigating racial discrimination in the war industries. The FEPC was underfunded and held little power to institute changes, so it had to rely on publicity and persuasion. The commission sometimes threatened to draft into the military those business owners who were shown to discriminate by hiring whites when more qualified blacks had applied. At first the FEPC was placed within the Office of Production Management (OPM). Then it was moved, first to the War Production Board (WPB), then to the War Manpower Commission (WMC), and finally in mid-1943 to the Executive Office of the President. There it became more aggressive in pursuing cases of discrimination. FEPC received eight thousand complaints and resolved about one-third of them until it was disbanded in 1946.

Anti-discrimination measures continue

Roosevelt's executive order helped reduce racial discrimination, but civil rights activists still had plenty of work to do. Polls in 1942 indicated that the majority of white Americans denied any race problems existed in the United States. They believed that blacks worked in inferior jobs because of personal shortcomings, not racial discrimination. Hoping to accelerate positive change on the home front, Americans in favor of ending racial segregation in public places formed the Committee on Racial Equality (CORE) in 1942. They organized various public demonstrations, including sit-ins (occupying seats in a racially segregated public place to protest discrimination) in movie theaters and restaurants.

Faced with unrelenting discrimination on the home front, black Americans adopted the Double V campaign in 1942. "Double V" stood for two victories: military victory overseas and home front victory over racial discrimination. The *Pittsburgh Courier,* a popular black newspaper, first announced the campaign in February 1942, encouraging readers to support both victory goals. The newspaper immediately received an overwhelming response from black Americans in support of the Double V idea. The paper was a staunch critic of Roosevelt and actually endorsed the Republican candidates for president against Roosevelt in 1940 and 1944. The *Courier* asserted that Roosevelt had failed to support civil rights and new leadership was needed. President Roosevelt and others in his administration worried that the aggressive tone of the Double V articles and the active campaigning to end racial discrimination that would appear in each issue of the paper could damage national unity—unity that was crucial to the home front war effort. The Double V campaign had succeeded in gaining the attention it sought.

Racial tensions

Worker shortages began to occur in 1943 as American men joined the military in increasing numbers. The shortages meant new job opportunities for black Americans, who eagerly moved to urban areas to work in the war industry. About seven hundred thousand blacks relocated during the war; roughly four hundred thousand of them came from the South. They settled mostly in large cities, including San Francisco and Los Angeles, California, where new industrial centers had sprung up, and Detroit, Michigan, home of the giant Willow Run plant where large bomber aircraft were produced. With housing in short supply in war industry centers, black workers were often forced to live in high-density ghettos such as the South Side of Chicago. Social services, like food and healthcare, for the impoverished and unemployed in these overcrowded areas were in short supply, and local officials did not go out of their way to provide housing relief for the overcrowded conditions.

Living in overcrowded areas and suffering from continued discrimination, blacks were frustrated. Whites were unwelcoming, partly because of racial prejudice and partly because the black newcomers stretched housing and other resources that were already scarce. Under these conditions, increased interactions between blacks and whites led to race riots and fighting. In 1943 major incidents occurred in Newark, New Jersey; El Paso, Texas; Centreville, Mississippi; Beaumont, Texas; and Camp Stewart, Georgia. When twelve black workers were promoted at a shipyard in Mobile, Alabama, white workers rioted and injured twenty blacks. In Philadelphia, Pennsylvania, white transit workers went on strike when eight black motormen were hired to drive the streetcars. President Roosevelt had to send armed troops to end the strike and to act as security guards on the cars.

The worst racial incident occurred in Detroit, where severe overcrowding led to increased tensions. In June 1943, during an intense heat wave, white teenagers and black teenagers began fighting in a crowded city park known as Belle Isle. The fighting escalated to a riot when a rumor spread that whites had thrown a black woman and her baby off a bridge. After dark, groups of blacks went through the city, looting (to rob by force) and fighting. After thirty-six hours of violence, U.S. troops were brought in to restore order. By the time calm was restored, thirty-four people had died, twenty-five of them black, and almost seven hundred had been injured. Some

Police shoot tear gas into a crowd of white rioters, seen fleeing from a black section of downtown, during the June 1943 race riots in Detroit, Michigan. © Bettmann/Corbis. Reproduced by permission.

$2 million of property damage had been done. Local police had done little to stop the beatings of blacks but did shoot several black looters. Another riot erupted two months later in August in New York City's Harlem district after a rumor started that police had killed a black soldier. Black mobs swept through the business district, smashing windows and looting. Six blacks were killed and three hundred injured. Following these riots various communities formed commissions to find ways to prevent further rioting.

Coverage of the riots in newspapers and on the radio brought public attention to the plight of black Americans, so whites became somewhat more aware of the problems faced by the black minority.

By 1944 the U.S. Employment Service, which helped find workers for critical war industries, quit accepting whites-only requests from employers, and the National Labor Relations Board stopped certifying unions that excluded blacks.

Home front gains

The number of employed blacks rose from 4.4 million in April 1940 to 5.3 million in April 1944 (1.2 million of these workers held industrial positions). By 1945 more than 8 percent of war industry jobs were held by blacks, up from 3 percent in 1942. The number of skilled black workers doubled as new trades opened up. Most of the increase in job opportunities came in the last years of the war. Blacks also increased their numbers in federal employment from 1942 to 1945—from sixty thousand to two hundred thousand—and received better-paying positions.

President Roosevelt provided little personal support to the cause of racial equality, neither through promoting legislation to protect the rights of blacks nor making racial equality a priority in his administration. He was much more interested in getting production rolling and winning the war. He did not want to get involved in controversial home front issues that would distract from these goals. As a result, discrimination still loomed large in the United States. Blacks were often the first to be laid off when war industries began cutting back. The Fair Employment Practices Commission (FEPC), which had been in charge of investigating racial discrimination in the war industry, ceased its existence in 1946. Many blacks felt there was still a need for this commission, even though the war industry jobs had come to an end.

World War II brought at least one major change to black Americans: Racial barriers in the military and in industry were lowered. Many blacks considered the war a turning point in their struggle to gain better jobs. In addition, increased black activism during wartime laid the foundation for the civil rights movement that would swell in numbers and eventually pressure Congress into passing major legislation in the mid-1960s to guarantee the exercise of certain basic rights, such as equal access to public places and relief from discriminatory voting requirements. The National Association for the Advancement of Colored People (NAACP) increased its membership during the war years, growing from fifty thousand to almost half a million.

Enemy aliens

After the fall of France to Germany in June 1940, fear of political radicals on the home front who might be sympathetic to Germany and Italy grew. On June 28, 1940, Congress passed the Smith Act, which made it illegal to promote the violent overthrow of the U.S. government. The act also required aliens (immigrants who are citizens of a foreign country) to register with the U.S. government, be fingerprinted, and list any organizations they belonged to. Aliens associated with Communist or Fascist organizations would be deported. (Communist organizations promote a political and economic system that bans private ownership of property and limits individual freedoms in order to maintain greater government control. Fascist organizations promote dictatorships based on strong nationalism and often racism. Both Communist and Fascist ideas conflict with America's political and economic systems, democracy and capitalism.) When the Smith Act was passed, aliens made up 3 percent of the U.S. population. A month before the Smith Act became law, President Roosevelt had authorized wiretaps on anyone suspected of subversive (working secretly to overthrow a government) activity. With the Smith Act in place, aliens were targeted for wiretapping. With fears of aliens growing, defense contractors refused to hire workers who looked like they might be from a foreign country, regardless of their citizenship. But when worker shortages began to grow in 1941, Roosevelt spoke out against such job discrimination. He stated that discriminating against aliens and immigrants was wrong and not helpful in the war effort. He asked the Fair Employment Practices Commission (FEPC) to make sure industry employers cooperated with the government's antidiscrimination policies.

After the surprise Japanese attack on U.S. military bases in Pearl Harbor, Hawaii, on December 7, 1941, the United States officially entered World War II. All Italian, German, and Japanese aliens in the United States were designated "enemy aliens." Enemy aliens could not possess shortwave radios or cameras, and they were restricted from traveling near important defense installations. They had to carry special identification and could be detained or even deported readily.

The Federal Bureau of Investigation (FBI) arrested some enemy aliens immediately after the attack on Pearl Harbor. They were often taken away abruptly, without any announcement or explanation to their families, and then placed in detention centers established by the U.S. Department of Justice. Eight of these detention centers—essentially prison camps—were located in Idaho, Montana, New Mexico, North Dakota, and Texas. Later the camps also held German and Japanese prisoners of war. Some Japanese Americans—who were U.S. citizens and not aliens—were taken to two Department of Justice centers called citizen isolation centers in Moab, Utah, and Leupp, Arizona.

In the next few months following Pearl Harbor, U.S. officials debated what to do with all the enemy aliens. Options included mass relocation or continuing detention. Finding little evidence of subversive activity, the government soon eased restrictions on Italian and German aliens. Japanese Americans faced a far more uncertain future.

Japanese Americans

Of all the various groups considered enemy aliens, Japanese Americans and aliens suffered the worst treatment by the U.S. government. The relatively small Japanese American population had always been the target of racial discrimination in the United States. Japanese Americans faced discrimination in hiring and housing. They were barred from marrying whites and were banned from some public places. They could not vote or own land, even if they were American citizens. About 127,000 Japanese Americans lived in the United States at the time of the Pearl Harbor attack. Most of them—approximately 112,000—lived in California and along the western coast. They made important contributions to the region's economy through their agricultural production and harvest (principally vegetables) and their ethnic businesses, such as restaurants. However, they held little political power. About 80,000 were Nisei (pronounced "NEE-say"), or native-born U.S. citizens; their children were called Sansei (pronounced "SAN-say"). Roughly 47,000 were Issei (pronounced "EE-say"), Japanese immigrants born in Japan who were not American citizens. Immigration laws passed in 1924 prevented Japanese immigrants from attaining U.S. citizenship.

Executive Order 9066

Because of widespread discrimination, Japanese Americans lived in isolated communities. That raised even more suspicion from outsiders. The surprise raid on Pearl Harbor, carried out by Japanese bombers, had taken the lives of 2,300 American military personnel. This created feelings of hatred against Japan and Japanese people, and some members of the public began to pressure the government to remove Japanese Americans from their West Coast homes. Local

A military police officer posts a notice requiring evacuation of all Japanese living on Bainbridge Island, Washington, in 1942.
© Bettman/Corbis. Reproduced by permission.

newspapers and politicians fanned the flames of hysteria by mentioning the possibility that Japanese Americans might be conducting espionage and

Japanese American children awaiting baggage inspection upon arrival at the assembly center in Turlock, California, May 2, 1945. After a temporary stay, they and their families will be transported to detention camps. *© Corbis. Reproduced by permission.*

sabotage. After initially resisting the pressure, Roosevelt finally signed the removal order, Executive Order 9066, on February 19, 1942. All Japanese Americans were affected, even those with only one grandparent of Japanese ancestry. To oversee the removal, the War Department established the War Relocation Authority (WRA), which was headed by Milton Eisenhower (1899–1985), brother of General Dwight Eisenhower (1890–1969). However,

Eisenhower left the position after only three months and was replaced by Dillon S. Meyer.

Under the presidential order Japanese Americans had to register at control stations by the end of March. Evacuation notices were posted in prominent public places in and around Japanese American communities. Each family was issued a number and advised what they could take and when to leave. A total of 120,000 Japanese Americans, including men, women, and children, were rounded up beginning in March 1942. Seventy percent of them were U.S. citizens. They could only bring what they could carry, and they had to leave their pets behind. Other Americans took advantage of their plight by buying the homes, cars, and stores from the Japanese Americans at very low prices. The removal of Japanese Americans eliminated some competition in agriculture and small business, a welcome consequence for their competitors. There was no evidence that Japanese Americans were a security threat to the United States. Their relocation was the government's attempt to eliminate a perceived threat.

About 150,000 Japanese Americans lived in Hawaii, making up one-third of the island's population. U.S. military commanders in Hawaii were less prejudiced against these Japanese Americans. They selected a few hundred whose loyalty to the United States was suspect and sent them to the U.S. mainland for detention.

Detained Japanese Americans were taken to temporary holding areas called assembly centers. These centers were located at fairgrounds, exposition centers, stockyards, and racetracks, and at camps no longer used by the Civilian Conservation Corps, a federal agency that provided jobs for young men during the Great Depression. Life drastically changed with the loss of privacy and freedom. For example, families held at racetracks, who not long ago lived in their comfortable homes, were now crowded into horse stalls that acted as their home. The average stay for a family at an assembly center was one hundred days before being transported to a detention camp. At the centers government officials gave the detainees loyalty tests to help determine who the troublemakers might be.

The WRA soon discovered that communities located inland, away from the coast, were unwilling to accept the detainees. Therefore, ten permanent detention camps were hastily constructed in seven states, well away from existing communities. The camps were situated in the barren desert country of California (two camps), Arizona (two camps), Utah, Wyoming, Colorado, and Idaho. The two other camps were located in Arkansas swamplands. Surrounded by barbed wire and armed guards, the bleak camps consisted of wooden barracks covered with tar paper. Bathing areas, toilets, and eating facilities were public, used by all the detainees, and sanitation was poor. Shocked by the lack of privacy, women wore swimsuits to take showers. The barracks were divided by thin walls into one-room apartments. The apartments were lit

Did you know?

- Some of the Japanese American relocation camps have been preserved and interpreted for the public to help guard against similar occurrences in the future. The camp of Manzanar in California has been designated a national historic site and is operated by the U.S. National Park Service. Only the foundations of buildings and traces of the Japanese-style gardens remain.

- On June 29, 2001, a national monument in Washington, D.C., was dedicated to the memory of Japanese Americans in World War II. The memorial contains the names of the eight hundred Japanese Americans who were killed in combat.

with bare lightbulbs and contained very little furniture except cots for sleeping. Each one-room apartment housed one family, but because the walls were so thin, there was no privacy; families could hear all that went on within their barracks. Outside temperatures ranged from suffocating heat in the summer to temperatures below zero in the winter. Sand would blow in through cracks in the thin walls.

Camp life was regimented. Children from elementary to high school age were expected to attend classes. Every morning all the detainees were required to attend the raising of

A view of the Manzanar War Relocation Center in California. Families were housed in the bleak, wooden barracks that line either side of the road. *The Library of Congress.*

the American flag and say the Pledge of Allegiance. Detainees were not allowed to do much else, so morale was very low. Some camp jobs were available, such as making camouflage netting for the military, but there was very little incentive to work. Mental depression became a major problem. Riots and fights sometimes would break out among the detainees.

Appalled by their undeserved detention and the deplorable conditions of the camps, several thousand Japanese Americans angrily renounced their U.S. citizenship. Eighteen thousand "disloyal" detainees were sent to camp at Tule Lake, California. Tule Lake, located on a dry lake bed in the desert, was the largest relocation camp. The smallest camp was Grenada in Colorado, which held just over 7,300 detainees. The Heart Mountain camp in Wyoming held 11,000 detainees; it was the third largest community in the state.

Detention camps close

By 1943 detainees who could show evidence of an employment offer were allowed to leave. Although it was

Remembering Life in Relocation Camps

Many books have been published that describe what life was like in the remote Japanese American relocation camps; some are firsthand accounts. The first such book, *Citizen 13660* by Mine Obuko, was published in 1946. Later publications include *I Am an American: A True Story of Japanese Internment* by Jerry Stanley (New York: Crown Publishers, 1994); *The Invisible Thread* by Yoshiko Uchida (New York: Beech Tree Paperback, 1995); *Only What We Could Carry: The Japanese American Internment Experience,* edited by Lawson Fusao Inada (Berkeley, CA: Heyday Books, 2000); *The*

Children of Topaz: The Story of a Japanese-American Internment Camp by Michael O. Tunnell and George W. Chilcoat (New York: Holiday House, 1996); *Remembering Manzanar: Life in a Japanese Relocation Camp* by Michael L. Cooper (New York: Clarion Books, 2002); and *Japanese American Internment during World War II: A History and Reference Guide* by Wendy Ng (Westport, CT: Greenwood Press, 2002). The Public Broadcasting Service (PBS) first televised a program titled *Children of the Camps* in 1999. Copies are available from the Asian American Telecommunications Association.

not an easy task to find an employer while living in such isolation, some thirty-five thousand detainees succeeded and were able to leave the camps by late 1944.

All the remaining detainees were released in December 1944 as the war was drawing to an end. (Many did not leave until later in 1945 when the camps actually closed.) However, for many of them life did not get much easier for a while. The government provided very little assistance for them to reenter society. Some were even fearful to return to U.S. society, because of the general hostility toward Japanese Americans. Many Japanese Americans were able to

integrate back into mainstream society, although their resentment and psychological distress lingered.

For almost three years, Japanese Americans had been stripped of their rights, their dignity, and their property, even though there was never any evidence that they were a security threat. No Japanese American was ever charged with anti-American activities. According to estimates, detainees lost some $400 million in property and income. When the detention was legally challenged, however, the U.S. Supreme Court, in 1944, sided with the government, saying that detention was judged a military necessity.

Japanese American soldiers from the 100th Battalion aboard the USS *General M.C. Meigs,* September 1, 1944. © *The Mariners' Museum/Corbis. Reproduced by permission.*

Japanese Americans in World War II

During World War II thirty-three thousand Japanese Americans were serving in the U.S. armed forces. In 1943 Nisei (native-born U.S. citizens) became eligible to join. The 442nd Regimental Combat Team was composed entirely of Japanese Americans. This group fought in Europe and became the most decorated army unit of World War II. One of the decorated Nisei veterans was Daniel Inouye (1924–), who would later represent Hawaii as a senator. In January 1944 Nisei became eligible for the military draft; two from the Heart Mountain detention camp were Medal of Honor winners. Ironically, they were fighting for the same government that imprisoned their families on the home front. Some detainees in the camps contributed to the war effort by making handmade blankets for the Red Cross or buying U.S. war bonds with the small government allowances they were given while detained.

In 1959 U.S. citizenship was restored to Japanese Americans who had renounced it in protest of their treatment. In 1988, more than four decades after the detention, President Ronald Reagan (1911–2004; served 1981–89) signed legislation authorizing payment of $20,000 to each surviving person who had been detained in the camps.

Mexican Americans

The war years provided jobs for Mexican Americans, who only a few years earlier had faced severe racial discrimination and even deportation. About 1.5 million Spanish-speaking people lived in the United States at the time the nation entered the war in 1941. Mexican Americans were by far the most numerous of the Spanish-speaking population. Most lived in the Southwest and West. Some 350,000 Mexican Americans served in the armed forces during World War II.

Like black Americans, Mexican Americans were not able to find jobs at the beginning of the war. For example, no Mexican Americans were employed in Los Angeles shipyards in 1941. However, worker shortages soon opened opportunities for minorities, and many Mexican Americans then took jobs in the war industries. Most worked in the West Coast shipyards and airplane factories. By 1944 seventeen thousand were employed in the Los Angeles shipyards. The hiring of Mexican Americans was also seen in other war industrial centers. To help Americans, including Mexican Americans, living in small isolated communities in the Southwest gain the skills needed for better-paying industrial jobs, the Department of Labor's Office of Education established vocational schools. These schools were located in various cities, including Santa Fe and Albuquerque, New Mexico, and training included plumbing, welding, and mechanics.

As many Americans left rural life for military service or higher-paying jobs in the war industry, farm workers grew scarce. U.S. growers looked to Mexico for aliens (immigrants who hold citizenship in a foreign country) who could assist with the work. However, because Mexican American aliens had suffered so much discrimination in the 1930s (through mass deportation to Mexico, including even those with U.S. citizenship who had never lived in Mexico), the Mexican government would not immediately agree to a new worker program. Instead, Mexican officials insisted that the workers' basic human rights be protected. They reached an agreement with the United States in 1942; the agreement provided for food, shelter, medical care, and transportation for alien workers. Several hundred thousand Mexican workers entered the United States through the new worker program, known as the Braceros program (*braceros* is a Spanish word meaning "day laborers" or "people who work with their arms"). Despite the safeguards, these workers still faced considerable discrimination and poor working conditions in America's fields.

Discrimination in housing, wages, and jobs was present in the industrial centers as well, and it contributed to the formation of Mexican American youth gangs who resented the dominant U.S. culture. Some Mexican American youths wore "zoot suits"—consisting of full coats reaching to mid-thigh, trousers flared at the knees but tight at the ankles, thick-soled shoes, felt "pancake" hats, and long key chains—as a symbol of cultural pride. These outfits were meant to intimidate white Americans because the outfits were different and defiant against standard U.S. cultural values. Violent clashes broke out when servicemen on leave in the cities made advances toward Mexican American young women, many of whom were girlfriends of the gang members. In June 1943 the "zoot suit riot" broke out in Los Angeles, California, when servicemen, claiming revenge, attacked and beat Mexican Americans wearing zoot suits. Civilians and military police stood by and watched as the fighting went on. The Los Angeles City Council eventually banned zoot suits in an attempt to head off further conflict. The Los Angeles incident and similar clashes in other cities raised awareness about prejudice against Mexican Americans. As a result, local citizen groups began working to reduce prejudice and improve the economic status of Mexican Americans.

"Americans All"

"Americans All" was a key slogan that was used to unite U.S. citizens during World War II. The phrase suggests that all Americans shared equal status. However, racial minorities in the United States were not treated as equals by most white Americans. They did not have the same opportunities as white Americans did to contribute to the war effort, on the home front or on the battlefield. Nonetheless, with the dramatic exception of the Japanese Americans, minorities did gain entrance into mainstream America during the war, by serving with distinction in the armed forces or by moving to urban areas where they could improve their economic status. The fears and suspicions of the war years inspired legislation like the Smith Act, but the United States continued to grant citizenship to qualified aliens—two million in all—throughout World War II.

Many black Americans and Mexican Americans who served in the military saw greater acceptance of racial diversity overseas. When they returned to the home front, they refused to accept discrimination any longer. For example, many blacks originally from the South chose to resettle elsewhere after returning. (The South had a lengthy, well-established tradition of racial discrimination extending back to the slavery days of the eighteenth and nineteenth centuries.) Black Americans worked hard to end discrimination, and their efforts built the foundation for the civil rights movement of the 1950s and 1960s.

For More Information

Books

Acuna, Rodolfo. *Occupied America: A History of Chicanos*. 5th ed. New York: Longman, 2003.

Cooper, Michael L. *Fighting for Honor: Japanese Americans and World War II*. New York: Clarion Books, 2000.

Daniels, Roger. *Prisoners without Trial: Japanese Americans in World War II*. New York: Hill & Wang, 1993.

Fremon, David K. *Japanese-American Internment in American History*. Springfield, NJ: Enslow Publishers, 1996.

Kelley, Robin D. G., and Earl Lewis. *To Make Our World Anew: A History of African Americans*. New York: Oxford University Press, 2000.

Murray, Alice Yang. *What Did the Internment of Japanese Americans Mean?* Boston: Bedford/St. Martin's, 2000.

Saunders, Kay, and Roger Daniels, eds. *Alien Justice: Wartime Internment in Australia and North America* Portland, OR: International Specialized Book Services, 2000.

Stanley, Jerry. *I Am an American: A True Story of Japanese Internment*. New York: Crown, 1994.

Takaki, Ronald T. *Democracy and Race: Asian Americans and World War II*. New York: Chelsea House, 1995.

Takaki, Ronald T. *Double Victory: A Multicultural History of America in World War II*. Boston: Little, Brown & Company, 2000.

Wynn, Neil A. *The Afro-American and the Second World War*. New York: Holmes & Meier Publishers, 1976.

Web Sites

Japanese American National Museum. http://www.janm.org (accessed on July 1, 2004).

National Archives and Records Administration. http://www.nara.gov (contains many digital images of Japanese American internment in section on War Relocation Authority) (accessed on July 1, 2004).

National Japanese American Historical Society. http://www.nikkeiheritage.org (accessed on July 1, 2004).

Mobilization of Women

7

At the start of World War II (1939–45) most Americans still held an old-fashioned notion of women's place in society; that is, they believed that a woman's proper role was in the home, working as a housewife, caring for her husband and children and handling the household chores. Husbands were expected to make the money on which a family lived; they controlled the household finances and held ultimate authority in the home. In U.S. society at large, men also controlled politics and the economy. World War II disrupted these patterns, thrusting men and women into new roles and activities related to the war. Between 1942 and 1945 about fifty million women over the age of fourteen lived in the United States. Roughly 90 percent of them were white, 9 percent were black, 0.3 percent were Native American, and 0.1 percent were Japanese American.

During the war women found new job opportunities in factories and shipyards. They also had increased opportunities to work as support personnel in governmental positions, such as in the many temporary federal agencies set up for wartime. Those who stayed at home to raise their families faced new challenges: The job was lonely and more difficult for anyone whose husband was serving overseas. Shopping for necessities was also more demanding because of the complicated wartime rationing system and shortages of various goods.

Work experience

U.S. employment records have been kept since the end of the 1930s, when the Social Security system was first established and activated. (Social Security is a federal program that provides economic assistance for citizens including the aged, retired, unemployed, and disabled.) Statistics show that by the late 1930s most women entered the workforce upon completion of their schooling and worked until they got married, while men entered the workforce and stayed. Men worked toward promotions and pay raises, but women generally did not. At the start of World War II women who already had work experience and those enrolled in high school and college would become the first women recruits for the wartime industry labor force.

Twelve million men left the U.S. labor force to join the military between 1940 and 1944. At the same time, industry was mobilizing to produce massive amounts of war materials. Approximately eighteen million additional workers would need to be hired to meet production goals. In 1940 there were still eight million Americans who were unemployed, a holdover from the Great Depression, the severe economic crisis of the 1930s.

The unemployed were the first people hired for war industry jobs. Experienced working women, women with a high school or college education, and older men were the next to be hired. In 1940 out of the approximately fifty million women in the United States, about twelve million were in the labor force. By 1945, over nineteen million women were employed. Women gained the most positions in clerical and retail sales, factories, and agriculture jobs (see Chapter 4: Agricultural Mobilization). Women also held many more federal government jobs. Fewer women held teaching positions and other professional jobs, and fewer women chose to work in domestic services. Women made an exodus from teaching when they saw that higher-paying war industry jobs were available. Some joined the military. Likewise, many women in domestic services, mostly black Americans employed as maids and cooks, moved into better jobs in war-related industries.

Propaganda campaign

Women who were already in the workforce in 1941, mostly single women, were the first to take wartime manufacturing positions. Dime store and department store clerks and restaurant employees left their low-paying jobs for work in aircraft and shipbuilding factories. Other women left school to take advantage of the wartime employment boom. Once these two groups had been hired, there were still many job openings, so government workforce experts went to

"Rosie the Riveter," the symbol of working women during World War II. *The Library of Congress.*

great lengths to urge married women to enter the workforce. Through the War Advertising Council and the media (magazines and newspapers), the federal government and the war industry mounted a giant propaganda campaign. The campaign attempted to end the cycle that American women had traditionally followed—attending school, working a year or two until marriage, and then having children.

"Rosie the Riveter" was the "poster girl" for the campaign. The idea for Rosie came from a wartime song called "Rosie the Riveter." Rosie's image appeared on posters and in magazines. Dressed in coveralls and displaying the muscle in her arm, Rosie was indeed a riveting character. People were not accustomed to seeing women dressed in pants, but factories seeking women workers advertised how glamorous their women employees looked in their spotless and nicely pressed slacks and shirts.

Between 1942 and 1945 between six million and seven million American women reentered the workforce or entered it for the first time. Many took jobs as typists, retail clerks, waitresses, and domestic workers, replacing those who had gone into war industries. Some were able to find factory positions. Fifteen percent of married women in the United States were employed in 1940; by war's end 25 percent were employed. Despite all the propaganda, most married women chose not to enter the workforce.

Very few young married women with children under six years of age

Painting the American insignia on airplane wings was a job that many women working in the war industry did with precision and skill. *The Library of Congress.*

entered the workforce. Young mothers were strongly encouraged to stay home and raise their children. Although the Federal Works Agency spent $50 million on daycare centers for working mothers, most were no more than half filled. Most Americans, women and men alike, looked on daycare centers with disdain, considering them harmful to child development. Working mothers preferred to leave their children with nonworking relatives.

It became quite common for male and female factory workers to work side by side during the World War II years. *Getty Images. Reproduced by permission.*

Factory work

Before the United States officially entered World War II in late 1941, American industry was already busy producing war materials for the Allied forces. However, few employers considered hiring women for factory jobs. Historically it was a common belief that women had no ability to do mechanical or technical jobs. Women and men were expected to fill stereotypical roles, so two labor markets existed—one for men and one for women. Women were given jobs as secretaries, office clerks, retail clerks, teachers, librarians, and nurses. Black women were relegated to domestic services. Factory jobs were for men only. However, when the United States entered the war and American men joined the military to serve overseas, a monumental attitude change was required. As millions of male workers left the workplace, the resulting labor shortage forced employers to begin hiring women for work traditionally handled by men.

The attitude of many employers changed quickly. Managers, often called foremen, began hiring women for factory jobs and were soon amazed: It was clear to them that women excelled in tasks requiring high degrees of dexterity and speed; women had patience for long-drawn-out jobs far surpassing that of male workers, such as installing complex electrical wiring systems in aircraft; and they were outstanding in production of instruments that required great accuracy in the measurements of components. Some munitions factories began hiring only women because of their fine motor skills (muscle control in arms and hands). Such skills were vital for wiring fuses for bombs or filling gun casings with gunpowder.

Foremen and eventually male coworkers began to accept inexperienced women workers who had been hired by necessity for factory jobs. Because women excelled at a variety of manufacturing tasks, they could quickly fill many unskilled positions with a minimum of training. For example, they easily mastered the repetitive motions of assembly line tasks. Most women war industry workers were employed in unskilled and semiskilled positions, leaving skilled positions to men.

Women were also good at inspecting jobs, for example, inspecting certain pieces before they moved on in the assembly line. Older women workers were especially good inspectors. Women did not often act as supervisors, except in textiles and clothing factories. Men consistently refused to work under a female supervisor. Women, too, showed a preference for male supervisors.

The riveters

National attention for women in the workforce focused on women employed in aircraft assembly, shipbuilding, munitions manufacturing, and directly related war industry jobs. The media glamorized women in this segment of the workforce. By early 1944 more than two and a half million women were employed in the war industries.

Walking through any U.S. manufacturing plant in November 1941, a person would have rarely, if ever, seen a woman in the factory rooms. Two years later nearly 35 percent of factory workers were women. War production efforts ended the idea that women could not do mechanical work. At Douglas Aircraft, 45 percent of workers were women, and it was the same at the Boeing and Glenn L. Martin aircraft plants. Some women moved up to

A woman works as a riveter on a bomber at Consolidated Aircraft Corp. in Fort Worth, Texas, in October 1942. *The Library of Congress.*

positions requiring higher skills. For example, the Glenn L. Martin plant had a female test crew that was responsible for the final ground testing of bomber planes; they adjusted every functioning part of the planes as needed. Theirs was the last test done before the plane was delivered to the military.

In 1939 thirty-six women worked in U.S. shipyards. By 1943 hundreds of thousands of women worked in shipyards across the country, doing work traditionally reserved for men. At the massive Kaiser shipyards women

What's a Riveter?

"Rosie the Riveter" was a government-sponsored artist's creation, a stylized drawing of a female war industry worker. Her image appeared on posters and in magazines across the nation; the government hoped the image would encourage women to join the workforce. Rosie the Riveter wore coveralls, rolled up at the sleeve to show her muscles, and her hair was tied in a scarf to protect it from factory machines. But what exactly did a riveter do?

Riveters assembled thousands of warplanes by joining together all the metal pieces of the aircraft. Riveting was actually a two-person job known as "riveting and bucking." Two women worked together: One woman shot rivets (metal pins with a head on one end used to fasten pieces of metal together) through the metal pieces with a riveting gun while the other flattened or "bucked" the protruding rivet on the other side to hold the pieces together. Thousands of riveting and bucking teams worked in war factories around the country.

operated the huge cranes that moved entire sections of ships into place for final assembly. Thousands worked as riveters (workers who join pieces of metal together by inserting and compressing metal pins, forming heads on both ends) and welders (workers who assembled sections of large ships by heating them and joining them together) in the war plants.

At munitions factories women operated machines involved in producing gun mechanisms. They wired fuses for bombs and filled bullets with powder. Some greased gun barrels, and others painted the barrels at the final production stage before the guns were shipped overseas.

In steel mills, where the structures and equipment dwarfed all humans, women were rebuilding furnaces, operating manipulating levers to move mill machinery, and performing chemical analysis and metal testing. In machine shops women were better able than men to assemble tiny parts for precision aircraft instruments. Women made up 50 percent of the production workers at the Sperry Gyroscope Company's plant on Long Island, New York. They made compasses, bombs and gun sights, and automatic pilots (electronic equipment that keeps aircraft flying at specific settings). At Eastman Kodak Company women rolled out film of all types.

Women also found jobs in logging and railroading, two industries that had previously hired men only—and only the toughest of men. Women worked for logging companies in the Northwest, the Southeast, and New England, replacing men who had joined the military. They cut branches off felled trees, directed logs through millponds, sorted logs, and drove the logging trucks. On the railroads, women worked side by side with men to maintain the railcars, the rail yards, and tracks.

Although women working in aircraft factories, shipyards, and munitions

Women welders at Ingalls Shipbuilding Corp, Pascagoula, Mississippi, in 1943. *National Archives photo no. 86-WWT-85-35 (World War II Photos).*

received the most attention from the media, women scientists also made significant contributions to the war effort. Before the war most scientific jobs were reserved for men. When the United States entered the war, women who had obtained undergraduate and advanced degrees in physics and engineering in the 1930s often found work for the first time. In defense plants they experimented with new scale models of ships and planes. Women chemists worked at Monsanto Chemical, Hercules Powder Company (manufacturers of explosive powder), and the Mellon Institute of Industrial Research in Pittsburgh. Many

industries set up programs with universities to train women to replace men who were in the military. Westinghouse Electric trained dozens of women in electrical engineering at Carnegie Institute of Technology. RCA and Purdue University cooperated to train women as radio engineering aides.

Difficulties for women in industry

Obtaining a job was only the first hurdle women faced. Once they had employment, their challenges

As the war progressed, women were slowly accepted into the traditionally male-oriented world of factory work. *The Library of Congress.*

multiplied. In newly opened war factories women generally started at the same pay rate as men. (Unions worked to maintain relatively equal pay for women and men in equivalent jobs, mainly because the unions feared that if women were paid less when hired, then the men's pay would also eventually be lowered.) However, women were usually hired for the lowest-paying jobs, and it was quite difficult for them to get promoted. Employers generally would not promote women workers until all male workers had been promoted as far as they could be; if any skilled jobs remained open at that point, an employer would consider promoting women to fill the positions.

Women also had difficulty with skilled male employees who refused to adequately train them. In the early 1940s, many men working in the war industries tended to resent female workers. They feared that women would work for lower wages, thus undermining men's wages. They also assumed that women would not take their jobs seriously and that they would not produce as much as men. Men resented any special privileges given to women, such as longer lunch or rest breaks. Women had to endure harassment, including sexual harassment, and insults from some men.

In addition to the immediate difficulties they faced on the job, women workers had to endure criticism from traditional-minded people, both men and women, who worried that war work would destroy women's femininity. Housewives chastised factory women for neglecting their own homes, wearing slacks (which were considered manly), and flirting with their men. Nevertheless, women workers generally won over their male coworkers in the same way they had won over management—with their hard work. Women worked and thrived, gained confidence in their skills, and saved their well-earned wages.

Outside the workplace, another difficulty existed for working women, particularly those who were married and those who had children. Most found it difficult and exhausting to manage their workload at home. Before, during, and after World War II, American women generally did all shopping, cleaning, and cooking for their families. Most war factories operated on a six-day, forty-eight-hour week, with round-the-clock shifts. Women often reported managing on six hours of sleep or less to get home duties done after work. Few wanted overtime work. Married women who had children often preferred evening or night shifts if their husbands worked the day shift; this way, one parent was always at home to care for the children. Working the evening shift also made it possible for women to shop at stores that were only open during the daytime. Working wives and working mothers had to juggle these tasks without any accommodation from their employers. There were no maternity or family benefits; in fact, if a working woman became pregnant, she was usually terminated.

Women and Labor Unions

Many of the war industries had contracts with labor unions, which meant that all the workers in those industries had to be union members. So, like their male coworkers, most women employed by factories during the war years were required to join a union and pay union dues. In 1940 labor unions were generally not in favor of admitting women as members. However, as the war progressed, they grudgingly admitted women, realizing that women were needed to fill the gaps left by men who were joining the military. Yet the unions spent little time explaining membership benefits to their new female members and even less time addressing issues such as childcare, maternity leave, and time off to deal with family illness.

Between 1940 and 1944 union membership increased overall from 7.5 million to 12.5 million; female members made up 3.5 million of this total. Male union members often opposed, even feared, female membership for a number of reasons. Women had little history with the labor movement, a group that had fought hard for its gains during the 1930s. Women generally had been willing to accept lower wages. Therefore, as women moved into job roles that had traditionally been held by men, men feared that women would pull down wages and be hired in place of men. Old stereotypes and attitudes persisted among some male union members. They believed that women could not produce as much as men, that married women belonged in the home, and that women should stay out of the toolroom. Male union members also questioned women's commitment to the labor cause, because women often had homes and children to tend to while not at work, and did not have time to attend union meetings and activities.

Generally unions fell into three categories with regard to female membership: (1) Some unions continued to bar women throughout the war; (2) some fought female membership but gave in as the war progressed; and (3) some were friendly to women as members. Unions in the first category included those in the construction, railroad, and mining industries. The second category—unions that began to allow female membership as the war continued—included unions for workers in aircraft production, shipbuilding, automobile manufacturing, furniture and lumber, machinery, utilities, and government postal service. In the friendly-to-women category were unions in food manufacturing, oil and chemical industries, electronics, retail and wholesale trade, clothing, and the hotel and restaurant business. When the war ended and layoffs were necessary, unions that had originally opposed female membership supported laying off women first. Most women in aircraft, shipbuilding, and munitions manufacturing were quickly laid off.

Black women in factories

By 1941, 40 to 50 percent of black American women were in the workforce as maids and cooks, both poorly paid jobs. At first, most employers in the war industries tried to avoid hiring black women. However, blacks began to hold protest demonstrations in front of defense plants that employed whites only. To avert a huge protest march on Washington, D.C., President Roosevelt issued Executive Order 8802 in June 1941. The order banned discrimination in the war industries. If companies failed to hire blacks, or if managers tolerated white workers who refused to work with blacks, they would lose their profitable defense orders.

Thousands of black women migrated to the Great Lakes region and to both coasts in search of war industry work. Many moved from jobs that paid $2.50 a week to employment paying $40 a week.

Many black women hired in the war industries were given the worst, most dangerous jobs. Author Elaine Tyler May, in the article "Pushing the Limits, 1940–1961" published in *No Small Courage: A History of Women in the United States,* edited by Nancy F. Cott, describes what many black women experienced: "In airplane assembly plants, black women worked in the 'dope rooms' filled with poisonous fumes of glue, while white women were in the well-ventilated sewing rooms. In every industry, the lowest-paying, most difficult, most dangerous, hottest, and most uncomfortable jobs

Thousands of black women, such as this riveter, migrated to both coasts of the United States in search of war industry work. *National Archives.*

went to black women—and they often worked the night shifts." In "Women at Work," an August 1944 article for *National Geographic Magazine,* LaVerne Bradley reports that at Bellevue Naval Magazine (in this case, "magazine" means a place where supplies are stored; often a warehouse for explosives) black women were working "in steel-barricaded rooms measuring and loading pom-pom mix, lead azide, TNT, tetryl, and fulminate of mercury [various explosive substances] . . . any snip of it could blow them to flinders [pieces]." Bradley's article notes that the women liked the job because they received an extra six cents an hour as hazard pay.

One black woman, Margaret Starks, saw a different type of opportunity in the war industry. As thousands of black Americans migrated to Richmond, California, to work in the Kaiser shipyards, she recognized a potential market for entertainment and established the most popular nightclub in North Richmond, Tappers Inn, for the growing black community. Starks also served as secretary for the Richmond branch of the National Association for the Advancement of Colored People (NAACP).

Federal civil service employment

The number of women in federal civil service—that is, women employed by the U.S. government—tripled between June 1940 and June 1942. In June 1940 there were 186,210 women in federal civil service. That number increased to 558,279 by June 1942, and about 8,000 women were added every week after that. About 60 percent of the federal government's female employees worked in the War and Navy Departments. However, most of them worked outside the Washington, D.C., area. They performed jobs at munitions manufacturing plants, proving grounds (a place for scientific testing), navy yards, flying fields, air stations, naval torpedo stations, and military bases. Women with

credentials in science often joined engineering groups and did research on chemical warfare.

Women in federal civil service held an amazing array of jobs—manufacturing gas masks, assembling delicate parts of time fuses in artillery shells, cleaning and grinding lenses for gun sights and bombsights, sewing fleece-lined suits for pilots, inspecting military clothing, and testing and repairing parachutes. Women could take courses sponsored by the U.S. Office of Education to train for these jobs. Government arsenals, navy yards, and air stations held training courses, and vocational schools and colleges throughout the country also offered training.

The Selective Service employed 16,000 women to enroll men and women who were enlisting or being drafted into the military. The Treasury Department employed 23,000 women to speed the sale of war bonds. About 24,000 women worked for the Office of Emergency Management, which guided the conversion of industry from consumer goods to war materials. The Department of Agriculture had more than 25,000 women employees; many were professionals working in food laboratories as nutritionists and chemists.

For college-trained women, who numbered about 3.5 million in 1941, thousands of federal government jobs were available in professional and scientific fields. Women served as doctors, nurses, lawyers, dietitians, economists, biologists, chemists, engineers, personnel officers, and public relations officers. Working in laboratories, they tested military clothing for resistance to mildew, conducted experiments to learn how to preserve food and increase nutritive values, and developed preventive vaccines.

The amount of paperwork created by the total war effort was overwhelming. As a result there was a tremendous increase in the need for stenographers and typists in the federal government. The government also needed telephone operators, file clerks, fingerprinters, and people to administer exams for civil service job applicants. To fill these positions, the Civil Service Commission recruited women from across the country, and thousands were brought to the nation's capital to work. The media dubbed them "Government girls." Magazines ran features on their daily lives in Washington, D.C., describing their experience in exciting, glamorous terms. However, because so many women had been recruited from afar, housing in the Washington, D.C., area was in critically short supply. Some women had to return home for lack of living quarters.

Housewives

"I was just a housewife during the war." This was the modest comment some women made after the war ended. Although "homemaker" was the preferred term by the end of the twentieth century, the word "housewife" was commonly used during the World War II and postwar years. Unlike

 ## "Be with Him at Every Mail Call"

"Be with him at every mail call" was a motto used by the U.S. government to encourage frequent letter writing to military men overseas. The U.S. military considered letters a powerful morale booster. Letter writers were told to be positive and "cheery," to provide details of home life but never to include information that might be useful to the enemy if the letters were captured. Magazines featured articles on the "do's and don'ts" of letter writing. Wives, mothers, sweethearts, grandmothers, sisters, aunts, nieces, and neighbors all wrote. For many it was a daily ritual. It usually took a letter six weeks by boat to reach the intended soldier.

Letters took up so much cargo space that the government developed V-mail. V-mail letters were written on special 8 $\frac{1}{2}$-by-11-inch forms that could be purchased at local stores or the post office. Once the letter was written, the form was then returned to the post office and sent to the military where it was photographed. The film was flown to a mail center near the recipient's position. There the film was developed, and the V-mail was delivered in the form of a 4-by-5 $\frac{1}{2}$-inch photograph.

Approximately seventeen hundred V-mail letters could fit in a cigarette packet. V-mails reached soldiers by air in twelve days or less. Over a billion V-mails were sent during the war. The V-mail process was the beginning of microfilming.

Victory gardens, found in backyards across America, helped feed families at a time when many foods were scarce or were being sent overseas to military personnel. *AP/Wide World Photos. Reproduced by permission.*

not a glamorous job, but the women who did it were the backbone of the country during the war.

At the peak of the war in 1943 and 1944, approximately 32.5 million married women worked at home, caring for their households. About 88 percent of these women had husbands at home during the war. Only 8 percent had husbands in the military, and 4 percent were separated or had been abandoned. The nuclear family of husband, wife, and children was the norm. The housewife went grocery shopping, prepared food, cleaned the house, provided childcare, washed and ironed clothes, and gave medical advice and minor first aid to family members. If she could find time, the housewife sometimes tended a victory garden (small private gardens planted in backyards or public places, such as parks, to supplement the production of food by commercial farms) in the backyard and canned its produce. She also volunteered to aid the war effort if she could.

Household challenges on the home front

During the war years housewives had to overcome significant challenges. Most of them had to deal with shortages of food and other essential items. In other cases, a husband or a whole family would have to relocate because of a job opportunity or military service; this would disrupt the entire household. Most family incomes went up during the war years, but

factory women, housewives were mostly ignored by the media. Running the average American household was fewer foods and goods were available to buy. Rationing (a system to make foods and other items of short supply available in limited amounts to ensure citizens receive a fair share) and poor-quality merchandise (often lower-quality materials were substituted for the main materials, which were needed by war industries) were a fact of life. So, just as they had done during the Great Depression of the 1930s, housewives found themselves "making do"—doing all they could with what they had at hand.

Shortly after the United States entered World War II, the federal government began issuing notices that production of various consumer goods would be limited and that some goods would not be made at all. Electric refrigerators, small appliances, vacuums, irons, radios, and even such items as can openers and kitchen knives became difficult to obtain. The raw materials normally used to make them were diverted to industries making war equipment. Newly married women had a difficult time putting together basic supplies for their households. Because new merchandise was unavailable, the repair of old items was essential. However, repairmen were hard to find, because many had gone off to war.

Keeping a family in clean clothes was very time-consuming. At least half of housewives washed all clothes by hand or used a hand-cranked machine. (To add to the challenge of laundry day, soap was scarce throughout the war.) Clothes were air dried on a clothesline and then ironed. Women who had automatic washing machines had their own troubles. If a machine broke down, repair or replacement was not an easy option because of scarce repair workers and limited production of machines and parts. Faced with a malfunctioning machine, housewives sometimes turned to professional laundries. However, many laundry workers had left for better-paying jobs, so service was slow and unreliable.

Shopping for clothes was unsatisfying as prices soared and quality plummeted. All wool items disappeared from department stores because wool went into military use for uniforms, blankets, and other items. Most women resorted to sewing much of their family's clothing, but material was hard to find. Even babies' rubber pants disappeared; all rubber was being used to make tires for military equipment. Likewise, the nation's supply of leather was used for military garb rather than civilians' shoes.

Wartime food shortages

What brought the war home to families more than anything else was food shortages and food rationing. Americans "tightened their belts" so soldiers could eat. People who complained were likely to hear a common refrain: "Don't you know there's a war on?" A nationwide food rationing system began in 1942 (see Chapter 3: Managing the Nation's Finances). Housewives became familiar with coupon ration books and tried to master the complicated rationing system. Each book contained blue stamps for processed foods,

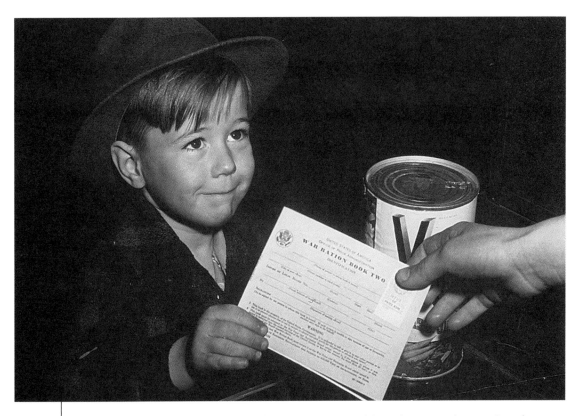

A young boy presents coupons from his War Ration Book in order to purchase rationed goods at a store. *National Archives photo no. 208-AA-322H-1 (World War II Photos).*

such as canned goods, and red stamps for meat, fats, and cheese. Each stamp was worth a set number of points and had an expiration date. Housewives kept close track of how many stamps or points they had and when the stamps or points expired. To purchase rationed food items, they had to present both cash and the proper stamps. Adding to the complexity, point values regularly changed as new items became scarce. Local newspapers published the ever-changing point values, which helped housewives plan (or replan) their shopping and meals. Beef was constantly in short supply. Choice cuts were rarely

available. Basic items such as sugar, coffee, canned goods, and dried beans and peas were all rationed.

Having limited ration points, a woman with growing teenagers or a husband doing heavy war industry work had a hard time keeping them fed. Ration points for war factory workers increased in mid-1943, but by October of that year, 50 percent of housewives still had difficulty getting enough food for their families. To fill their stomachs, many adults ate baby food, a nonrationed item. About 70 percent of housewives canned vegetables (grown in their victory gardens), fruits, meat products, jams, and jellies. To do the canning, housewives sometimes had to walk all over town looking for sugar, a rationed item. Using the car for such shopping expeditions was a rare event, because gas was tightly rationed. In big cities, housewives rode public transportation, which was always overcrowded. Often lugging children along, they became accustomed to standing in long lines for both food and transportation.

Despite the wartime food shortages, housewives were able to provide better nutrition for their families than they had during the Great Depression. This was partly because their husbands were earning higher wages, giving them more to spend on food, and partly because the rationing system required careful meal planning. Overall, the war years demanded more effort on the household front, but housewives stayed flexible and were willing to adjust. They dutifully followed the government's frequently heard advice, "Use It Up, Wear It Out, Make It Do, Or Do Without."

War brides and wives left alone

Hollywood movies during the war years may have exaggerated the wartime separation of lovers, but, in reality, only 8 percent of American wives, about two and a half million women, had husbands in the military. However, the percentage was higher in certain age groups. For example, 40 percent of wives under age twenty had husbands in the military.

 "Allotment Annies"

Instead of working for a living, a few women took advantage of a different wartime opportunity. They defrauded the government by collecting multiple allotment checks (a monthly stipend that the government sent to servicemen's families while the men were overseas). To do this they had to marry multiple servicemen. Allotment Annies hung around military bases. When the opportunity presented itself, an Annie romanced and married an unsuspecting serviceman. She then tearfully saw her soldier off as he headed overseas. As she began to collect his $50 monthly allotment check, she was already waiting to trap the next soldier. Some Annies collected six or seven checks per month, although authorities did eventually catch up with them.

Not all military husbands had to face combat. Twenty-nine percent never left the United States, and only one-fourth of the married soldiers who went overseas actually went into combat. Nevertheless, wives experienced great loneliness when their husbands were away in the military, and their husbands also suffered from the separation. If a husband left when his wife was pregnant, he often did not see his child until the child was one or two years old. Daily letter writing sustained both husbands and wives. Overseas servicemen's wives received monthly

$50 allotment checks to pay for basic necessities. To supplement this income, women married to servicemen were much more likely to enter the labor force than married women with working husbands at home.

Military husbands and their wives usually tried to stay together as long as the husband remained in the United States. Wives, along with their children, traveled from base to base as servicemen were constantly transferred. They rode crowded trains and often found little in the way of housing at their destinations. They rented rooms or lived in trailers near the bases. Once their men were sent overseas, the wives generally returned to their parents' homes to live until their husbands returned. Having a loved one overseas, possibly in combat, caused great anxiety. Of the 15 million American servicemen who served in the military during World War II, 300,000 were killed, and another 700,000 were injured so severely that they were disabled or impaired to varying degrees.

For More Information

Books

Campbell, D'Ann Mae. *Wives, Workers, and Womanhoods: America during World War II.* Ann Arbor, MI: University Microfilms International, 1979.

Cott, Nancy F., ed. *No Small Courage: A History of Women in the United States.* New York: Oxford University Press, 2000.

Gluck, Sherna Berger. *Rosie the Riveter Revisited: Women, the War, and Social Change.* Boston: Twayne Publishers, 1987.

Hartmann, Susan M. *The Home Front and Beyond: American Women in the 1940s.* Boston: Twayne Publishers, 1982.

Lingeman, Richard R. *Don't You Know There's a War On? The American Home Front, 1941–1945.* New York: G. P. Putnam's Sons, 1970.

Litoff, Judy B., and David C. Smith, eds. *Since You Went Away: World War II Letters from American Women on the Home Front.* New York: Oxford University Press, 1991.

McMillan, Lucille F. *The Second Year: Study of Women's Participation in War Activities of the Federal Government.* Washington, DC: U.S. Government Printing Office, 1943.

Zeinert, Karen. *Those Incredible Women of World War II.* Brookfield, CT: Millbrook Press, 1994.

Periodicals

Bradley, LaVerne. "Women at Work." *National Geographic Magazine* (August 1944) pp. 193–220.

Web Sites

Rosie the Riveter and Other Women World War II Heroes. http://www.u.arizona. edu/~kari/rosie.htm (accessed on July 8, 2004).

Rosie the Riveter Trust. http://www.rosietheriveter. org (accessed on July 8, 2004).

What Did You Do in the War, Grandma? http://www.stg.brown.edu/projects/WWII_Women/WWTWref.htm (accessed on July 8, 2004).

Women and the Home Front during World War II. http://www.teacheroz.com/WWIIHomefront.htm (accessed on July 8, 2004).

Civil Defense

8

As airplanes first began to appear in warfare in the early years of the twentieth century, war's destruction suddenly extended beyond the battlefields to towns and cities. Increasingly, government leaders and the general public worried that enemy nations might bomb civilian populations. No organizations existed to protect civilian populations during wars, but in 1916, just before the United States entered World War I (1914–18), the U.S. government began to plan for home front defense. Congress created the Council of National Defense (CND), and the CND encouraged states to create state defense councils, which in turn encouraged creation of local defense councils.

World War II (1939–45) spurred much more extensive home front defense efforts; most of the defense strategies that were developed were built on the concept of civil defense. Civil defense refers to a system of defensive measures designed to protect civilians and their property from enemy attack. The U.S. civil defense system included bomb shelters, air raid warning systems, patrols along the nation's borders, and distribution of information on emergency survival. Citizens who had

SERVICE ON THE HOME FRONT

★ CITIZENS DEFENSE CORPS
★ CITIZENS SERVICE CORPS
★ AMERICAN UNITY
★ SALVAGE PROGRAM
★ VICTORY GARDENS

There's a job for every Pennsylvanian in these CIVILIAN DEFENSE EFFORTS

PENNSYLVANIA STATE COUNCIL OF DEFENSE
CAPITOL BUILDING,   HARRISBURG, PENNA.

A poster from the Pennsylvania State Council of Defense encouraging participation in civil defense efforts in the local community. *The Library of Congress.*

not joined the nation's armed forces were eager to support the war effort in any way they could. They joined civil defense organizations in their local communities, volunteering to help construct bomb shelters and distribute survival tips. Fortunately, the bomb shelters and emergency plans were never called into service. Few actual enemy attacks occurred on the U.S. mainland. The ones that did occur happened primarily on the West Coast. Unlike most other nations involved in World War II, the United States was spared the destructive forces of war on its home soil.

Office of Civil Defense

When World War II broke out in Europe in September 1939, the United States did not immediately join the fighting. Instead, the U.S. government agreed to provide support to the Allied forces who were battling Germany's aggressive troops. Initially President Franklin D. Roosevelt (1882–1945; served 1933–45) simply warned the civilian population to keep an eye out for possible espionage and sabotage activities on the home front. Meanwhile the war continued to expand in Europe and in Asia. By the summer of 1940, Germany had captured France and soon began a prolonged bombing campaign on Great Britain. In Asia, Japanese military expansion threatened the U.S. territories of Guam and the Philippines.

In the spring of 1941, witnessing the expanding war, President Roosevelt prepared to issue an "unlimited" national emergency declaration, giving the president extensive wartime powers to mobilize the nation and take actions, economic and military, against foreign nations, while still not being officially entered into the war. Roosevelt also decided to step up home front defense. In preparation for possible war, Roosevelt advised communities to reestablish or organize their own local civil defense councils, which had waned substantially in the years since World War I due, in large part, to the economic crisis of the Great Depression (1929–41). To coordinate and assist the new civil defense system, Roosevelt replaced the CND with the Office of Civil Defense (OCD) on May 20, 1941. He hoped that the OCD's activities would boost public support for the upcoming war effort. Roosevelt named New York mayor Fiorello La Guardia (1882–1947) as the first director of OCD. La Guardia also served as director of the New York City Office of Civilian Defense. He established nine OCD regional offices to coordinate state and local efforts.

For the first several months of 1941, little public enthusiasm existed for civil defense. In addition, state governors opposed any centralized federal control over civil defense. Therefore, each state was told to set up its own civil defense system. The states created various organizations that could be called upon for emergency help; specialists such as public health personnel and auxiliary firemen were recruited and placed on standby. By November 1941 all the states had civil defense organizations, and almost six thousand towns and cities had defense councils. However, Congress was slow in providing money to the states for civil defense. The various local organizations, and the OCD as well, had minimal equipment and supplies. Few air raid shelters existed.

The surprise Japanese air attack on the military bases at Pearl Harbor, Hawaii, on December 7, 1941, dramatically changed the American public's attitude toward civil defense. The attack had killed more than twenty-three hundred U.S. servicemen, and American citizens were angered and ready to join the war effort in any way they could. The Pearl Harbor attack also triggered public fear of attacks on the U.S. mainland, by air or by sea, particularly on the West Coast. Many more local civil defense units quickly formed. OCD was suddenly overwhelmed with requests for information and assistance. In Chicago, Illinois, for example, twenty-three thousand civil defense volunteers were sworn in at one time. Civil defense would soon grow into a significant network of home front organizations.

Air raid protection was one of the top concerns for civil defense organizations. To assist them, the OCD published a booklet called "What to Do in an Air Raid." OCD printed some fifty-seven million copies. Newspapers published the information as well. The booklet advised Americans to identify a central refuge room in their homes and to have stout tables on hand that they could crawl under if air raids occurred. Preparations for air raids varied greatly from one city to another. Construction of new shelters was limited, because most building materials were designated for military use. In Seattle, Washington, numerous barrage balloons (small balloons supporting nets and tethered by cables to the ground over cities protecting against enemy air attacks) were put up over the city, sandboxes were placed on each

World War II poster encouraging the American public's participation in the war efforts on the home front. *The Library of Congress.*

corner to put out possible fires, and certain buildings were chosen and prominently marked as air raid shelters.

President Roosevelt and Mayor La Guardia, the director of the OCD, disagreed about the priorities of the civil defense program. In September 1941 the president appointed his wife, Eleanor Roosevelt (1884–1962), as La Guardia's deputy, hoping she could increase opportunities for women to volunteer. Mrs. Roosevelt directed the Volunteer Participation Program, which focused on physical fitness, childcare, health, welfare, and morale for all, including children. However, in February 1942 the program came under fire by critics in Congress, who claimed it was a waste of federal funds. The First Lady soon resigned, followed by La Guardia. Roosevelt replaced La Guardia with James Landis, dean of the Harvard Law School. Soon thereafter, issues surrounding the civil defense program were resolved and Congress resumed funding in March for civil defense equipment. Despite La Guardia's quick departure, much had been accomplished under his brief leadership: By the end of January 1942 after only eight months since the establishment of the OCD, 8,478 local civil defense councils were established. There were also 334,666 auxiliary police, 670,673 air raid wardens, and 265,580 medical staff. In all, more than five million volunteers worked in civil defense.

Volunteerism

To help organize the civilian volunteer efforts and provide adequate

Posters sprung up all over America's big cities and small towns informing people about important wartime issues, such as air raid protection. *The Library of Congress.*

training for volunteers, the U.S. Citizens Defense Corps was established within the OCD in April 1942. Locally designated wardens and various auxiliary emergency workers were the core of the civil defense system. Specialists included air raid wardens, auxiliary firemen, auxiliary police, emergency food and housing personnel, chaplains, air patrol workers, decontamination specialists, demolition experts, fire watchers, instructors, medical corps,

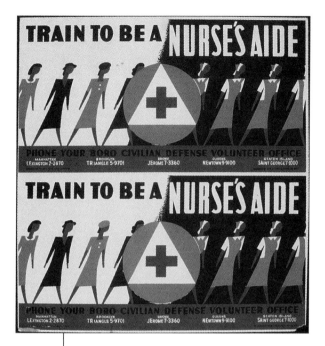

Nurses' aides was just one of many civil defense organizations recruiting volunteers during World War II. *The Library of Congress.*

drivers, messengers, nurses' aides, rescue squads, road repair crews, and utility road squads. Members of civil defense organizations wore insignias on their helmets and armbands to identify their specialty. The OCD symbol was a white triangle inside a blue circle. Specialists' armbands displayed a unique insignia within the OCD symbol.

The Civilian Voluntary Service organized a variety of volunteer efforts, including scrap drives (a public program of gathering discarded or unused items made of materials needed by the defense industry, such as rubber tires, metal pots and pans, and nylon hose), victory speakers (people who gave speeches on government policies), victory gardens (small private gardens planted in backyards or public places such as parks to supplement the production of food by commercial farms), and neighborhood block leaders (individuals who took responsibility for overseeing the war effort on a single city block). The responsibilities of a neighborhood block leader included explaining government programs that required the residents' cooperation (such as rationing), finding salespeople for war bonds and war stamps, checking on housing needs, and recruiting women for openings in local war factories. Armed with a kit supplied by the federal government, block leaders called on each household in their block to provide helpful information. Many housewives volunteered as block captains. Not to be left out, a Junior Service Corps was formed for youths under fifteen years of age. They helped with scrap drives and local community civil defense projects including promoting the sales of war bonds.

Many people gained a sense of contribution to the war effort by participating as volunteers in civil defense. Others got involved by taking classes on emergency preparedness. First aid classes were made available to hundreds of thousands of civilians, and classes on how to survive air raids were highly popular. By the summer of 1942 there were 11,000 local defense councils and more than seven million volunteers. By July 1943 there were twelve million registered volunteers.

Guides for Citizens

One key responsibility of the Office of Civil Defense (OCD) was getting survival information out to the public. The OCD's publications in 1941 included "Handbook for Air Raid Wardens" and "Handbook for First Aid," the latter in cooperation with the American Red Cross. In 1942 OCD published "What Can I Do? The Citizens' Handbook for War." The OCD also supported publications by other agencies, such as "Share the Meat for Victory" (1942), a guide published by the U.S. Office of Defense, Health, and Welfare Services. "How to Keep Warm and Save Fuel in Wartime" (1942), published by the Office of Price Administration, was another guide that supplemented OCD publications. Private businesses also offered helpful information. The Frigidaire Division of General Motors published "Wartime Suggestions," which provided handy advice on how to use and maintain refrigerators. (New refrigerators were not available during the war; government restrictions had forced refrigerator manufacturers to stop production so that the war industry could use their materials.)

OCD also encouraged local civil defense chapters to publish their own materials. Two months before the air attack on Pearl Harbor, a handbook titled "The Air Raid Protection (A.R.P.) Organization" was published in Forest Hills, New York. The Queens Civilian Defense Volunteer Office in New York City published a one-page leaflet titled "What to Do in an Air Raid." The Civilian Defense Volunteer Office in Forest Hills, New York, published "Block Organizations," which described how to set up civil defense volunteer organizations. It included instructions on how to salvage materials important for the war industries and listed locations where the materials could be dropped off.

Aircraft Warning Service

One of the first organizations formed by the OCD in 1941 was the Aircraft Warning Service (AWS). It was the first large-scale organization within the civil defense system that accepted citizen volunteers. The goal of the AWS was to protect the coastal regions of the United States from foreign attack. Many were convinced such a strike would eventually hit the U.S. mainland.

However, the technology of radar was still in the development stage in 1941 and the coverage provided by existing radar installations did not extend to many coastal areas. Consequently the government had to rely on individuals to watch the skies for enemy aircraft. Overall more than one and a half million volunteers would serve AWS. They were determined to do whatever was necessary to protect the coastline from attack.

Men and women who kept watch for enemy aircraft were called spotters; they were part of the Ground Observer Corps within AWS. Spotters also watched for wildfires during the summer months. Though most spotters were unpaid volunteers, the U.S. Forest Service and the U.S. Coast Guard provided some compensation for those stationed in remote areas of the coast, such as the forested mountains of Southwest Oregon. In these areas spotters worked round-the-clock in two twelve-hour shifts seven days a week. In the first year turnover was high, but over time, spotters stayed at the job for lengthy periods.

The accommodations for spotters were primitive. Carpenters built two-room cabins in the woods at the lookout locations. In some areas spotters had to pack in their supplies; during the winter months they had to hike on snowshoes pulling loaded toboggans. Firewood had to be cut and split. Spotters who were injured by accidents or who had a sudden illness had problems getting to physicians quickly because of the spotters' remote locations.

Spotters reported all aircraft to a nearby headquarters. At each headquarters the AWS had three telephone operators and a supervisor to compile reports from spotters. Headquarters relayed the information to the U.S. Army's Filter Centers, located in major coastal cities. About six hundred thousand spotters served the country under AWS. Though no enemy airplanes were ever spotted, the AWS and its spotters ended rumors of enemy attacks by keeping a vigilant watch on the skies and defusing the public's fears of air attacks just with their presence.

The Coast Guard Auxiliary and Reserve

When World War II began in September 1939, the United States initially declared itself a neutral country. President Roosevelt immediately assigned the U.S. Coast Guard to carry out "neutrality patrols" along the U.S. coastline. He wanted to make sure the war stayed away from America's shores. When France fell to Germany in June 1940, Roosevelt feared Germany would become bolder in its military and operation. Therefore he increased coastal security by ordering port security measures. The Coast Guard was to monitor all movement of ships in U.S. waters and protect harbors. Roosevelt knew that German submarines were near the American coast, lying in wait to attack Allied ships that were carrying American-made supplies back to Europe. (Even though the United States was still officially neutral, the government had agreed to supply Allied countries with war materials; however, the Allies had to transport the materials themselves.) In November 1941 Roosevelt made the Coast Guard part of the U.S. Navy so Coast Guard crews could actively protect ships by intercepting German submarines on the open seas. The navy was very limited in capabilities prior to industrial mobilization in 1942 and enemy attacks on shipping were escalating. Help was needed. After the United States officially entered the war in December 1941, the navy continued to be spread very thin and was primarily assigned to more direct combat roles overseas. On the home front the Coast Guard still retained its responsibility to patrol the coasts and beaches and prevent foreign landings of submarines.

The duties of the Coast Guard expanded again when the United States officially entered the war in late 1941. Filling in for the U.S. Navy in its traditional naval roles, the Coast Guard needed a backup as well to perform its traditional roles of coastal patrols and sea rescues. To supplement the existing Coast Guard Reserves, civilian volunteers organized the Coast Guard Auxiliary to assist in Coast Guard duties on the home front. The threat of approaching war also led to the reorganization of the Coast Guard Reserves. (Congress originally established the Reserves in June 1939. The growth of pleasure boating in the 1930s created a greater demand on the Coast Guard to respond to boating emergencies. The Reserves, a group made up of private boaters, aided in rescues and promoted boating safety.) Duties were often shared between the Auxiliary and the Reserves with the Reserves concentrating on Coast Guard tasks that were too demanding for the Auxiliary volunteers, such as escorting large ships in U.S. waters. Many of the Auxiliary volunteers were men who did not qualify for military service in the Coast Guard Reserves because of age or physical capabilities.

From 1941 to 1945 the Auxiliary was a key home front arm of the Coast Guard, patrolling the coastline for enemy ships and guarding port facilities in addition to the traditional duties of sea rescue. Its first action came on the evening of December 7, 1941, the day Pearl Harbor was bombed. As a rumor spread that the Japanese might attack the U.S. mainland, the Auxiliary launched patrol cruises out of Seattle, Washington. Such patrols would continue throughout the war, though the navy was able to assume many of the coastal defense duties once its increased level of wartime forces had been reached through the next two years. All of the Auxiliary's boats were privately owned craft of various shapes and sizes, either owned by the Auxiliary volunteer or loaned in a patriotic gesture by others. To distinguish their craft from other private boats, they painted CGR (Coast Guard Reserves) on their bows.

Some of the Auxiliary's activities became more formalized as time went on. When President Roosevelt established the Volunteer Port Security Force in February 1942, the Auxiliary was assigned a key role in home front defense. Armed with machine guns, pistols, and rifles, Auxiliary volunteers were to assist the Reserves in protecting ports, warehouses, piers, and other waterfront facilities from sabotage. Together, the Auxiliary and the Reserves had some twenty thousand volunteers involved in port patrols. About two thousand women handled the port security paperwork. The Reserves and the Auxiliary became almost indistinguishable in many instances as the two groups worked side by side on various

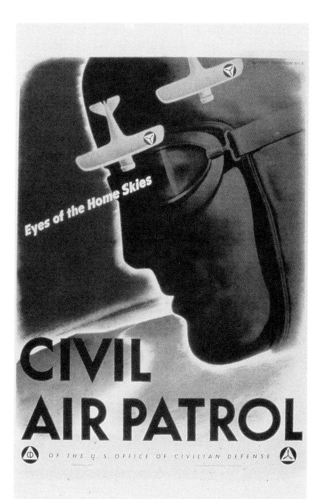

The Civil Air Patrol, activated just days after the Pearl Harbor attack, was a way for private citizens to help patrol the skies and waters on the home front. © *Corbis. Reproduced by permission.*

(1894–1979), who helped patrol Boston Harbor in Massachusetts.

During the war, in addition to patrols, the Auxiliary aided in rescues, trained potential recruits for the Reserves, provided public education on boating safety, and continued shore patrols. Auxiliary members even patrolled beaches on horseback, keeping an eye out for any possible landings by enemy spies. By the end of the war in 1945, the Auxiliary had 67,533 members performing shore and port patrols and other duties. Many others temporarily served in the Reserves. In January 1946 the Coast Guard was returned to the U.S. Transportation Department. The Auxiliary continued its activities.

Civil Air Patrol

The Civil Air Patrol (CAP) was a major part of civil defense during World War II. When war first broke out in Europe and Asia, Gill Robb Wilson, an aviation advocate from New Jersey, began promoting the idea of private aviators supplementing U.S. military operations. With key assistance from OCD director Fiorello La Guardia, CAP was officially established on December 1, 1941, less than a week before Japan's surprise attack on Pearl Harbor. Immediately after the Pearl Harbor attack, all civilian planes were grounded so that any enemy planes over the home front could be spotted more easily. A few days later, on December 11, CAP was activated.

The first CAP base was established in Atlantic City, New Jersey. CAP

assignments. Notable volunteers included Hollywood actor Humphrey Bogart (1899–1957), who operated his yacht on several patrols out of Los Angeles, California; and Boston Pops Orchestra conductor Arthur Fiedler pilots were given two hundred hours of special training, and by March 1942 they were on patrol duty looking for enemy submarines. Their first interception of a German submarine occurred off Cape May, New Jersey. An unarmed CAP plane dove in mock bombing attacks, forcing a German submarine to break away from its intended target and run back to deeper ocean. CAP pilots used their own airplanes for patrols, but they received government money for living expenses while on duty, as well as additional airplane insurance and a rental fee for the use of their planes.

CAP pilots became known as the Flying Minutemen of World War II, a reference to the volunteer private militia of the American Revolution (1775–83). CAP's insignia was a three-bladed red propeller within the OCD's white triangle in a blue circle. The insignia began appearing on small private planes throughout the United States.

Like the Coast Guard Auxiliary, CAP filled in on the home front when U.S. military resources and personnel started going overseas. At first, CAP pilots flew only as messengers or to conduct reconnaissance (information-gathering) of the nation's borders and coastlines. However, German submarines became increasingly bolder, attacking U.S. and Allied ships off the U.S. coast. By July 1942 the military authorized CAP planes to carry bombs and depth charges (an antisubmarine weapon consisting of drums filled with explosives dropped from a ship designed to explode underwater at a certain depth). CAP pilots had a very hazardous job, flying as far as one hundred miles out over frigid ocean waters in rough winter weather.

CAP eventually had eighty thousand volunteers. During World War II the CAP coastal patrol flew 24 million miles and logged half a million hours of flying time. CAP planes spotted 173 enemy submarines and attacked 57 of them. They hit 10 submarines and sank 2. Sixty-four CAP pilots lost their lives while on duty. Acknowledging CAP's success and critical role in home front defense, President Roosevelt made CAP a formal auxiliary of the Army Air Force within the War Department in 1943. (Congress formed the U.S. Army Air Corps in 1926 as airplanes began to take a more prominent role in military arsenals. In 1941 Congress made the Air Corps more independent and renamed it the Army Air Force, which it remained throughout the war. In 1947 the armed forces were restructured and the U.S. Air Force was made a fully distinct military service.)

Besides patrolling and attacking enemy submarines, CAP pilots flew search-and-rescue missions, saving hundreds of lives. They also ferried civilian and military personnel involved in the war effort, transported small cargo, such as critical materials for industrial production, and towed targets for military pilot training. CAP pilots participated in air raid drills by dropping flour-filled sacks (which acted as mock "bombs") into public areas. They also trained twenty thousand

Patrolling the Nation's Coasts

In addition to the Civil Air Patrol (CAP), large U.S. Navy blimps assisted with coastal air patrol. Housed in giant hangars, they operated out of several locations on both coasts. The blimps flew hundreds of feet above the ocean's surface, looking for mines, survivors of torpedoed boats, and any suspicious bubbles or periscope wakes left by enemy submarines. Under good conditions they could spot the shadow of an enemy submarine up to 90 feet below the surface. The blimps would often carry several homing pigeons, birds that could fly messages back to the home station in case of emergencies or radio communications blackouts.

youths between fifteen and eighteen years of age as future pilots.

After the war, in mid-1946, Congress passed an act making CAP a permanent peacetime organization. In 1948 Congress made CAP an auxiliary to the newly formed U.S. Air Force. CAP expanded its duties to include disaster relief, and in 1985 CAP pilots renewed their reconnaissance of U.S. borders, working with the U.S. Customs Service to combat drug trafficking. In 1999 CAP flew sixty-five hundred missions to fight illegal drug trade. It also saved eighty-nine lives that year through its search-and-rescue efforts.

Enemy attacks on the home front

Immediately after the Pearl Harbor attack, nearly every American feared that enemy attacks would occur on the mainland. At the time, the United States was ill prepared to respond to air or sea attacks. California's coast had some defensive guns, but the Atlantic Coast was largely undefended. Additionally, because of the attack on Pearl Harbor, the United States had decided to enter the war. This meant that millions of military personnel were needed immediately, so President Roosevelt federalized (to bring under control of the federal government) the National Guard of each state to serve in the U.S. military. As a result, the states had no means of protecting their citizens in case of subversive activity, civil unrest, or emergency. Each state established a State Guard to temporarily replace the National Guard. State Guards recruited men with draft deferments (those excused from military service, often due to health or physical conditions), those too young for military service, and older men up to sixty-five years of age. To assist state efforts, Georgia used convicts to build bridges and improve roads so that men and supplies could be transported more readily to the coast in case of invasion.

In January and February 1942 German submarines were seen operating along the eastern coast. However, the federal government censored news of their presence so as not to alarm the public or unintentionally aid the enemy by announcing their ships' positions and activities. At night residents and tourists along the coast saw flashes and heard rumbles from explosions in the distance. They sometimes found debris (and occasionally a body) that had washed ashore. Rumors began spreading about German submarines landing at night and letting off spies.

Meanwhile, along the western coastline the Japanese carried out several very limited attacks. The attacks did not receive much publicity as the government did not want to alarm citizens or encourage further Japanese efforts. The first incident occurred in February 1942, two months after the attack on Pearl Harbor. A Japanese submarine briefly shelled a coastal oil field in the vicinity of Santa Barbara, California. In June a similar incident occurred on the Oregon coast, when another Japanese submarine shelled a fort, damaging a baseball backstop.

With enemy submarines appearing along both coasts, the OCD enforced dimouts along the coasts. Extending up to 16 miles inland along the Atlantic coast, dimouts were in effect from Maryland southward to Florida in March 1942. The OCD prohibited lights from being shone directly toward the sea during dimouts. Even drivers had to turn off their car headlights if they were traveling toward the ocean. Dimout rules also banned leaving unused lights on after dark. People who violated the dimout rules could be sentenced to up to one year in prison and fined up to $5,000. In June 1942 New York City was dimmed out and outdoor, lighted advertising banned.

With the absence of the usual glitter, attendance at Broadway shows declined, as did city nightlife in general. Blackout drills—periods when all lights had to be turned out—were also required. San Francisco had seven blackout drills in the first month after the Pearl Harbor attack. By November 1942 dimout rules had become even stricter. People living along the coast had to hang heavy curtains in windows facing the shoreline, and coastal towns had to shield streetlights so that they could not be seen from the ocean. *House and Garden,* a popular magazine, published tips on how to stylishly decorate a home using blackout materials.

Daring raids

The most daring raid on the U.S. mainland during World War II came on September 9, 1942. A small Japanese floatplane dropped incendiary bombs (small bombs designed to start fires) in the remote forested mountains of southwest Oregon, 10 miles northeast of the coastal town of Brookings. The modified plane was transported in a small watertight hangar attached to the deck of a submarine. Five months earlier, on April 18, the U.S. military had carried out a bombing raid on Tokyo, Japan, led by Jimmy Doolittle (1896–1993). Partly in response to that raid, Nobuo Fujita (1912–1997), the pilot of the tiny Japanese seaplane, carried out the raid near Brookings. Fujita used the Cape Blanco lighthouse as a guide. Spotters were stationed there, but he went undetected.

Two women hang heavy blackout curtains over a window to prevent light from shining out toward the Atlantic coastline. © *Bettmann/Corbis. Reproduced by permission.*

U.S. military intelligence was caught completely off guard by this enemy attack on the home front. The ambitious goal of the Japanese mission was to start massive forest fires that would distract the United States from its war effort. Unfortunately for the Japanese, several rainy days preceding the bombing had left the ground and trees wet, so the bombs started only a few small forest fires. Fujita got back to the submarine just before it came under fire; a U.S. Navy patrol aircraft forced the submarine to hide on the ocean floor just off the Oregon coast. Three weeks later Fujita flew a second mission, with little success.

The target area of Fujita's initial raid was very remote, so most Americans were unaware of the attack for a day or two. Though it did minimal damage, the raid was a propaganda victory for Japan because it made U.S. newspaper headlines. Fujita's small-scale attacks caused some public concern about the vulnerability of the West Coast to enemy raids; however, the public did not panic. U.S. government censorship of the news media kept the reports fairly limited. No other similar attacks were attempted during the war.

Japanese balloon bombs

The most ingenious enemy assault on the U.S. home front began in November 1944 and lasted for months. The Japanese launched thousands of large, hydrogen-filled balloons that carried incendiary and antipersonnel bombs across the Pacific Ocean to North America. Japan hoped that the balloon bombs would demoralize the U.S. home front by randomly killing civilians, destroying buildings, and starting wildfires. Riding the swift winds of the jet stream, the balloons took three days to cross the ocean. The Japanese Ninth Army Technical Research Laboratory, led by Technical Major Teiji Takada, developed the

balloon bombs, and some fifteen thousand balloon bombs were made. The balloons, about 33 feet in diameter, carried 1,000 pounds of gear, including the bombs. The balloons were first made of rubber, but for better retention of the hydrogen the Japanese switched to a tough paper skin made from mulberry bushes.

The Japanese launched nine thousand balloons between the fall of 1944 and the spring of 1945, taking advantage of winter's strong jet stream conditions. Released with great fanfare at Japanese weapons plants to boost the morale of Japanese workers, the balloons flew at an altitude of over 30,000 feet and traveled about 5,000 miles. An automatic control system kept the balloon afloat at the proper altitude and timed the release of the bombs on the third day.

Some three hundred balloon bombs were observed in various locations in North America, from California to Alaska along the western coast. At least fifty were observed in one day in Washington State. One balloon traveled as far as the Detroit, Michigan, area, but most fell in the West.

At first, U.S. citizens and military officials did not believe the balloons could fly so far. They assumed the Japanese had released the balloons from close by, either from their submarines or from West Coast beaches. However, a chemical analysis of the sand used to weight the balloons indicated that the balloons were of Japanese origin since the sand composition uniquely matched that from certain

Home Front War Casualties

Though no major enemy attacks occurred on the U.S. mainland during World War II, several small isolated incidents did occur. One incident led to several civilian casualties. In May 1945 a Japanese balloon bomb killed six people in southern Oregon. The bomb landed about 200 miles inland. On a pleasant Sunday afternoon the Reverend Archie Mitchell and his wife took five children, ages eleven to thirteen, from their church to the nearby mountains for a picnic. As Mrs. Mitchell and the kids hiked over a hill to the picnic spot, the reverend drove the car ahead to meet them with the food. As he got out of his car, he heard the children shouting that they had found a balloon. Though the U.S. Office of Censorship withheld news of Japanese balloon bombs, the reverend had heard of them. Before he could yell out a warning, a loud explosion tore through the peaceful mountain setting. Mitchell rushed to the scene and found all six people dead. They had gathered around an unexploded Japanese bomb and accidentally set it off by handling it. Two Forest Service employees in the area arrived moments later to find the six bodies and the distraught reverend. The Office of Censorship kept the news media from publicizing the incident for a month; then it decided it would be best to forewarn others and allowed the information to be released. The one adult and five children were the only known fatalities caused by enemy attack on the U.S. mainland during World War II.

beaches in Japan. In response, the U.S. government created a secret operation called "Fire Fly," which directed U.S. fighter pilots to shoot down the balloons. A U.S. military fighter plane shot down one balloon near Santa Rosa, California. However, because the balloons floated very fast at a high altitude, few of them (less than twenty) were ever intercepted by U.S. warplanes. Under Operation Fire Fly, firefighters had orders to combat any fires caused by the balloons. The firefighters involved in the operation were part of the 555th Parachute Infantry Battalion; they were the first smoke jumpers used in the United States.

Because it was a wet time of year, the balloons did not start many fires, and very little property damage occurred. However, six American civilians were killed in one incident in southern Oregon (see sidebar). The U.S. military feared Japan would begin putting biological or chemical weapons in the balloons rather than using conventional bombs. However, it appears that the Japanese made no attempt to do so.

In its January 1, 1945, issue *Newsweek* magazine published an article titled "Balloon Mystery." Fearing widespread panic among the U.S. population, the U.S. Office of Censorship immediately banned any further publicity about the balloons. Thus the only news reports on the subject came from Japan, where the media reported great fires and ten thousand casualties. These reports caused a general panic on the U.S. home front, exactly what the Office of Censorship was trying to avoid. Shortly after the deaths in southern Oregon, the Office of Censorship lifted the news blackout (prohibition against giving certain information to the public) to protect other citizens who might accidentally discover unexploded bombs. Japan stopped launching the balloons in April 1945. One of the last balloons observed on the home front appeared on March 10. It descended on power lines at Hanford, Washington, shutting down a secret nuclear reactor. Ironically, the reactor was producing plutonium for the atomic bomb that would hit Nagasaki, Japan, several months later.

For More Information

Books

Elliott, Lawrence. *Little Flower: The Life and Times of Fiorello La Guardia.* New York: Morrow, 1983.

Fujita: Flying Samurai. Medford, OR: Webb Research Group, 2000.

Web Sites

Civil Air Patrol. http://www.cap.gov/about/history.html (accessed on July 7, 2004).

Coast Guard Auxiliary History. http://www.uscg.mil/hq/g-cp/history/Auxiliary%20History.html (accessed on July 7, 2004).

Women in Uniform

The only women serving in the U.S. military when Pearl Harbor was attacked on December 7, 1941, were a few thousand in the Army Nurse Corps and Navy Nurse Corps. By the end of World War II (1939–45), more than 350,000 women had served in the U.S. military. Women in the military supported the total American war effort by carrying out essential noncombat responsibilities. The idea of women serving in the military in any role outside of nursing was a new concept for the American public, a concept that was difficult for many Americans to accept.

After much debate in the U.S. House of Representatives and the Senate, Congress created the Women's Army Auxiliary Corps (WAAC) in May 1942. On July 30, 1942, President Franklin D. Roosevelt (1882–1945; served 1933–45) signed a bill authorizing the navy, Coast Guard, and marines to accept women. That same day the U.S. Navy established the Women Accepted for Volunteer Emergency Service, or WAVES. In November 1942 the Coast Guard created its women's reserve, known as SPAR (the name SPAR came from the Coast Guard motto: Semper Paratus—Always Ready). In February 1943 the

Armed Services' recruiting poster aimed at women, circa 1943. *National Archives photo no. 44-PA-820 (World War II Posters, 1942–1945).*

Marine Corps established the Marine Corps Women's Reserve. On July 3, 1943, the army dropped the term "Auxiliary" from the official name of its women's reserve, so the WAAC became simply the Women's Army Corps (WAC). Together the Army Nurse Corps and Navy Nurse Corps accepted approximately sixty thousand women during the war years. Additionally, more than one thousand women served in the Women's Airforce Service Pilots (WASP), ferrying new planes to locations where the military received them for war service, towing targets for antiaircraft firing practice, and testing repaired aircraft.

When women first joined the military, they were assigned to clerical tasks most of the time; this was the typical role assigned to female workers in the civilian world as well. Women in the military often served as typists and file clerks, freeing male recruits for other tasks. Soon women showed they were capable of performing almost any task, and the military began to assign them to a variety of positions, from auto and aircraft mechanics to air traffic controllers. To solve its manpower shortage, the military could not simply bring in civilian women to do these tasks. They had to officially admit the women to the military so they could be subject to military orders that might assign them to different jobs and locations as needs arose. Even if it had been practical from a military standpoint to hire civilian women, the military could not have afforded the higher wages civilian workers commanded in the wartime economy.

Nurses in the army and navy and other women in the army were never prohibited from overseas assignment. However, in the beginning, WAVES, SPARS, and women marines were banned from serving outside the continental United States. In late 1944 Congress approved a bill allowing limited assignments to Alaska, Hawaii, and the Caribbean. In early 1945 a few WAVES, SPARS, and women marines served in Alaska and Hawaii.

WAC: Women's Army Corps

When the United States officially entered World War II after the attack on Pearl Harbor, U.S. military personnel was put to full use. The military needed more recruits—fast. Many people serving in Congress and many in the general population did not think women belonged in the military. However, General George Marshall (1880–1959), army chief of staff, saw no reason to train men how to type, file, and operate telephone switchboards when thousands of women were already skilled in these areas. He supported a bill that sought to establish a women's army corps; the bill had been presented in the House by Massachusetts representative Edith Nourse Rogers (1881–1960). President Roosevelt's wife, Eleanor Roosevelt (1884–1962), also supported this legislation.

Although many in the House of Representatives and the Senate firmly opposed Rogers's bill, the legislation

VICTORY WAITS ON YOUR FINGERS –

KEEP 'EM FLYING, MISS U.S.A.

UNCLE SAM NEEDS STENOGRAPHERS! ★ GET CIVIL SERVICE INFORMATION AT YOUR LOCAL POST OFFICE
U.S. CIVIL SERVICE COMMISSION, WASHINGTON, D.C.

When women first joined the military, they often served as typists and file clerks, freeing male recruits for other tasks. *National Archives.*

Eager to do their part in the war, thousands of women submitted applications at WAAC recruiting centers such as this one. *AP/Wide World Photos. Reproduced by permission.*

comparable rank in the regular army and would not receive continuing veterans' benefits such as life insurance, medical coverage, and death benefits. The bill did not prohibit women from being sent overseas; however, if WAACs were captured by the enemy, they would not be given the prisoner-of-war protections that men in the regular army were guaranteed. With this bill, Rogers achieved some standing for women within an organized army corps, but many protections were still lacking. Despite the inadequacies, women were eager to participate in the war effort, and they readily joined the WAAC.

General Marshall asked Oveta Culp Hobby (1905–1995) of Texas to head the WAAC. A lawyer, successful media executive, civic leader, and mother, Hobby had been serving as head of the Women's Interest Section in the War Department since the United States entered the war. Hobby pursued her new position with great zeal. To attract women for WAAC, Hobby had to convince the U.S. public that women who served in the WAAC could still be "ladies"—that is, truly feminine by society's standards. Hobby set up an officers training school at Fort Des Moines, Iowa. Applicants for officers training had to be between twenty-one and forty-five years of age, with no children. Hobby received 35,000 applications and selected 440 women for the first officers training class, which began on July 20, 1942. The average age of the women in training was twenty-five; most had attended college and had been working as office managers, teachers, or executive secretaries.

passed and became law on May 15, 1942. The bill, a compromise worked out with army leaders, created the Women's Army Auxiliary Corps (WAAC). WAAC's stated purpose was to "release a man for combat duty." WAAC would make women available to serve in the army, but it would not be part of the regular, permanent army. WAAC would function as a separate, temporary unit for women. The army would provide uniforms, food, living quarters, and medical care. However, the women would receive lower pay than men of

The first "auxiliaries"—nonofficers equivalent to privates in the regular army—began training on August 29. New training centers were soon established in Daytona Beach, Florida; Fort Oglethorpe, Georgia; and Fort Devens, Massachusetts.

Patriotism was the main reason women volunteered to serve in the WAAC. Sometimes they volunteered because there were no men of fighting age in their family; in other cases, they wanted to show support for a male family member in the service. Several of the first group of volunteers were widows from the Pearl Harbor attack. Many volunteers saw the WAAC as a chance to combine adventure and patriotic service. WAAC volunteers came from all over the country. Hometown newspapers interviewed local WAACs and published the letters when WAACs wrote home.

The first deployment of WAACs in the field was to Aircraft Warning Service (AWS) stations along the East Coast. The WAACs replaced volunteer civilians in monitoring aircraft positions within each station area. WAACs were also sent to army bases throughout the country, where they worked as typists and file clerks, answered telephones, or took over the drivers' positions in base motor pools. The army quickly realized that the women could do almost any job men could do.

About 40 percent of WAACs went to the army branch known as the Army Air Force (AAF). Roughly half of them were assigned to be weather forecasters, cryptographers (code breakers who helped decipher German and Japanese messages), radio communication specialists, mechanics and maintenance specialists for army equipment, and air traffic controllers. Another 40 percent of WAACs went to the Army Service Forces; there they worked in munitions production as electricians, mechanics, and draftsmen. WAACs also served in the Transportation Corps, processing soldiers who were heading overseas and issuing them weapons. WAACs served in the laboratories of the Chemical Warfare Service, in the Quartermaster Corps (where they kept track of supplies stored across the country), in the Signal Corps, and in the Army Medical Department. A number of WAACs assisted with the Manhattan Project, the project to develop the country's first atomic bomb. About 20 percent of WAACs served in the Army Ground Forces (AGF), which had long resisted having women in their ranks. AGF relegated most WAACs to clerical duty.

In November 1942 Lieutenant General Dwight D. Eisenhower (1890–1969) requested WAACs for overseas service in North Africa; later WAACs would be asked to go across the Mediterranean into Italy. Overseas they performed similar duties to those they were trained for on the home front including weather forecasters, cryptographers, radio communication specialists, mechanics, and air traffic controllers. With WAACs moving overseas into combat zones, Congress passed a bill on July 3, 1943, converting the WAAC into the Women's Army Corps (WAC). The bill established the

Major Charity Adams inspects members of the black women's unit of the Women's Army Auxiliary Corps (WAAC). *National Archives.*

WAC as a full member of the regular army. WACs would receive the same pay, rank, privileges, and protections as men did in the regular army.

The army needed more women in the program, so the recruitment campaigns accelerated in late 1943. However, several factors hampered recruitment. First, American women were more eager to take high-paying war industry jobs if they could find them. Also, some women were already volunteering in the other armed services. Worst of all, the program was suffering from an "image" scandal that started

earlier in 1943 before the congressional bill was passed. A slander campaign swept through the army and across the country. Rumors abounded that 90 percent of WAACs were prostitutes and that 40 percent of overseas WAACs were pregnant. In some U.S. communities residents complained that large groups of WAACs stationed at local bases were overwhelming restaurants and beauty shops; these complaints most likely came from disgruntled Americans who had opposed the idea of women in the military. Also, many enlisted soldiers stationed in the United States did not want to be freed

Black Women in Uniform

Black women were accepted into WAAC from its beginning in the summer of 1942. About 80 percent of the black women accepted for officer training had attended college and had been working as teachers or in offices. While they were in training, black officer-candidates attended classes with white candidates and ate meals with them, too. However, almost all social activities were strictly segregated; for example, the army set up separate service clubs and beauty shops for blacks and whites. At graduation blacks were assigned to all-black auxiliary units. A black women's unit did not deploy overseas until February 1945. The 6888th Central Postal Battalion, commanded by Major (later Lieutenant Colonel) Charity Adams (1918–2002), first went to England and then settled in Paris, France. Working around the clock in three shifts and seven days a week, the eight hundred black women in the battalion were responsible for getting mail to all members of the U.S. military in Europe. Military personnel assigned to Europe moved constantly, so the battalion had to keep an address update card for each one.

Black women were not admitted into the U.S. Navy WAVES or the Coast Guard SPAR until November 1944. By July 1945 there were seventy-two black enlisted women and two black officers in the WAVES. Four black women had been accepted by SPAR. Black women were never accepted into the Marine Corps Women's Reserve or the Women's Airforce Service Pilots (WASP).

for overseas duty; their family members and friends did not want them sent overseas either. These people resented the WAACs. Because of the general public's growing negative perception of the WAACs, Congress asked the program's director, Oveta Culp Hobby, to produce statistics of pregnancies and sexually transmitted diseases. Statistics showed that there was no truth to the rumors.

Most WACs remained in the United States, but by mid-1944 the military was sending many abroad. About 5,500 were sent to Australia and several South Pacific islands. About 400 WACs went to the China-Burma-India war region. By June 1945, 7,600 WACs were stationed throughout Europe.

By mid-1945, near the war's end, 150,000 women had served in either WAC or WAAC. By the end of the war, 657 WACs had been honored with medals and citations for outstanding service. Army leaders recognized the ongoing value of women in the army, and in 1946 they requested that Congress make the WAC a permanent corps. Political conservatives, long

Women serving in WAVES were granted the same wages, benefits, and rank as navy men received. *The Library of Congress.*

since that time only a few hundred women had served in the Navy Nurse Corps. Like the army, the navy needed an ever-increasing number of personnel as World War II progressed. However, people in the navy were not eager to have women in their ranks. Nevertheless, President Roosevelt signed a bill on July 30, 1942, authorizing the navy, the Coast Guard, and the marines to recruit women. That same day, resigned to the fact that women would be a wartime necessity, the navy established its women's branch, WAVES, which stands for Women Accepted for Volunteer Emergency Service. Navy leaders made WAVES a full part of the navy, not just an auxiliary unit. Therefore, women serving in the navy would receive the same wages, benefits, and rank as navy men did.

The navy set high standards for female applicants. To gain admittance, women had to have a college degree, or at least two years of college, and two years of professional experience. For the first time in its history the navy commissioned a female officer on August 3, 1942. Mildred McAfee (1900–1994), president of the prestigious Wellesley College, a women's college, was commissioned as a naval reserve lieutenant commander. As director of WAVES, McAfee immediately began recruiting women; she also set up training facilities and had uniforms designed. Ultimately about ninety thousand women became WAVES; eight thousand of them were officers. Officers trained at the Naval Reserve Midshipmen's School at Smith College and Mount Holyoke College in

opposed to women in the military, delayed the bill. It finally passed on June 12, 1948, and the WAC became a permanent branch of the U.S. Army.

WAVES: Women of the U.S. Navy

About fifteen thousand women served in the navy or the marines during World War I (1914–18)—often doing clerical staff work and radio communications, but also serving as air traffic controllers and aircraft mechanics—but

Massachusetts. Enlisted WAVES attended boot camp at the U.S. Naval Training Center, located at Hunter College in the Bronx, New York. WAVES represented 2.5 percent of the navy's total strength. By mid-1943 WAVES made up the majority of personnel at many home front naval air stations. Their purpose was to handle shore duty so navy men could be freed up for sea duty.

Most WAVES took clerical positions, but thousands also did jobs previously never associated with women. All 246 shore jobs open to naval enlisted men were also open to WAVES. Navy women had the opportunity to work as air navigators, plotting out routes for planes; as air traffic controllers and aircraft mechanics; in communications, intelligence, science, and technology; and in naval law courts of the Judge Advocate General Corps. Many women remained in the navy after the war.

SPAR: U.S. Coast Guard Women's Reserve

On November 23, 1942, the U.S. Coast Guard established its women's reserve, known as SPAR. The director of SPAR was Dorothy C. Stratton, on leave from her position as dean of women at Purdue University. Stratton, a lieutenant in the WAVES, was assigned to lead the new temporary war program. The Coast Guard was assisting the navy in its duties on the home front. Stratton coined the name SPAR from the initials of the Coast Guard motto: <u>S</u>emper <u>P</u>aratus—<u>A</u>lways <u>R</u>eady. In doing

Approximately ninety thousand women became WAVES during World War II, representing 2.5 percent of the navy's total strength. *Naval Historical Foundation. Reproduced by permission.*

so, she saved the women from being named "Worcogs" (Women's Reserve of the Coast Guard)—the only name the Coast Guard men had come up with. For the first time in its history, the Coast Guard began to enroll women into its enlisted and officer ranks. By the end of the war more than ten thousand women had volunteered to be SPARS.

SPAR officers were trained at the Naval Midshipman School in Northampton, Massachusetts, or the Coast Guard Academy in New London, Connecticut. Those at the Coast Guard Academy were the first women to attend a U.S. military academy. The average SPAR officer applicant was a twenty-nine-year-old college graduate who had worked seven years in a management, teaching, or government position.

SPAR training centers for enlisted women were at Oklahoma's A & M College, which later became Oklahoma State University, in Stillwater; Iowa State Teachers College in Cedar Falls; and the U.S. Naval Training Center at Hunter College in the Bronx, New York. By June 1943 the Biltmore Hotel in Palm Beach, Florida, was converted for use as another SPAR training center. The average SPAR enlistee was a single, twenty-two-year-old high school graduate who had worked in a clerical or retail sales job.

SPAR officers and enlistees were assigned to all Coast Guard stations in the continental United States. SPAR officers held general-duty assignments, working in administrative and supervisory roles throughout the Coast Guard. They also served as communications officers, pay officers, supply barracks officers, and recruiting officers. A large percentage of enlisted SPARS served as yeomen (secretaries) and storekeepers (bookkeepers). However,

others received assignments as chaplains' assistants, boatswains' mates (people who help with the ship's hull maintenance), ship cooks, vehicle drivers, pharmacists' mates, and medical assistants. A select few were parachute riggers, air control tower operators, flight instructors, and radio operators. A handful of SPARS participated in a top-secret military communications project known as Loran (Long-Range Aid to Navigation). Loran monitoring stations, located along U.S. coastlines, operated twenty-four hours a day; these stations made calculations to determine the exact location of ships and planes in transit. In 1943 an all-SPAR crew operated a Loran station at Chatham, Massachusetts.

Demobilization of SPARS began at the end of World War II in August 1945, and it was fully disbanded on June 30, 1946. SPARS left the Coast Guard knowing they had played an important role in the Allied victory.

U.S. Marine Corps Women's Reserve

Although in 1918 women in the United States did not have the right to vote, in August of that year they began enlisting in the Marine Corps. Women who enlisted at that time were known as Marinettes. Marinettes took over clerical jobs to free up marines for overseas combat in World War I (1914–18). Twenty-five years later, on February 13, 1943, in the midst of World War II, the Marine

Corps Women's Reserve was founded. Approximately twenty-three thousand women joined the Reserve.

The Women's Reserve was headed by Ruth Cheney Streeter (1895–1990). The women under her command did not have a special name like the U.S. Navy WAVES or the Coast Guard SPARS; they certainly did not wish to be called Marinettes as they had been labeled in World War I. They would be known simply as marines, and they would wear uniforms of forest green, just as male marines did. The recruitment slogan for the Women's Reserve was "Free a man to fight."

Camp Lejeune in North Carolina served as boot camp to the vast majority of women marines. After boot camp they fanned out to all marine posts in the United States. By June 1944 women marines made up roughly two-thirds of the personnel at Marine Corps posts. They performed clerical jobs, working as typists, file clerks, and telephone operators; they also worked as auto and airplane mechanics, welders, painters, and motor pool drivers. Some were radio operators, parachute riggers, mapmakers, aerial photographers, or control tower operators. When male marines began coming back to the United States, the Women's Reserve staffed relocation centers, where the marines were assigned to home front duties until their discharge. At the end of the war the Women's Reserve was rapidly demobilized. Only about one thousand women marines remained in the service by July 1946.

Army Nurse Corps

The Army Nurse Corps (ANC) was founded in 1901. In late 1941, at the time of the Pearl Harbor attack, the ANC had less than one thousand nurses. Six months later, twelve thousand nurses were enlisted; however, the army estimated that it needed about sixty thousand. The army gave the American Red Cross the responsibility of recruiting civilian nurses, and eventually roughly 43 percent of civilian nurses volunteered to enlist.

Despite all-out recruiting efforts, the army could not fill its need for nurses quickly enough. Only single women were eligible to serve; that rule alone limited the number of potential recruits. Furthermore, there was already a nationwide shortage of nurses. This was not due to lack of interest in nursing; it had to do with cost: Most women did not have the funds to pay for several years of nursing school.

As civilian nurses began volunteering for military service, the nursing shortage in U.S. hospitals reached a crisis point. Entire hospital wings had to be shut down in many hospitals across America as a result. In response Congress passed the Bolton Act in June 1943, establishing the Cadet Nurse Corps program. The program provided for government subsidy (a grant of money) for nursing education. In return for their education, cadets had to promise to serve in essential military or civilian nursing for the duration of the war. During their last six months of training, they were assigned to home front

U.S. Army nurses depart a troop ship en route to an overseas assignment during World War II. *The Library of Congress.*

facilities of the army, navy, Veterans Administration, Public Health Service, and Bureau of Indian Affairs, and to civilian hospitals.

The civilian nurses who volunteered for the Army Nurse Corps had no previous military experience and therefore no knowledge of army methods and protocol; they had no training in battlefield conditions either. However, in July 1943 the army finally established a training course for all new army nurses. During an intensive, four-week period at fifteen U.S. training centers, nurses learned how to follow army rules, how to cope during an attack, and how to requisition supplies.

In June 1944 the army announced that nurses would receive officers' commissions and full veterans' retirement privileges. By war's end approximately 59,000 women had served in the Army Nurse Corps. They were deployed in every war zone around the world. They served in field hospitals just behind front lines, in evacuation hospitals, and aboard medical flights. More than 200 were killed, and several hundred were prisoners of war (most in the Philippines).

More than 1,600 army nurses received medals honoring their service.

Navy Nurse Corps

The Navy Nurse Corps (NNC) grew from several hundred at the start of World War II to 11,086 by 1943. Navy nurses were not deployed in combat zones until the war was almost over. Instead, male medics treated soldiers in the field. Navy nurses served on twelve U.S. hospital ships, caring for soldiers brought in from the battle fronts. They were also aboard air evacuation missions to stateside hospitals. In the United States they served in 40 hospitals, 176 dispensaries, and 6 schools for corpsmen in medic training.

Black army nurses

The army remained segregated during the war, and by war's end, when the Army Nurse Corps (ANC) had a total of about 50,000 nurses, only 479 of them were black women. The army deliberately held down the number of blacks in its ranks by setting a low quota (proportional share) of black enlistees. Only 160 black enrollees were admitted in 1943. The army argued that black nurses were not as versatile: They could only provide care for black soldiers, because they could only serve in black wards or all-black hospitals. The first black nurses were deployed to Liberia, Africa. Eventually they served in other parts of Africa, Burma, the South Pacific, and England. Under public pressure, the army ended the quota in 1944, allowing 2,000 black students into the Cadet Nurse Corps educational program. Black women were not admitted into the Navy Nurse Corps until January 1945. Only four black women served in the NNC.

Opening doors for women pilots

During the early 1930s Amelia Earhart (1897–1937) became the first woman to fly solo across the Atlantic Ocean. At that time flying lessons were very expensive, so only people from wealthy families were able to take lessons. Soon, however, the opportunity to fly opened up to considerably more men and women. In 1939 the army established the Civilian Pilot Training (CPT) program. (At that time, all pilots were part of the army. The U.S. Air Force was not established until 1947.) The stated purpose of CPT was to acquaint young people with flight; the unstated purpose was to develop a larger pool of trained pilots, potential recruits in case of war. World War II had broken out in Europe and Asia that same year, and U.S. leaders believed that the United States might eventually be drawn into the conflict. Open to men and women in college, CPT charged only a $40 fee for flight instruction that led to a beginning pilot's license. Approximately nine thousand college men and women signed up, about one woman for every ten men.

By 1941 roughly three thousand American women had learned to fly. Some U.S. women who wanted to use their flying skills in the military went to England to work for the Air Transport Auxiliary (ATA). Jacqueline Cochran (c.1906–1980), a famous U.S. pilot who held numerous speed records, was instrumental in recruiting twenty-four American female pilots for ATA. They ferried new planes from the factory to the armed services and moved planes off the ground during air raids. Earlier in 1939, Cochran had approached U.S. government officials about setting up a women's ferrying service in the United States, but her idea was brushed aside.

Finding a role

Persisting in her idea for a ferrying service in the United States, Cochran attracted publicity by ferrying a plane from Montreal, Canada, to an air base in Scotland in June 1941. When Cochran returned to the United States, President Franklin D. Roosevelt (1882–1945; served 1933–45) and his wife, Eleanor Roosevelt (1884–1962), invited her to dinner. Mrs. Roosevelt was an avid supporter of women pilots. President Roosevelt listened to Cochran's explanation of all the activities women were carrying out in England and asked her to formulate a proposal for a similar program for the United States.

Meanwhile, another American pilot, Nancy Love (1914–1976), was developing a plan for highly experienced women pilots to ferry planes. The daughter of a wealthy doctor,

Nancy had learned to fly as a teenager. She and her husband, Bob Love, operated an aircraft sales company in Boston, Massachusetts. Nancy Love had been ferrying planes to Canada since early 1940. From there the planes were flown to France for the war effort. She had written to the army about her plans, but her letter was ignored.

Within a few months of the U.S. entrance into World War II, it became clear that the army would need help delivering thousands of planes to air bases and ports. General Henry "Hap" Arnold (1886–1950), chief of the Army Air Corps, was aware of both Love's and Cochran's plans. On September 10, 1942, the army put Nancy Love's plan into action, creating a women's ferrying group called the Women's Auxiliary Ferrying Squadron (WAFS). At the same time, Cochran worked with General Arnold to plan a program for training women to fly military planes. Cochran's training program was first known as the Women's Flying Training Detachment (WFTD), or "Woofteddies."

WAFS and Woofteddies were not official branches of the army. These organizations simply worked for the army. Their pilots were paid less than male pilots in the army who did the same type of work. The women did not have army titles or army uniforms, and they were not covered under army insurance. Nevertheless, both Love and Cochran accepted these terms in order to get their women on the job or in training immediately.

Alice Rhonie, one of the first female pilots of WAFS (Women's Auxiliary Ferrying Squadron), trains at the Delaware air base in 1942. © *Bettmann/Corbis. Reproduced by permission.*

WAFS

Nancy Love's ferry squadron required fliers to be at least twenty-one years old. They also had to be high school graduates and have five hundred hours of flying time, twice as many hours as men doing the same job. The twenty-eight original WAFS recruits had plenty of flying time under their belts—an average of one thousand hours. When those twenty-eight arrived at New Castle Army Air Base at Wilmington, Delaware, they had to pass a physical and a flying test and then learn army rules and regulations

for a couple of weeks; after that their mission would begin. The army first assigned WAFS to ferry Piper Cubs, small aircraft used for training and surveillance. Soon WAFS who were performing exceptionally well began ferrying the much larger PT-17 and PT-19, both training aircraft.

WFTD: "Woofteddies"

Jacqueline Cochran's WFTD training program was for women who knew how to fly but were not as experienced as the WAFS. The program

Women in the Military: Postwar

The Army Nurse Corps and the Navy Nurse Corps remained active after the war. Injured soldiers still needed care, so the demand for nurses continued. Many women serving in the WAVES (Women Accepted for Volunteer Emergency Service) remained uniformed naval personnel after the war. However, like women in the civilian workforce, military women were often forced to accept lesser roles in the postwar period, such as clerical office positions rather than pilots. Nevertheless, a foundation was in place for women's future involvement in the military. On June 12, 1948, Congress passed a bill making the WAC (Women's Army Corps) a permanent branch of the U.S. Army. By 2000, about 10 percent of all military personnel, across all military services, were women.

The Women's Airforce Service Pilots (WASP) program provides an example of women's struggle to gain broader acceptance in the military. WASPs filled an important need during the war by ferrying military planes to their destinations. However, in June 1944 Congress defeated a bill that would have attached WASPs to the Army Air Forces. Then in December of that year, as military victory appeared well in hand, Congress ended

provided training to fly military aircraft. Out of 25,000 applicants, 1,830 passed all requirements and were accepted into the program. Ultimately 1,074 successfully graduated from the program.

Cochran's first class of thirty women began training at Avenger Field in Sweetwater, Texas. Eventually eighteen classes would train at Avenger for five to six months each.

WASP: Women's Airforce Service Pilots

Love's pilots set up ferrying units at New Castle Army Air Base in Wilmington, Delaware, and in Long Beach, California; Dallas, Texas; and Romulus, Michigan. Each unit was located near a large aircraft manufacturing facility. Major destinations included Newark, New Jersey, where planes left for Europe; Alameda, California, for planes going to the South Pacific; and Great Falls, Montana, for planes headed to the Soviet Union for Soviet pilots. By spring 1943 the first graduates of Cochran's training program joined Love's pilots. The role of women pilots for the military was steadily expanding. In recognition of their larger roles, on August 4, 1943, the Army Air Force combined the WAFS and WFTD into a single organization, the Women's Airforce Service Pilots (WASP).

the WASP program. In the following years the women pilots of World War II started a WASP organization to stay in touch and hold reunions. Many of the pilots moved on to new careers, although some remained in the aviation field. Dora Dougherty, who ferried warplanes during the war and in May 1944 was selected to fly the new B-29 bombers, became an aircraft company official.

The air force, navy, and army did not accept women into pilot training until the 1970s. During the mid-1970s the former WASPs sought formal recognition from Congress that their flights were official military missions that ought to give them war veteran status. Their campaign for recognition proved successful, and 1977 was declared The Year of the WASP. On November 23, 1977, President Jimmy Carter (1924– ; served 1977–81) signed into law a bill that recognized that WASPs had flown on active duty for the U.S. armed forces during the war. All WASPs would receive honorable discharges and veterans' benefits. This recognition led to increased public awareness of the WASPs. A number of museum exhibits about their service were developed, including one at the National Air and Space Museum in Washington, D.C.

By late 1943 the army was training WASPs to ferry fighters and bombers. WASPs flew seventy-seven different aircraft, including the B-17 Flying Fortress and the enormous B-29 Superfortress. WASPs flew 60 million miles and made about 12,400 deliveries before the army ended the WASP program on December 20, 1944.

Although they never became an official part of any U.S. military service, eleven hundred female pilots participated in WASP. About three hundred WASPs worked for the army during the war years, assisting in the effort to ferry thousands of newly produced aircraft from factories to military bases and ports. Others served as tow-target pilots, pulling targets behind their planes so soldiers could practice antiaircraft firing. WASPs also tested aircraft that were in for repair. WASPs flew only noncombat missions and never flew outside the continental United States; however, their participation in home front duties allowed more male pilots to perform combat duty.

For More Information

Books

Merryman, Molly. *Clipped Wings: The Rise and Fall of the Women Airforce Service Pilots (WASPs) of World War II.* New York: New York University Press, 1998.

Nathan, Amy. *Yankee Doodle Gals: Women Pilots of World War II*. Washington, DC: National Geographic Society, 2001.

Poulos, Paula Nassen, ed. *A Woman's War Too: U.S. Women in the Military in World War II*. Washington, DC: National Archives and Records Administration, 1996.

Zeinert, Karen. *The Incredible Women of World War II*. Brookfield, CT: Millbrook Press, 1994.

Web Sites

The Army Nurse Corps. http://www.army.mil/cmh-pg/books/wwii/72-14/72-14.htm (accessed on July 9, 2004).

Army Women's Museum, Fort Lee, Virginia. http://www.awm.lee.army.mil (accessed on July 9, 2004).

The Coast Guard and the Women's Reserve in World War II. http://www.uscg.mil/hq/g-cp/history/h_wmnres.html (accessed on July 9, 2004).

Fly Girls. http://www.pbs.org/wgbh/amex/flygirls.htm (accessed on July 9, 2004).

WASP on the Web. http://www.wasp-wwii.org/wasp/home.htm (accessed on July 9, 2004).

The WASP WWII Museum. http://www.wasp-wwii.org/museum/home.htm (accessed on July 9, 2004).

The Women's Army Corps: A Commemoration of World War II Service. http://www.army.mil/cmh-pg/brochures/wac/wac.htm (accessed on July 9, 2004).

Women of the WAVES. http://www.womenofthewaves.com (accessed on July 9, 2004).

World War II Era WAVES. http://www.history.navy.mil/photos/prs-tpic/females/wave-ww2.htm (accessed on July 9, 2004).

Home Front Organizations and Services

During the war years two civilian organizations provided fundamental support for U.S. soldiers and their families: the American Red Cross and the United Service Organizations (USO). These organizations had centers throughout the United States and carried out their activities with the help of millions of volunteers. Each organization also had centers overseas, as near to the U.S. troops as possible. By providing relief and comfort, the Red Cross and the USO bolstered morale on the home front and on the front lines. Responsibility for maintaining the physical health of military personnel and the American public fell to the U.S. Public Health Service. During the war years the Public Health Service concentrated its efforts on treating war-related diseases and maintaining adequate vaccines for Americans at home.

American Red Cross

The American Red Cross, founded by Clara Barton (1821–1912) in 1881, established the following goals as its mission: to care for sick and wounded soldiers during wartime,

American Red Cross Wartime Statistics

The following table comes from the Red Cross Web site at http://www.redcross.org/museum/ww2a.html.

Total contributions received during war years	$784,992,995
Greatest number of chapters (1943 and 1944)	3,757
Greatest number of adult members (1945)	36,645,333
Greatest number of Junior Red Cross members (1945)	19,905,400
Greatest number of volunteers (1945)	7,500,700
Greatest number of paid staff (1945)	24,378
Number of Red Cross certified nurses in service with the military	71,000
Number of service personnel receiving Red Cross aid	16,113,000
Messages between military personnel and families	42,000,000
Families aided by the Home Service	1,700,000
Tons of supplies shipped overseas	300,460
Pints of blood collected for military use	13,400,000
Number of blood donors	6,600,000
Number of foreign countries where Red Cross operated	more than 50
American Red Cross war casualties (deaths)–male	52
American Red Cross war casualties (deaths)–female	34

to help U.S. military personnel overseas communicate with their families, and to provide relief during natural disasters such as floods, hurricanes, and fires. During World War II (1939–45), the Red Cross was the largest civilian organization providing vital services to military personnel and their families. By 1945, the last year of the war, the Red Cross had 36.7 million adult members, 19.9 million Junior Red Cross members, 7.5 million volunteers, and 24,378 paid staff. Almost every household in the United States participated in some way in Red Cross activities. Between 1941 and 1946, when the average yearly U.S. family income was roughly $3,000, Americans contributed about $785 million to the Red Cross war fund. Each year contributions exceeded goals set by the Red Cross.

Services to the Armed Forces (SAF)

SAF was a division of the Red Cross that focused on the well-being of military personnel, both in the United States and abroad. SAF assistance was generally delivered by paid staff and was divided into several categories: Camp Service, Home Service, Club Service, and Hospital Service. Through the Camp Service program, the Red Cross sent 3,250 field directors and assistant field directors to live wherever military personnel were based.

Camp Service workers maintained mail services on base so military personnel could communicate with their families They also kept soldiers informed of any difficulties their families were encountering, provided counseling, and aided families with grants and loans in cases of emergency.

Home Service staff members were in constant contact with Camp Service personnel to facilitate communication between family members and troops. Like Camp personnel, they provided guidance counseling and emergency financial aid to military families struggling at home. If a family member became gravely ill or died on the home front, Home Service workers were often the ones to deliver the news to the serviceman. They also helped military families and soldiers by explaining health benefits and pensions. In addition, Home Service personnel helped military officials decide when a discharge or furlough (leave of absence from military duty) was necessary. The Red Cross estimates that its Home Service program aided forty-two million (mostly written) communications between military personnel and their families and provided some $38 million in emergency financial aid.

The Club Service of SAF offered rest and recreation to U.S. troops in the European and Pacific war zones. The Club Service operated both large and small clubs. For example, the Rainbow Corner Club in London, England, was open twenty-four hours a day, had overnight facilities, and could serve sixty thousand meals a day. Donut Dugouts were much smaller operations,

Red Cross workers prepare to ship Christmas gift boxes, packed by volunteers from the Production Corps, to U.S. servicemen fighting in World War II. *© Corbis. Reproduced by permission.*

providing doughnuts and coffee to U.S. military camps. The Club Service also maintained special clubs for soldiers who were suffering from psychological stress, sometimes called combat fatigue. Soldiers were assigned to these clubs by their military service.

The Hospital Service division of SAF provided social workers and recreational activities at all military hospitals, including veterans hospitals, in the United States and overseas. Hospital Service social workers offered psychiatric assistance, identifying problems related to an injured soldier's recovery, confidentially consulting with families at home concerning their soldier's mental state, and helping medical staff members determine the best course of action for each individual. With the help of many volunteers, the Hospital Service also provided recreational activities for recovering soldiers, from card games to movies to small theatrical productions. These activities speeded recovery and contributed to the well-being of the soldiers.

Volunteer Special Services

Volunteer Special Services, also called the Volunteer Corps, was another division of the Red Cross. It provided home front services with the help of millions of volunteers throughout the country. The Volunteer Corps had eleven different programs to utilize Americans' generosity and desire to help. The largest program by far was the Production Corps. At its peak in 1942–43, more than three and a half million volunteers repaired pieces of military clothing, wound rolls of bandages for military use, and packed boxes of personal care and comfort items for U.S. and Allied soldiers and civilian war victims. Production Corps members across the country, many of them wives, mothers, and daughters of servicemen, gathered together to work on their assigned tasks. As they worked, they shared stories of how they coped with loved ones being far away and discussed the daily challenges they faced at home, such as food shortages and rationing. Another vital volunteer

corps was the Motor Corps. Women made up the bulk of this corps. They drove their own cars more than 61 million miles throughout the United States, transporting supplies, nurses, and volunteers to various posts and moving sick and wounded soldiers to hospitals and home. The Red Cross estimates that forty-five thousand women participated in the Motor Corps. Many of them took courses to learn how to repair and maintain their cars.

Three more large volunteer programs were the Canteen Corps, the Staff Assistance Corps, and the Volunteer Nurses Aide Corps. The Canteen Corps, 105,571 volunteers strong in 1942–43, served coffee, doughnuts, meals, and snacks to traveling troops at railroad stations, airports, and embarkation posts; they also served personnel at military bases and people donating blood at Red Cross donor centers. On its Web site, www. redcross.org, the Red Cross reports that the Canteen Corps served "163 million cups of coffee, 254 million doughnuts, and 121 million meals" during the World War II years. The Staff Assistance Corps provided office or clerical support at all Red Cross facilities. The Volunteer Nurses Aide Corps provided assistance in twenty-five hundred civilian and military hospitals. Their help was especially valuable because nurses were in short supply on the home front. Members of the Hospital and Recreation Corps served at more than one thousand military and veterans hospitals. They read to patients, helped them write letters home, shopped for personal care items, and staffed recreation facilities.

The three smallest corps under Volunteer Special Services were the Arts and Skills Corps (volunteers who helped rehabilitate wounded soldiers), the Volunteer Dietitians Aide Corps (people who provided assistance in hospital dietary departments), and the Braille Corps (volunteers who copied books and magazines into Braille for the blind); the Braille Corps disbanded in 1942, when more advanced transcription methods came into use. Rounding out the eleven Volunteer Special Services programs were the Administration Corps (volunteers who oversaw and directed all the corps programs) and the Home Service Corps (volunteers working in the SAF Home Service division).

Specialized Wartime Services

Specialized Wartime Services filled specific wartime needs. The two largest programs were the Blood Donor Service and the War Funds campaign. The U.S. military asked the American Red Cross to begin a blood donor service in January 1941. By September 1945 thirty-five donor centers and sixty-three mobile units, operated by paid Red Cross medical personnel, had collected 13.4 million pints of blood. The wartime donor service continued after the war, and at the beginning of the twenty-first century, the Red Cross was still the largest blood donor service in the United States.

The War Funds campaign set fundraising goals each year from 1941 through 1946 to support its war programs, and contributions exceeded goals every year. During those years

A Red Cross poster promoting the Volunteer Nurses Aide Corps. *The Library of Congress.*

the total goal was $675 million, but Americans contributed almost $785 million to support the many Red Cross programs.

Another program under Specialized Wartime Services responded to the urgent needs of 1.4 million U.S. and Allied prisoners of war in European camps. Volunteers at centers in Chicago, New York City, Philadelphia,

American Red Cross nurses arriving in London, England, to set up a hospital for U.S. servicemen. © Corbis. Reproduced by permission.

and St. Louis assembled over twenty-seven million packages, mostly food packages measuring a specific 10 inches by 10 inches by 4.5 inches and weighing 11 pounds. The food packages contained foods that would not spoil, such as dried fruits, canned meats, and dried milk. Unfortunately packages were not utilized in the Pacific war zone, because Japanese authorities refused to cooperate. Civilian War Relief, a similar program in the Specialized Services division, distributed relief goods worth over $152 million to the people of war-ravaged Europe. At the end of the war when prisoners of war were released, their unused relief packages were included in these civilian distributions.

Other programs of the Specialized Services included Victory Book Campaigns, which collected reading material for soldiers, and Aid to Rescued Seamen and Evacuees, which helped victims whose vessels had sunk at sea and civilian evacuees from other countries. Another program, called War Brides, helped foreign wives of U.S. soldiers adjust to life in the United States; about sixty-five thousand foreign women married American servicemen overseas and came to the United States during World War II. Finally, a service called Civilian War Aid established 49,700 shelters across the country that could feed and house millions of Americans if the U.S. mainland was attacked.

War-Related Services

Some services provided by the Red Cross were related directly to battlefront activities. One of the most important duties of the Red Cross during the war was recruiting and certifying nurses for military service. The Nursing Service provided nurses for the Army Nurse Corps and the Navy Nurse Corps. Approximately 90 percent of military nurses, both on the home front and abroad, came through the Nursing Service.

In the late twentieth century the First Aid and Water Safety program taught millions of American youths how to swim and millions of adults how to administer first aid. During the war years this program was in charge of teaching soldiers, sailors, and airmen how to escape from a sinking ship or plane. Program staff members taught servicemen how to swim carrying full packs and amid burning fuel. Later in the war the program provided rehabilitation swimming activities for wounded soldiers.

Programs for Youth and Young Adults

Still other programs provided means for those too young or otherwise not serving in the military to fully participate in Red Cross activities. By 1945 approximately 75 percent of U.S. schoolchildren were members of the Junior Red Cross. Children and teens were just as eager as adults to do their part for the war effort, and the Red Cross provided an excellent avenue. The Junior Red Cross had local branches that held regular meetings. Members assembled comfort boxes (boxes containing food and other items familiar to the servicemen to remind them of home) for soldiers, gathered metal for scrap drives, and helped adult Red Cross groups with other war-related activities. They also concentrated on helping children in war-torn Europe by sending gift boxes and raising money for the National Children's Fund, an organization providing aid to distressed children worldwide. For college-age youth, 187 colleges and universities offered College Red Cross Units. Students enthusiastically volunteered for various Red Cross

Navy personnel dancing at a USO servicemen's club in San Francisco, California. *The Library of Congress.*

programs and raised money for the War Funds campaign.

In the twenty-first century the Red Cross is primarily recognized as a blood collection agency and a disaster response organization. During World War II, however, it provided daily assistance to civilians and soldiers alike, on the home front and overseas. Red Cross services affected the lives of millions of Americans during the war

Comedian Bob Hope, on tour with the USO, entertaining troops stationed in the South Pacific.
AP/Wide World Photos. Reproduced by permission.

years, sustaining them through difficult and dangerous times.

United Service Organizations (USO)

Beginning in 1940 the number of Americans in the military escalated rapidly. Only fifty thousand strong in 1940, U.S. troops numbered twelve million by the end of 1944. Many of the troops were young men who were away from home for the first time. During leave time they needed places to gather for recreation and friendship. President Franklin D. Roosevelt (1882–1945; served 1933–45) asked private groups in local communities to provide for the soldiers' needs. Answering the president's call were six well-established civilian organizations: National Catholic Community Services, the National Jewish Welfare Board, the National Travelers Aid Association, the Salvation Army, the Young Men's Christian Association (YMCA), and the Young Women's Christian Association (YWCA). Together they formed a nonprofit, private organization called United Service Organizations (USO). USO was not a government agency and was totally

Four-Legged Recruits

During World War II the U.S. military needed a few good dogs. Actually, the military needed thousands of very good dogs. The U.S. Army and Coast Guard recruited many canines through a New York City organization called Dogs for Defense (DFD). DFD members were patriotic civilian dog lovers ready to enlist their pets for wartime service. Great Britain, France, Russia, Germany. and Japan had been breeding and training dogs in war duties for many years. Germany and Japan—enemies of the Allies during the war—were believed to have canine armies totaling at least 150,000 dogs.

In the 1940s about twelve million dogs lived in the United States. Many of their owners filled out official enrollment applications to see if their dogs would be accepted for military service. The application required the owner's signature and the dog's paw print. The Coast Guard accepted only German shepherds. The army accepted various breeds, including Airedales, Afghans, boxers, Dalmatians, Dobermans, Newfoundlands, and German shepherds. Like every soldier, each dog had to pass a physical. Dogs in the best of health were then sent to war dog training camps. One of the largest camps was located in the Blue Ridge Mountains of Virginia. Another was near Philadelphia.

The war dog training camps were rather plush, at least by dog standards. Each canine teamed up with his or her

U.S. Marine "Raiders" and their dogs, which were used for scouting and running messages, in the Philippine jungle, November 1943. *National Archives photo no. 127-GR-84-68407 (World War II Photos).*

trainer, an army or Coast Guard soldier. Each day they drilled together, at first learning basic commands and then learning specific skills they would use for their assigned duty. Each dog had his or her own wooden kennel house; trainers returned the dogs to their kennels by late afternoon, when the much-anticipated food wagon rolled through the dog village. Trainers fed, played with, petted, and brushed their dogs. They gave baths and pedicures, and if it was rainy, they carefully rubbed their dogs dry at bedtime. Veterinarians provided the best of care.

Picturing dogs in basic training brought smiles to Americans' faces, but training days at dog camp were as serious and strict as any boot camps for human soldiers. Some of the best trainers early on were naturalized U.S. citizens who had served as dog trainers for European armies during World War I (1914–18). They shared their extensive knowledge with army and Coast Guard soldiers so the soldiers could serve as dog trainers in the camps. Dogs could be trained for four different duties. On the home front they were usually put on guard duty or patrol duty. Usually drawing night duty and rarely spotted by the general public, guard dogs and their army trainers watched over storage depots, port areas, bridges, and factories. The Coast Guard used patrol dogs extensively to patrol beaches from Maine to Florida, around the Gulf of Mexico, and along the western coastline up to Oregon and Washington. Each patrol dog went out every night with a Coast Guard sentry, the same person who had trained the dog since boot camp. Together they walked the lonely beaches. Guard and patrol dogs were friendly tail-waggers by day, but while they were on duty, they were suspicious of anyone other than their trainers at base camp.

Dogs could also be trained as messengers or as locators, for service on the battlefield. These dogs were taught to be totally loyal to their trainers, who provided food, play, and shelter. At dog war camp they learned to maneuver through and over obstacles, to ignore cats, squirrels, and other live distractions, and to not fear the sound of firing guns and explosions, which they would have to endure on the front lines. They learned to follow trails or scents, leave messages, and return to their trainers.

Messenger dogs wore leather collars fitted with small hollow aluminum tubes that could carry messages. Messages were generally orders from base camps to the front lines; on the return trip, dogs would deliver soldiers' requests to the base camp. Dogs traveled much faster than men, ran silently and low to the ground, and were a much less likely target than a soldier would be.

Locator dogs were sent out to search for wounded soldiers. Each dog had a short stick, known as a "brinsell," attached to his or her collar. If a locator dog found a wounded soldier, the dog would return to base camp with the brinsell in his or her mouth. Seeing this signal, soldiers at base camp would take a stretcher and follow the dog back to the wounded man. Many wounded soldiers returned home ready to tell the story of how they were saved by a canine in the U.S. Army.

Air Carrier Contract Personnel

The commercial airline business was still in its infancy at the beginning of World War II (1939–45). Most ordinary Americans had never been on a commercial flight, but they were excited about the possibility of one day boarding a shiny silver plane and flying across the country. However, the shiny silver commercial airplane all but disappeared from civilian airports by the early 1940s. Most planes had been painted a dull military grey and pressed into military service. The majority of commercial pilots, navigators, radio operators, and maintenance workers had become part of the Air Carrier Contract Personnel of the U.S. Army Air Forces Air Transport Command (all air force duties were carried out by the army at that time; the U.S. Air Force was not established until 1947). The commercial airmen helped the army train pilots and develop a worldwide transport system for troops and supplies. During the war they could be found at home front bases and at Allied bases overseas. Eventually they organized an air transport system larger than the combined U.S. military and U.S. civilian airline systems as they existed prior to the Pearl Harbor attack on December 7, 1941.

funded by gifts from citizens and businesses. However, the president of the United States was its honorary chairman, and the organization would work closely with the military to look after the welfare, spirits, and recreational needs of America's military personnel. The USO billed itself as delivering a "touch of home" for every soldier. Volunteers from local communities located buildings in their towns that could be turned into USO clubs. Church basements, unused houses and stores, existing clubs of all sorts, even museums and barns were turned into USO facilities. Given the strong patriotic unity within the United States at the time, USOs always had plenty of volunteers. Everyone was interested in the welfare of American soldiers. Local young women, carefully screened for their moral character, served as hostesses and dance partners. Like the military, the USO segregated soldiers by race. There were USO facilities for white soldiers and separate USOs for black soldiers.

Soldiers who went to any USO found warmth, smiles, and friendship. Coffee and doughnuts were always on hand at every USO. Besides snacking, soldiers could eat a full meal, read a favorite magazine, see a movie, dance, and socialize. USOs also had quiet areas for letter writing or, if a soldier desired it, religious counseling. By 1944 there were three thousand USOs in communities across the country, usually close to a military base or sometimes actually on the base. The first overseas USO, for American soldiers abroad, was established in Rome, Italy, in 1943. It was known as a "USO Canteen." Soon volunteers set up USOs worldwide, in every outpost where it was feasible. Some USO facilities were large, and some were tiny.

In October 1941 USO established Camp Shows, Inc. Through this program, entertainers volunteered to put on shows for soldiers at USO centers. Between 1941 and 1947 more than seven thousand entertainers performed live for soldiers at USOs in the United States and overseas. Comedian Bob Hope (1903–2003) made his first overseas USO Camp Show tour in 1942. Hope would continue participating in USO tours for five decades. By 1947 U.S. soldiers worldwide had been treated to an amazing 428,521 USO shows.

At the end of World War II, USO estimated that 1.5 million volunteers had given their time, encouragement, and friendship to soldiers at USO centers. On December 31, 1947, President Harry S. Truman (1884–1972; served 1945–53) gave the USO an "honorable discharge," and all its facilities were closed. However, USO reactivated during the Korean War (1950–53) and continued its mission into the twenty-first century. In 2003 USO operated twenty-one centers worldwide plus five mobile centers. The USO World Headquarters is in Washington, D.C.

U.S. Public Health Service

In 1939 President Roosevelt moved the U.S. Public Health Service under the Federal Security Agency and gave it responsibility for the health of all U.S. military personnel and civilians. The Public Health Service worked closely with the army and navy to control diseases associated with military service. Deployment overseas exposed soldiers to malaria, typhus, and tuberculosis; soldiers also contracted sexually transmitted diseases, on the home front and abroad. The Public Health Service established major research and development programs to study disease control, and many home front scientists and medical personnel labored to find practical prevention and treatment for these diseases. Much of the research was carried out at the National Institutes of Health main campus in Bethesda, Maryland. The Public Health Service also maintained the nation's supply of vaccines for military and civilian use. The Communicable Disease Center, later called the Centers for Disease Control and Prevention, was formed after the war, in 1946, and was an outgrowth of Public Health Service studies.

Public Health Service research included studies of illness among American war industry workers. The chemicals and metal materials used in war production factories were highly toxic and led to illness and disease in many workers. Investigations to learn about occupational hazards were part of the industrial health program within the Public Health Service.

The Public Health Service worked closely with many government war agencies to protect workers on the job. For example, it coordinated with the War Production Board (to minimize hazards to workers), the War Manpower Commission (to ensure placement of workers in jobs suitable to their physical abilities), the War Shipping Administration (to monitor conditions aboard crowded oceangoing vessels), and the Office of Civil Defense (to protect civilian lives and property from attack). In fall 1943 the Public Health Service established the Division of Nurse Training to address a critical nationwide shortage of nursing staff. The army and navy were requesting twenty-five hundred additional nurses each month, leaving home front hospitals desperately short on personnel. The nurse training division aimed to recruit sixty-five thousand new cadet nurses and offered refresher courses for those wishing to return to a nursing career.

For More Information

Books

Andrews, Maxene. *Over Here, Over There: The Andrews Sisters and the USO Stars in World War II*. New York: Kensington Publishing, 1993.

Hurd, Charles. *The Compact History of the American Red Cross*. New York: Hawthorne Books, 1959.

Warren, James R. *The War Years: A Chronicle of Washington State in World War II*. Seattle: University of Washington Press, 2000.

Periodicals

King, Elizabeth W. "Heroes of Wartime Science and Mercy." *National Geographic Magazine* (December 1943): pp. 715–739.

Simpich, Frederick. "Your Dog Joins Up." *National Geographic Magazine* (January 1943): pp. 93–113.

Web Sites

American Red Cross. www.redcross.org (accessed on July 14, 2004).

National Library of Medicine. http://www.nlm.nih.gov (accessed on July 14, 2004).

United Service Organizations. http://www.uso.org (accessed on July 14, 2004).

Wartime in U.S. Communities

For the United States, World War II lasted from December 8, 1941, until September 2, 1945. During this period, communities across the country felt the impact of war in various ways. This chapter describes how the war affected San Diego, California; Washington, D.C.; the states of Michigan and Washington; North Platte, Nebraska; and the U.S. territory of Hawaii. The business of war significantly altered life on the home front in nearly every part of the nation; the communities described in this chapter serve as examples. From tiny North Platte to the boomtown of San Diego, citizens saw their communities transformed by the new wartime economy.

San Diego: Boomtown

With several large military facilities and an ever-expanding aircraft industry, San Diego turned into a boomtown during the war years. San Diego, a beautiful temperate Southern California city with a deepwater port, became one of the most important naval centers of the world. The city was home to a huge naval hospital and supply depot; a destroyer,

Something in Common

In communities across the United States, big and small, a common sight could be seen. When a family member, such as a son or daughter, joined military service, a service flag with a blue star was hung in a window of the family home, where it could be seen by the public. If the son or daughter was killed in service, a gold star replaced the blue star.

submarine, and light cruiser operating base; an advanced training center; and one of the largest U.S. naval bases for aircraft. At North Island Naval Air Station, located along the coastal section of the city, the U.S. Navy maintained facilities to repair airplanes. The Marine Corps also had facilities in San Diego, and U.S. Army personnel were at Fort Rosecrans and Camp Callan. Soldiers and sailors were everywhere on the streets of San Diego. Their paychecks brought a huge influx of money into the city's economy.

In 1917 a naval aviator named Reuben Fleet (1887–1975) graduated from the North Island Naval Air Station. Fleet established Consolidated Aircraft Company in the state of New York but moved the company to San Diego in 1933. The navy awarded him contracts for patrol planes, and the army placed regular orders for pursuit planes. To fulfill these orders Consolidated expanded from 900 employees in 1935

to 3,700 in 1936. In March 1939 Consolidated developed a bomber for the army, the B-24. When Germany invaded Poland in September of that year, the company anticipated that more military contracts would be coming, so it leased seventeen more acres to add to its plant. By March 1940 Great Britain was embroiled in the war and ordered 344 B-24s. That same month, President Franklin Roosevelt (1882–1945; served 1933–45) asked U.S. aircraft manufacturers to build a total of fifty thousand planes per year. Consolidated, 5,700 employees strong, had $70 million in backlogged orders, so it began adding 150 new workers each week. The B-24, Consolidated's major product, became one of the outstanding aircraft of World War II. San Diego was on its way to becoming a booming war industry town.

Linda Vista

The continuing influx of military personnel and the arrival of new war industry workers exhausted San Diego's supply of housing. Reuben Fleet recognized that his company's success hinged on having enough employees available to fill the military's orders; he also knew these potential employees had to have somewhere to live. Fleet decided to go to Washington, D.C., to request funding for a new housing development in San Diego. In October 1940 he met with Secretary of the Treasury Henry Morgenthau Jr. (1891–1967) and secured grant money through the Lanham Act for National Defense Housing. By early 1941 the new housing development, called Linda Vista,

The Linda Vista housing development in San Diego, California, circa 1943. © *Corbis. Reproduced by permission.*

was under construction. Linda Vista was a $9 million project featuring three thousand new houses; it was the largest construction project in San Diego history and the world's largest low-cost modern prefabricated tract housing development at the time. The original three thousand houses were to be built in three hundred days. At the peak of construction, builders finished forty homes a day. The floor plans for all the houses were identical, but buyers could choose from twenty-five different exteriors. The first tract housing development in the United States, called Edgemoor Terrace, was built in 1939 in Wilmington, Delaware. The term "tract housing" refers to similarly constructed homes built on a defined piece (tract) of land. Though it became a familiar sight in the mid-twentieth century, tract housing was still a new concept to most Americans in the 1940s.

The first homes in Linda Vista opened to residents on March 6, 1941. The first Linda Vista childcare center opened in spring 1942, as did Kearny High School. The development included a Safeway grocery store and Linda Vista Department Store. The department store was located in the first planned shopping center in San Diego. By April 1943, 4,416 families—16,245 people—lived at Linda Vista.

In one row after another, new houses continued creeping up and over San Diego's hills. Hundreds of trailers were brought in for living spaces. Construction workers flocked to the city, and many of their families lived in tents until they could find housing. Schools were seriously over-crowded. Classes met in every available space, including lunchrooms, until schools could be expanded. As the city struggled to keep up with its popula-tion boom, piles of lumber awaiting delivery to construction sites were con-tinuously stacked high in front of the San Diego civic center, known as the Embarcadero, a waterfront area where ships unloaded their cargo.

So many jobs

Consolidated Aircraft Com-pany employed 23,089 male and female workers in 1941, and by 1943 it had 45,000 workers on its payroll. New employees were trained at a twenty-four-hour vocational (training for a specific trade or technical task) school, a first in education history. Workers no longer needed to search for jobs; instead, employers were desperately searching for workers. Tourists in San Diego complained about being offered jobs while they were simply trying to relax on a park bench and enjoy the sun. Consolidated Aircraft workers averaged $47.50 for a fifty-hour week; minimum pay was $27.50 per week.

Only a few years earlier, a sleepy San Diego had closed down by 10 or 11 P.M., but by 1942 theaters and restaurants remained open all night to serve the around-the-clock workforce. Military bases gobbled up more and more land within the city. Ships moved continuously through the harbor water-ways while military planes rumbled overhead. The home front city of San Diego had been changed forever by the booming wartime economy.

Washington, D.C., in wartime

During World War II a visitor to Washington, D.C., would have found many famous public areas of the nation's capital filled with an array of temporary buildings, commonly refer-red to as "tempos." Between the Capitol Building and Lincoln Memorial, 53 acres of open green space gave way to tempo-rary wooden office buildings. Gazing from the Lincoln Memorial to the Washington Monument, a visitor would have seen two separate wooden spans crossing over the reflecting pools and connecting temporary navy office build-ings located on opposite sides of the pools. Washington, D.C., along with nearby areas of Virginia and Maryland, was headquarters for the massive busi-ness of war. Every available bit of office space was needed to hold new and tem-porary workers and mountains of war-related paperwork.

Federal war agencies and the military services filled tempos with thousands of war workers as fast as the

"Government girl" hostesses at a United Services Organization (USO) center in Washington, D.C., entertain servicemen with a game. *The Library of Congress.*

buildings could be constructed. In addition to the many tempos, the government leased all or parts of more than two hundred private office buildings. The former occupants, businesses or government agencies not considered essential for the war effort, moved to other areas outside the capital or to other cities. For example, the Patent Office headed to Richmond, Virginia, and the Railroad Retirement Board moved to Chicago, Illinois.

During the war years the White House and its grounds were closed to tourists. Iron fencing prevented trespassing, and armed soldiers stood guard. Troops guarding the White House area lived in temporary army barracks on the Ellipse, right by the president's home. The White House acquired the historic Blair House across the street to house its guests; the guest list included many government officials from all over the world, who were streaming into Washington to discuss wartime plans.

Between 1940 and 1943 the population in the Washington, D.C., area increased 25 percent. Approximately 283,000 federal workers, double the number employed by the government during World War I (1914–18), crowded stores, restaurants, theaters, and all forms of public transportation. Housing was virtually impossible to find. The War Department and the Treasury employed the largest number of civilian workers in Washington. Temporary war agencies such as the War Production Board (WPB), War Manpower Commission (WMC), and Office of War Information (OWI) also employed thousands. Downtown Washington streets were locked in traffic throughout the day. Over one hundred thousand civilian workers and military men and women moved through Union Station every twenty-four hours on their way to catch various commuter trains. Most federal workers had forty-eight-hour workweeks, and their working hours were varied to improve street traffic, train, and pedestrian flow. Before the war most stores were not open at night. However, many Washington-area stores began staying open until 9 P.M. on Thursdays to allow people who worked a day shift more time to shop. After the war and into the 1950s it became customary for department stores across the country to stay open on Thursday nights.

Housing relief

After the United States entered the war, thousands of young women flocked to Washington, D.C., hoping to fill government jobs newly created by the administrative needs of the war effort. Many of these young women did find employment, but they also found housing in Washington extremely scarce. In an effort to ease the housing shortage, the government began the Arlington Farms project, a housing project on the grounds of Arlington National Cemetery. The government built ten dormitories, each named after a state. The ten dorms accommodated about six thousand "government girls," as the working young women were called. Each room was pleasantly and comfortably decorated and rented for $24.50 a month. There was a central restaurant that seated eighteen hundred, gathering rooms (for social activities such as card games), and ironing rooms. The complex also had recreational areas, a department store, a huge beauty shop, and an infirmary. Four additional dorms housed military women. Three more dormitories—Alcott Hall, Barton Hall, and Curie Hall—were built in West Potomac Park. At nearby Langston Air Base in Virginia, two dormitories (Midway and Wake) housed black American young women who worked for the government.

In Arlington, Virginia, federal housing agencies built temporary dorms and family units to accommodate 4,400. Private builders added 8,500 homes. Arlington transformed from a quiet rural town to a busy suburban arm of the nation's capital. In Alexandria, Virginia, 371 apartment buildings with 2,300 apartments were built on 323 acres. In the northwest section of Washington, D.C., new apartment projects and nine residence halls for unmarried individuals were finished in 1943.

Women waiting for a bus at Arlington Farms, a housing project for female government employees, Arlington, Virginia, June 1943. © *Corbis. Reproduced by permission.*

New permanent buildings

The most impressive building constructed during the war years was the Pentagon. A massive concrete structure—definitely not a tempo—the Pentagon would house the huge War Department. (War Department offices had previously been scattered in several different buildings.) The Army Corps of Engineers chose a 320-acre site across the Potomac River in Virginia, about three miles from the White House. Construction began in September 1941, and the building was finished sixteen months later, in January 1943. Sixteen and a half miles of corridors led to almost 4 million square feet of office and storage space. More than 55,000 meals, 25,000 cups of coffee, 3,250 quarts of milk, and 17,000 carbonated beverages were sold every day in the Pentagon's eating areas. A large shopping area within the structure, complete with bank and health facilities, served those working at the Pentagon. The American Red Cross set up a permanent blood donor center there. The telephone system within the Pentagon was the size of a small city's service.

Civilian employees of the War Department relax in the courtyard, which is nicknamed "Pentagon Beach," at the Pentagon in Washington, D.C. *© Bettmann/Corbis. Reproduced by permission.*

Another permanent building completed during the war was the Jefferson Memorial. Although it had no connection to war activities, Americans proudly viewed it as a symbol of "Life, Liberty, and the Pursuit of Happiness," that is, the ideals Americans were fighting for in the war.

The Washington National Airport (later called Reagan National, named after President Ronald Reagan, 1911–2004; served 1981–89) was completed and opened in June 1941. It was close to the Pentagon and just 3.5 miles from downtown Washington.

By February 1942, fifty thousand passengers were arriving and departing from National daily. However, only a year later commercial flights decreased because pilots were leaving civilian work to join the Army Air Forces. Many of the silver passenger planes were repainted in a dull military grey and put to use by the Air Transport Command.

Also completed during wartime was the National Naval Medical Center near Bethesda, Maryland. Navy, marine, and Coast Guard servicemen who had been wounded in action were treated there. A 270-foot white tower centered the structure and was visible for miles around. The medical center also housed research and study facilities.

Michigan: Wartime powerhouse

The Great Lakes region provided a prime example of a region converting its industry to production of wartime needs and the social changes that accompanied the conversion. Michigan's automobile industry led the way in the state's conversion from a peacetime economy to a wartime economy. The U.S. government banned production of civilian automobiles in early 1942, to force the industry to switch to the production of aircraft, aircraft parts, military trucks, tanks, and marine equipment. For example, landing craft known as "ducks," which had propellers for water and six wheels for land, moved along the assembly lines at General Motors' Truck Division. Automobile mogul Henry Ford built a gigantic aircraft plant called Willow Run in a rural area west of Detroit, completed in early 1942. The plant offered thousands of jobs building B-24s.

To supplement the war production of Detroit's automotive giants (Ford, Chrysler, and General Motors), thousands of small manufacturers across the state contracted with the big manufacturers and the federal government to make smaller parts. Their facilities ranged in size from converted garages to small plants. The city of Detroit also became the largest producer of munitions in the world.

War industry wages were very good, averaging $62 a week in the Detroit area and $56 a week for the entire state. These wages were considerably better than those paid in the aircraft industry in Southern California, where the average wage was $47.50 a week. However, there was a general shortage of available workers, especially in the Detroit area, so manufacturers recruited thousands from Kentucky, Tennessee, Oklahoma, and Texas. To avoid workforce shortages in neighboring states, the War Manpower Commission, a federal agency, prohibited Michigan from recruiting workers in the bordering states of Indiana, Illinois, Ohio, and Wisconsin. Detroit was growing by 13,500 people per month in 1942 and 1943. The population in the greater metropolitan area increased by 600,000 to hit a total of 2.4 million. So many new workers came from Tennessee and Kentucky that people began to joke about it, saying that there were only forty-six states in America because Tennessee and Kentucky were now in Michigan. (At this time, there were only forty-eight U.S. states.)

Social change

The large, rapid increase in population presented numerous challenges in Michigan. The most pressing social concern was housing. For example, the rural area where Willow Run was located lacked adequate housing and transportation. Nearby communities such as Ypsilanti were already bursting at the seams with Willow Run workers. The federal government built some housing in the area, including

North Platte Canteen

From December 25, 1941, until April 1, 1946, seven months after the end of World War II, the train station on Front Street in North Platte, Nebraska, was much more than a place to catch trains. The station was transformed into the North Platte Canteen. North Platte was a farming community of twelve thousand, located on the Midwestern plains and hours from the nearest urban centers. The tracks that ran through the town were a main east-west line of Union Pacific Railroad. The trains carried thousands of soldiers to ports on the East and West coasts where they would embark for war zones in Europe or the Pacific. On a freezing Christmas Day in 1941, a handful of North Platte citizens decided to offer the soldiers moving through the station a home-cooked meal and treats. The news about the food and treats spread rapidly, and more and more volunteers came forth. Soon the station was a warm, welcoming canteen where soldiers could enjoy food, magazines, and even live piano music. Canteen staff members also offered smiles, words of encouragement, and thanks to the young soldiers.

North Platte Canteen volunteers met every train that came through the station, beginning at 5 A.M. and staying until the last train passed through around midnight—and they did this every single day, from that first Christmas until a few months after the war ended (at that point, they were serving soldiers who were headed home). Groups from 125 communities in Nebraska and Colorado participated regularly in an organized schedule to staff the canteen. Farming communities donated thousands of eggs and vast quantities of milk and vegetables. Homemade cakes and cookies arrived daily. Meanwhile troop trains were constantly coming in and out of the station. Early in the war between 3,000 and 5,000 soldiers moved through North Platte on the busiest days. Toward the end of the war as many as 8,000 a day passed through on peak days. Although stops lasted only ten to fifteen minutes, the soldiers poured off the train into the canteen. Eventually 600,000 soldiers received the kindness of the North Platte Canteen.

dormitories for unmarried workers. A privately financed subdivision between Willow Run and Dearborn advertised a $100 move-in cost for permanent homes. Additionally, hundreds of temporary duplexes were built on several acres near Willow Run. Some workers lived in trailers along the highways. In nearby communities, zoning ordinances were frequently ignored as residents rented out rooms in their homes to Willow Run workers and their families. Still, most Willow Run workers had to commute long distances to work every day. Carpooling and combining gas ration coupons, many drove their cars

During World War II, some industries opened daycare centers on site to accommodate families where both the mother and father worked outside the home. *The Library of Congress.*

up to an hour each way from areas east and west of Detroit.

Because of wartime gas shortages and rationing, workers commuting within Detroit also had trouble obtaining enough gasoline for their trips to work. The gas shortage affected the city's transportation pattern. Before the war, most Detroit residents drove their own cars to work and to the stores. During the war, almost all of them crowded onto streetcars and buses, and those public transportation systems became severely overcrowded.

As more and more women took jobs in the region's war industries,

Michigan's social service agencies recognized a considerable number of children were becoming "latchkey kids." With no parent at home, these children carried keys on string around their necks so they could let themselves into their homes or apartments after school. Concerned about the safety and welfare of these children, local schools, agencies, and recreation centers opened snack bars and created small social clubs, hoping latchkey kids would spend time there rather than staying home alone. Social services agencies also attempted to oversee privately run nursery schools opened for working mothers with preschool children. Concern for latchkey kids and youngsters in daycare was prevalent in most large war industry centers where mothers as well as dads joined the workforce.

Michigan residents not only experienced lifestyle adjustments to accommodate wartime employment but also changed their recreational habits. Movie houses, bowling alleys, and restaurants stayed open around the clock. It was apparent when shift changed occurred, because long lines formed outside movie houses, even at such odd hours as 8:00 A.M. Because of gas rationing, Detroit residents no longer jumped in their cars and headed to northern Michigan for fishing and other recreational activities. Resorts close to the industrial centers still thrived, but most of those that required long drives were forced to close. Tourism, especially fishing and hunting, had been a major industry in Michigan before the war, but it dropped off significantly during wartime.

Just as other citizens across the nation, Michigan residents spent many hours volunteering for war effort activities. Volunteering for responsibilities such as air raid warden within the local branch of the Office of Civilian Defense attracted considerable numbers of people. Studies had been released in local papers showing that Michigan's war industries were within range of German bombers. Cooperating with local civil defense organizations, communities and neighborhoods prepared with practice air raid alerts.

Another highly popular war activity was planting victory gardens (private gardens planted by individual families to add to the nation's wartime food supply). Michigan residents planted more land in victory gardens than was planted in the entire state for commercial vegetable crops. Diligently caring for their crops, Michigan victory gardeners produced 500,000 tons of vegetables, worth $20 million, in 1943 alone. A different type of wartime agricultural project occurred in northern Michigan near Petoskey. Milkweed grew wild there, and scientists thought it might be an excellent substitute for kapok, a fiber that was used as a buoyant material for life jackets. Before the war the United States had imported kapok from Southeast Asia; however, all U.S. trade with that region ceased during wartime. In a 1943 experiment, milkweed was collected (with the aid of schoolchildren), dried, and tested in scientific laboratories. It was found to have the same properties as kapok. In 1944 project leaders organized twenty-nine states to collect milkweed. The pods went to Petoskey for processing.

The state of Washington

The wartime economy played a significant role in every state. In some states, such as California and Michigan, war industry contracts from the U.S. government had profound effects on local communities. Washington was another state affected by war production contracts. In July 1942 the War Production Board (WPB) announced that the aircraft industry in the

Seattle-Tacoma-Bremerton area of western Washington had been awarded contracts worth $1 billion. To fulfill these contracts, the Seattle aircraft plants, including the giant Boeing Company, quintupled their square footage, reaching an expanse of 4.1 million square feet at the beginning of 1943. The WPB also announced that Seattle shipyards had received $709 million in government contracts, more than one hundred times the amount awarded in 1939. According to the census of 1940 the state of Washington had a population of 1,736,191. The war industries quickly added 250,000 individuals to that number.

To support its aircraft and shipyard industries, the state of Washington produced essential metals such as aluminum, lead, zinc, copper, and tungsten. Washington had produced no aluminum in 1939, but by 1942 it was producing one-third of all U.S. aluminum. The Grand Coulee and Bonneville Dams, both built during the 1930s, provided the tremendous amounts of energy needed for aluminum production. Washington's lumber, fishing, and agricultural industries hit all-time production highs. Lumber was used in a variety of wartime construction projects, from barracks to barges to whole factories. The army and navy bought up the entire supply of Northwest canned salmon, a nonperishable item that could be shipped to troops overseas. The army and navy also purchased much of the state's farm produce.

The population centers in Washington State experienced the same problems of overcrowding that plagued San Diego, Washington, D.C., Detroit, and many other U.S. cities. New housing developments sprouted almost overnight, but many families lived in temporary trailer parks. Hospitals, local city services, and schools were severely strained. The military presence in the state contributed to the population boom. By 1944 approximately fifteen army bases and twenty-one stations for the Army Air Forces were located throughout the state. There were also eight navy stations, including the Puget Sound Navy Yard. Hanford Atomic Works, the nuclear plant that would purify plutonium for the first U.S. atomic bomb, also brought an influx of new workers to the state. The facilities were built along the Columbia River in southeastern Washington.

Affected towns and cities

Spokane, a town in eastern Washington, provides one example of how military bases affected small-to medium-sized U.S. towns. Two small bases, Fort Wright and Felts Field, were already established in Spokane when the United States went to war. Geiger Field, Fairchild Air Force Base (originally known as Galena), Baxter Hospital for wounded soldiers, and Velox Naval Supply Depot were added during the war years. Just across the Idaho-Washington border from Spokane was Farragut Naval Station, the navy's second-largest training center.

Thousands of civilian positions within the military provided new job

Rising Telephone Use

During the war years only about one-half of American homes had telephones. Before the war residents and civilian businesses rarely made long-distance calls. Long-distance calling did not become common until U.S. military personnel were separated from their loved ones during World War II. The number of long-distance calls placed in the United States tripled between 1939 and 1945. There was no direct dial; all calls went through a live long-distance operator who connected callers to the numbers they requested. Government and military calls had priority over all others.

Bell Telephone, later known as AT&T, employed 171,439 long-distance operators during the war. Approximately 600,000 long-distance calls were placed every day in 1945.

opportunities and greatly brightened the employment picture in Spokane. The military leased numerous civilian buildings in Spokane, including a closed department store, and used them for office space to build the new military bases. The military then hired Spokane residents into civilian clerical and administrative jobs. To build the new military bases, approximately thirty thousand male residents were needed. Women took over jobs in the town, such as bus drivers, that those men had previously held. Two new

aluminum-producing plants were built in the area requiring construction workers and, later on, regular employees. The Spokane public school system had hired only single schoolteachers before the war but many of those teachers left for the war jobs. Soon the schools were hiring married teachers as fast as they could.

The war also affected Spokane's service organizations and social life. The residents of Spokane established welcoming centers and recreational facilities for the thousands of soldiers in town. Several USO (United Service Organizations) centers opened, including the George Washington Carver Club for black military personnel. USO centers, operated by local volunteers, provided food and social activities to servicemen. USOs strove to be a "home away from home" for those in the military. Church groups sponsored dinners, dances, and other social events. Many residents rented rooms to wives of servicemen, who usually wanted to stay close to the military bases.

Tacoma, a city just south of Seattle, was also a military hub and a war industry center. Its two army bases, Fort Lewis and McCord Air Field, expanded rapidly. McCord was the largest bomber training facility in the United States by 1943. By late 1941, when the United States entered the war, Fort Lewis could train fifty thousand soldiers at a time. The Fort Lewis Hospital eventually became the immense Madigan Medical Center for wounded servicemen. After the war Fort Lewis and Madigan remained as permanent military centers and were still at the center of Tacoma's economy in the early twenty-first century.

War's impact on Washington's schools

The Washington legislature provided funding in 1941 for new school construction. However, despite the funding, there was an acute shortage of school facilities throughout the state because building materials were scarce and student numbers continued to rise. Teachers held classes in every nook of the school, including hallways and lunchrooms. Schools needed twice the number of teachers they had needed in 1940. At the same time, many teachers were leaving their profession to take higher-paying jobs in the war industry. Because regular certified teachers were not available in sufficient numbers, the state of Washington began issuing War Emergency Certificates, teaching certificates that allowed noncredentialed people to teach in the public school system.

Schools also struggled with transportation and scheduling. Because of wartime restrictions on the use of important materials such as metal and rubber, no new school buses were built during the war years. As old buses broke down, they had to be fixed or let go. Therefore, schools often had to stagger student arrivals and departures, because there were not enough buses to transport all of them at one time. In areas near war production plants, schools sometimes adjusted their hours so the oldest students could work in the factories but still finish high school. Many public schools offered intensive vocational classes, classes that were open to the general public, which taught students the technical skills they needed to work in the aircraft and shipyard industries. Approximately 110,000 people went through these programs.

At the University of Washington in Seattle, many departments quickly adjusted to the needs of the military and the war industry. For example, the chemistry department researched chemical warfare and explosives. The newly established Applied Physics Laboratory worked with the U.S. Navy on weapons projects. The oceanography department worked with the navy and government agencies on secret investigations. The Department of Mines experimented with minerals used in the war industries. The engineering department found better ways of welding ships and investigated aerodynamics in wind tunnels. The foreign language department began offering courses in Chinese, Japanese, Korean, and Russian. The home economics department taught students how to prepare huge quantities of food, in case they ever needed to literally feed an army (or any of the other armed services).

Enrollment at the University of Washington and Washington State University in Pullman (southeastern Washington) dropped during the war years; men's dormitories and fraternities emptied out as students enlisted. However, the dorms were soon filled with military personnel who attended special classes set up just for them. For example, at Washington State the Army Signal Corps, Army Veterinary Corps, and Army Air Forces all conducted classes on campus. Like other colleges and universities across the country, Washington's schools had significantly lower enrollments of regular students during the war years. However, at the war's end, in the fall of 1945, veterans, under the GI Bill, began to enroll by the thousands. (See Chapter 5: Wartime Politics.)

Lifestyle changes in Hawaii

Before 1959, Hawaii was a U.S. territory, not a state. However, its residents were U.S. citizens. After the Japanese attacked the U.S. military base at Pearl Harbor, Hawaii, on December 7, 1941, Hawaii's residents faced more-significant daily lifestyle changes than any other U.S. citizens.

After the Pearl Harbor attack, people living in Hawaii continued to work, attend school, and carry out daily activities. However, sun-loving tourists soon gave way to military personnel. Soldiers and sailors were everywhere. Barbed wire barricades lined Waikiki Beach. Women who used to weave flower leis for guests began to weave miles of camouflage nets used to conceal military equipment on the battlefront. Schoolchildren learned how to use gas masks. Air raid sirens regularly went off in Honolulu to signal practice drills and blackouts. Golf courses were dotted with obstructions to prevent enemy airplanes from landing on them.

Residents of Hawaii lived under a state of martial law (military rule),

and this was widely accepted as a wartime necessity. Instead of a civilian governor, a U.S. military governor was in charge. From government offices, U.S. military leaders issued rules and laws and ordered all basic foodstuffs for island use. Both army officers and civilians worked within government headquarters to ensure island security. Security was deemed necessary because most residents of Hawaii thought there would be another attack.

For identification purposes all 425,000 residents were fingerprinted. Everyone was immunized against typhoid fever, typhus, smallpox, and diphtheria to prevent epidemics in case of another attack and disruption to regular medical care. Regular American money was replaced with scrip (temporary paper money) to prevent the Japanese from possibly seizing and using American currency. Hawaii's military government officials took other measures and established many temporary laws to ensure safety and order during wartime. Lieutenant Frederick Simpich listed several of the more interesting laws in a *National Geographic Magazine* article titled "Life on the Hawaii 'Front.'" Published in October 1942, his list included the following rules:

> Dogs must be confined during blackouts.
>
> Unemployed men must register for employment.
>
> Owners of pigeons must register them with the military.
>
> One must obtain a permit to buy his ration of one bottle of liquor a week.

A U.S. soldier guards a deserted Hawaiian beach during World War II. *National Archives photo no. 111-SC221867.*

Wartime shortages were more noticeable in Hawaii than on the U.S. mainland. Nearly everything was scarce, including food, gasoline, phonograph records, and magazines. Hawaii had plenty of pineapples and sugar but few other crops, so residents depended on ships from the U.S. mainland to bring almost all their basic necessities. However, the military had first use of all ships so that servicemen and their supplies could be transported to Hawaii.

Therefore, shipping of civilian supplies was greatly curtailed.

Like people on the U.S. mainland, residents of Hawaii generously volunteered to aid the war effort. Women wrapped bandages for the American Red Cross. Working with the army and local civilian police, Honolulu men formed emergency reserve units that helped carry out police duties. Sugar and pineapple companies, the largest employers in Hawaii before the war, allowed employees time to work on defense projects. Many high school students left school for defense jobs. Some schools shortened their daily schedules so school buildings could be used in the afternoons for war-related purposes, including fingerprinting, vaccinations, and the issuing of food ration books.

Japanese citizens in Hawaii

Approximately 35,000 Japanese aliens (immigrants who hold citizenship in a foreign country) lived in Hawaii in 1942. Many of their children and grandchildren—about 124,000—had been born in Hawaii and were therefore U.S. citizens. After the Japanese attacked Pearl Harbor, Japanese aliens and Japanese American citizens on the U.S. mainland were rounded up and sent to internment camps (guarded camps built in remote areas of the United States for the placement of Japanese Americans and Japanese aliens during the war). However, most Japanese people in Hawaii remained free to go about their lives. They faced some restrictions for travel, and they could not possess any item considered useful for spying or sabotage, such as guns, explosives, shortwave radios, or cameras. Some on the islands urged a stricter policy, but many believed that the Japanese were so intertwined in the community and the economy that it was neither necessary nor practical to follow the internment policies carried out on the U.S. mainland.

For More Information

Books

Greene, Bob. *Once Upon a Town: The Miracle of the North Platte Canteen.* New York: William Morrow, 1992.

Warren, James R. *The War Years: A Chronicle of Washington State in World War II.* Seattle: University of Washington Press, 2000.

Periodicals

Klemmer, Harvey. "Michigan Fights." *National Geographic Magazine* (December 1944): pp. 676–715.

Nicholas, William H. "Wartime Washington." *National Geographic Magazine* (September 1943): pp. 257–290.

Simpich, Frederick. "Life on the Hawaii 'Front.'" *National Geographic Magazine* (October 1942): pp. 541–560.

Simpich, Frederick. "San Diego Can't Believe It." *National Geographic Magazine* (January 1942): pp. 45–80.

Simpich, Frederick. "Wartime in the Pacific Northwest." *National Geographic Magazine* (October 1942): pp. 421–464.

Web sites

Reuben Fleet. http://history.acusd.edu/gen/WW2Timeline/fleet.html (accessed on July 14, 2004).

Information and Entertainment

12

During World War II (1939–45) people on the U.S. home front faced gas rationing, shortages of certain foods, overcrowded public transportation, and bans on pleasure driving. Unaccustomed to such restrictions and inconveniences, Americans found some comfort in various forms of media, including radio, movies, newspapers, books, and popular music. These forms of mass communication provided not only entertainment but important war-related information. Early in the war President Franklin D. Roosevelt (1882–1945; served 1933–45) declared that movies and even certain sporting events were essential for maintaining morale on the home front. The U.S. government used these media and others to communicate with the American public. Government messages included statements about the nation's war goals, suggestions for what citizens could do to contribute to the war effort, and reports on the progress of the war. Government communication of this sort is often called propaganda. Propaganda is information designed to shape public opinion. Radio, movies, and all the other popular media provided the U.S. government with an effective means of funneling wartime information to the public. At the same time, these media forms

Movie theaters became places where Americans could escape from their troubles and also get news of the war in Europe. *The Library of Congress.*

gave people on the home front a welcome escape from the war.

Hollywood movies on the eve of war

In the late 1930s many people in the Hollywood movie industry's upper management were Jewish. They strongly supported the war against Germany because German leader Adolf Hitler (1889–1945) and his Nazi government were persecuting Jews in Europe. Long before the United States entered the war, the movie industry produced several films that criticized Nazi Germany. The most notable was *Confessions of a Nazi Spy,* released in early 1939. In the film the German-born director exposed Hitler's plans for European conquest. *Confessions of a Nazi Spy* was the first anti-Nazi film and a commercial hit.

Other movies also promoted the idea of the United States entering World War II. *Sergeant York* (1941), a movie about fighting Germany in World War I (1914–18), is one example. The movie revived the notion of Germany as an enemy of democracy and freedom. Another example is *A Yank in the RAF* (1941). This movie tells the story of an American pilot in the British Royal Air Force. It promoted the idea of Americans, even individually, helping Great Britain in its fight against German military expansion.

When Congress established a military draft in 1940, the film industry formed the Motion Picture Committee Cooperating for National Defense. Its purpose was to distribute and show films that encouraged Americans to participate in the war effort. (The United States had not yet entered the war, but it was supporting the fight against Germany by manufacturing war materials for the Allies.) One of these films was called *Women in Defense* (1941). Written by Eleanor Roosevelt (1884–1962) and narrated by Hollywood actress Katharine Hepburn (1907–2003), the film encouraged women to find jobs in the war industries or to join military services.

Although some of the movies that promoted the war were hits, the American public was not eager for the United States to enter the war. Isolationism (the policy of avoiding formal foreign commitments and involvement in foreign conflicts) had been Americans' preferred foreign policy since the end of World War I (1914–18). Members of Congress also held isolationist views, and they disapproved of Hollywood's pro-war stance. In 1941, before the nation entered the war, senators in Congress began an investigation of Hollywood. They charged that the movie industry, led by Jewish film company executives, was misleading the public by producing pro-war propaganda designed to gain public support for entering the war against Germany.

On the lighter side, Hollywood was also producing war-related comedies, which helped put to ease, at least fleetingly, the rising tensions of the public over the threat of war. *Buck Privates* (1941) and *In the Navy* (1941), both starring comedians Bud Abbott (1895–1974) and Lou Costello (1906–1959), are two examples of war-related comedy films.

Controlling war information

During wartime the government often controls what news and information the public hears or sees. When World War II broke out in Europe in September 1939, President Roosevelt immediately began establishing some information controls. First the president established the Office of Government Reports. This agency was supposed to coordinate the release of information about U.S. preparations for possible involvement in the war. By March 1941 the war in Europe had greatly expanded, so the Office of Emergency Management also became involved in controlling public information about the government's growing defense activities. Because these two agencies had similar responsibilities, Roosevelt created the Office of Facts and Figures to coordinate their activities. He appointed Archibald MacLeish (1892–1982), best known as an American poet, to head the office. To filter information from overseas,

Elmer Davis, named head of the Office of War Information in 1942. *AP/Wide World Photos. Reproduced by permission.*

the Foreign Information Service was created in August 1941.

Having so many new information control organizations created some confusion for the public and within government. Nonetheless, censorship of military information proved effective in blocking selected information from the public. When the Japanese attacked Pearl Harbor in December 1941, for example, the government withheld a great deal of information from the public, including the casualty list, which was not released for a year. The thinking was that the U.S.

government did not want to encourage the Japanese over the destruction wrought, and, also, alarm the public any more than it was already.

Shortly after the attack on Pearl Harbor, President Roosevelt asserted that motion pictures were important for informing and entertaining American citizens on the home front. He also claimed that movies should be relatively free of censorship. A short time later the government officially ruled that motion pictures were an essential service to the war effort and that production should continue. Hollywood war movies quickly went into production.

The president soon directly approached Hollywood about using certain motion pictures for propaganda purposes. Warner Brothers released *Mission to Moscow* in 1943 in response to a presidential request. Roosevelt wanted to maintain public support for U.S. military aid to the Soviet Union. Based on the experiences of Joseph E. Davies (1876–1958), the U.S. ambassador to the Soviet Union from 1936 to 1938, the movie portrays the Soviet dictator Joseph Stalin (1879–1953) as a great defender of democracy. The movie became a major embarrassment to the studio when the public later learned about Stalin's brutal reign of terror on Soviet citizens.

Office of War Information

To resolve the confusion and chaos of overlapping government information offices, Roosevelt created the Office of War Information (OWI) in June 1942. The OWI took over the role of all the other information organizations. The president named popular CBS news commentator Elmer Davis (1890–1958) as head of the OWI. Besides overseeing the information released to the public, the OWI produced radio messages, leaflets, booklets, films, and a glossy magazine titled *Victory*. In addition, the new agency sought to influence the entertainment industry. The OWI issued guidelines urging advertisers, corporations, and publishers, among others, to produce positive, inspiring messages that showed confidence in the future. America was to be portrayed in a highly favorable light at all times.

Bureau of Motion Pictures

To coordinate and produce government films, the OWI created the Bureau of Motion Pictures (BMP) branch, headed by White House assistant Lowell Mellett. The BMP established three offices, in Washington, D.C., New York, and Los Angeles.

The New York office, under the direction of playwright Sam Spewack (1899–1971), made government informational films. The films trumpeted America's successes, such as its home front industrial production miracles. One such film, *Autobiography of a Jeep*, was released in sixteen different languages. BMP also produced fifty-two informational short films called the *America Speaks* series. The OWI staff wrote half of these films and Hollywood studios the other half. (The twenty-six films written by OWI were also known as "Victory Films.")

The BMP films were supposed to be shown along with the regular movie features. The BMP also made 16-millimeter films for showing at churches, schools, and other community centers. These films actually reached a larger audience than the "Victory Films." By January 1943 about 4.7 million people had seen one or more of the 16-millimeter films.

The military also produced informational films, in coordination with the BMP. During World War II one-third of the male workers in the film industry entered the armed forces, where many of them produced educational and informational films. In addition, noted Hollywood director Frank Capra (1897–1991) volunteered to make a series of soldier indoctrination films for the U.S. Army; the series was called *Why We Fight*. Army commanders liked the films so much that they insisted the films be shown to the general public, too. As a result, these Capra films were shown in movie theaters around the country. Capra himself directed the first film of the series, *Prelude to War*, which included footage from captured enemy film and newsreels. *Prelude to War* explained the series of events in Europe and Asia that had led to war, the character of the German and Japanese governments, and the reasons why the United States had entered the war. Capra's series and various other military inspirational films were quite popular with the public and attracted a large audience in war factories and community centers as well as movie theaters.

Wartime Baseball

Throughout World War II, going to the ballpark was a favorite pastime on the home front. In January 1942, just over a month after the United States entered the war, President Franklin Roosevelt declared that major-league baseball could serve as a big morale booster for the American public. The country was at war, but the 1942 baseball season would proceed. Major-league baseball did its part for the war effort by sponsoring scrap drives. Kids who brought metal and rubber items to the ballpark for recycling were admitted to the game for free. Sometimes baseball fans could get free admission with the purchase of a war bond.

Four thousand professional baseball players—about 70 percent of the league—joined the armed services during the war, including Joe DiMaggio (1914–1999), Ted Williams (1918–2002), and Bob Feller (1918–). As a result, many unknown names filled the league rosters. Despite this fact, attendance rose to the highest it had ever been in major-league history to that point. The wartime stand-ins were old-timers, foreign players recruited from Latin America, and men who had not passed the physical requirements for U.S. military service. Pete Gray (1915–2002), a one-armed outfielder, was a big attraction. To many war veterans who had lost limbs in combat, Gray was an inspiring figure.

Minor-league baseball was also a popular attraction, although only nine out of forty-one minor leagues continued to play during the war. Some of the players were defense workers who played in their off hours. A professional league of female ballplayers formed in 1943; it was called the All-American Girls Professional Baseball League. Women's baseball games drew a good attendance, but the league folded in 1954.

Not everyone liked the OWI/BMP productions. Republicans in Congress were highly critical of the inspirational war films and OWI's *Victory* magazine. They charged that these productions were merely propaganda, designed to support the potential reelection bid of President Roosevelt, a Democrat, in 1944. In May 1943 Congress cut back funding for OWI, eliminating most of OWI's home front activities. Only the Washington, D.C., office of OWI survived.

Hollywood goes to war

Nelson Poynter (1903–1978) in BMP's Hollywood office was the agency's lead contact with the movie industry. He advised Hollywood on how it could assist in the war effort. BMP also wanted to make sure Hollywood was portraying the war effort and American culture in a positive way. To help Hollywood comply, the BMP issued *The Government Information Manual for the Motion Picture*. The manual spelled out official government policy to guide moviemakers. For example, it recommended that an occasional war message, something to promote home front unity, be worked into movie dialogue. The manual also suggested that producers ask themselves a key question, "Will this picture help win the war?"

Hoping to avoid formal censorship measures by Congress, Hollywood executives formed the War Activities Committee and agreed among themselves to cooperate with the BMP and other government agencies. They allowed the BMP to review scripts submitted by studios and to make suggestions about how to portray proper (that is, government-approved) images of America. Sometimes BMP suggested changes in dialogue or emphasis. In some cases it requested that a movie not be produced or that it be held back until after the war. National unity was the government's chief concern, so the BMP wanted films to avoid topics such as crime, poverty, and racism. The BMP banned scenes showing war heroes winning battles single-handedly because they did not want the public to think that combat was easy or that the war would be over soon. Filmmakers were never to show Americans surrendering, but rather fighting stubbornly to the end when overrun by superior forces. Gangster movies, which were popular during the 1930s, were banned because of their negative portrayal of Americans, unless the gangsters were fighting Nazis, such as *All Through the Night* (1942) and *Lucky Jordan* (1942). Citizens of Allied countries were not to be shown in an offensive manner, such as unkempt in appearance, offensive behavior, or involved in crime. The BMP reviewed about 1,650 scripts. Conformance with BMP recommendations varied among the movie studios, but most usually complied. The BMP review of Hollywood movies and film productions ceased when funding was reduced for OWI in May 1943.

Between July and October 1942, thirty-eight of the eighty-six movies in production were war movies. Filming the movies during wartime was a challenge. Film was rationed, materials for building sets were limited, beaches and open seas were off-limits for filming because of safety and security concerns, and many skilled technicians, such as electricians, were drafted. The loud resonating noises of military aircraft made outdoor filming chancy. Furthermore, like every other business enterprise in the nation, film studios had extra responsibilities during the war; for example, to protect staff members and Hollywood stars, they built sandbag air raid shelters on their lots. The war also affected some of the ceremony of a movie's opening night: Due to dimout and blackout requirements early in the war, Hollywood had to quit using flashing searchlights for world premieres.

Thirty Seconds Over Tokyo (1944) was a popular World War II movie. *The Library of Congress.*

Wartime movies

The first combat film, *Wake Island*, was released in September 1942, less than nine months after the battles it portrays. Director John Farrow (1904–1963) won an Academy Award for the film. Other early war movies portraying actual combat events include *Battle of Midway* (1942) and *The Flying Tigers* (1942). Twenty-four of the initial thirty-eight early war movies were about espionage and sabotage on the home front. Noting this trend, the OWI became concerned about raising public fears. The FBI gave reassurances to the public

that very little of such activity was actually going on.

Twenty-eight percent of all Hollywood pictures produced between 1942 and the end of 1944 dealt with the war in some way. *Action in the North Atlantic* (1943) tells the story of the merchant marines (officers and crews of U.S. vessels that engaged in commerce). *Guadalcanal Diary*, released in 1943, is based on Richard Tregaskis's 1942 book about the fierce fighting that took place between U.S. and Japanese ground forces on the small Pacific island of Guadalcanal. *Thirty Seconds Over Tokyo* (1944) dramatizes a

U.S. bombing raid over the Japanese capital city that occurred in April 1942. Other popular combat movies were *Bataan* (1943) and *Memphis Belle* (1944). War themes appeared even in lighter movies, including Sherlock Holmes tracking Nazi spies in London in *Sherlock Holmes and the Secret Weapon* (1942). The cartoon character Donald Duck was shown collecting scrap metal for the war effort.

Hollywood combat movies stressed teamwork on the home front and the battlefield and emphasized the diversity of Americans involved in the war effort. Women were shown going beyond established boundaries, such as going from homemaking to working in factories, but Hollywood was careful not to challenge American norms and maintained traditional femininity, including being clean with makeup, wearing hose and neatly pressed clothing, and generally sporting a bright supportive spirit. Similarly, Hollywood walked a fine line in its portrayals of black and working-class Americans; movies celebrated the contributions of both but largely stayed with traditional white middle-class values and steered away from controversial issues of race or class so as to provide a positive image of America. Of course, films touted the bravery of Allied combat soldiers and demonized the German and Japanese enemy. Movies generally portrayed the Japanese as sneaky and dishonest, such as in *God Is My Co-Pilot* (1945) and *Across the Pacific* (1942), and the Germans as stupid and ineffective such as in *Invisible Agent* (1942)

and *How to Operate Behind Enemy Lines* (1943).

Early in the worldwide conflict, movies avoided showing the grim side of war. However, the BMP suggested more realistic portrayals by late 1943, hoping to guard against home front overconfidence. Newsreels also became more graphic by 1944. Though made by private companies, the newsreels reported war news that was approved by the government.

Hollywood's escapism

Most box office hits did not directly address the war. *Mrs. Miniver*, released in early 1942, was a highly popular film that won several Academy Awards including best picture. It was also a favorite of the BMP for its strongly pro-British perspective. *Casablanca* (1942), starring Humphrey Bogart (1899–1957) and Ingrid Bergman (1915–1982), avoided the main issues of the war, even though the story involved the French struggle against Nazi Germany.

Moviegoers grew tired of war movies by 1943. They wanted an escape from serious subjects and turned to romances, musicals, comedies, adventure stories, and animated films for a break from day-to-day problems. Walt Disney's animated movies—including *Fantasia* (1940), *Dumbo* (1941), and *Bambi* (1942)—quickly gained popularity. Disney also produced short cartoons for the government, including "Donald Gets Drafted" (1942), "Out of the Frying Pan into the

Firing Line" (1942), and "Der Fuehrer's Face" (1942).

Attendance at movie theaters rose significantly during the war. More than ninety million Americans attended the movies every week, up 33 percent from before the war. The American movie industry made more than a billion dollars annually through the peak war years. By late 1944, when the Allied forces had liberated much of Western Europe and the Pacific, some 40 percent of Hollywood's gross receipts came from abroad as, once again, Hollywood movies were shown in Europe.

Radio

Before television, radio was the main medium for informing Americans of world events. Radio was also the main source of entertainment at home. Families would gather around the radio for news or comedy-variety programs. The average listener tuned in for 4.5 hours a day. Because so many people listened to the radio, radio broadcasts were an essential part of the government's wartime information campaign.

Just after the Japanese attack on Pearl Harbor in December 1941, the National Association of Broadcasters created a set of codes banning certain types of broadcasts. Included were broadcasts that might cause undue alarm on the home front, such as dramatizations of war events. Weather reports were discontinued until the fall of 1943 so that enemy pilots would not have weather information to aid them.

Security at radio stations was increased to protect against enemy infiltration.

Government radio programs

Making use of the airwaves, in February 1942 the White House introduced plans for a series of radio programs called *This Is War*. The half-hour programs were created by the major networks and broadcast simultaneously every week for thirteen weeks. The programs aimed to maintain calm and boost morale on the home front, because the war was not going well for the United States through the early part of 1942. The first release in the series was titled "How It Was with Us." In a calm and reassuring voice, the narrator of the film reminded Americans that they were on the right side in the battle against evil (Nazi Germany and Japan) and that it was right to go to war. Other programs paid tribute to the army, navy, Army Air Corps, and War Production Board. Twenty million listeners regularly tuned in to the series.

The OWI's Domestic Radio Bureau also provided war information on the radio in various forms. One series, *Uncle Sam Speaks*, featured the Uncle Sam, a fictitious character representing the U.S. government, talking about hope for the future.

Two of the most noted radio writers for home front morale-boosting programs were Norman Corwin (1910–) and Ronald MacDougall. Corwin introduced sound effects, background music, and voice documentaries (radio programs featuring ordinary citizens talking about their perspectives on different war issues). MacDougall wrote *The Man behind the Gun,* a series about American soldiers in combat. The government also produced short spot announcements for war bonds, scrap drives, and V-mail (personal letters written to servicemen overseas on government forms that were photographed by the post office on a smaller format and delivered overseas by air mail). These war messages were broadcast during all varieties of programming, from kids' afternoon serial programs to evening adventure dramas.

The amount of airtime devoted to news rose dramatically through the war years. For example, the National Broadcasting Company (NBC) increased news reporting from 4 percent of air time in 1939 to 20 percent through the war years. Firsthand live accounts quickly became popular, beginning in 1938 when William L. Shirer (1904–1993) reported from Czechoslovakia about Nazi Germany's takeover of that country. Speaking from distant locations about somber and significant world events, radio war reporters had a certain glamour and attained star status with home front listeners. Memorable moments included Edward R. Murrow (1908–1965) reporting live from a B-17 bomber while flying over Berlin.

Besides news, radio provided music and entertainment, allowing listeners some escape from the war. Soap operas, quiz shows, sportscasts, drama and mystery stories, children's programs, and variety shows were popular. The most popular radio personalities included comedians Red Skelton

News correspondent Edward R. Murrow in London, England, circa 1940. *AP/Wide World Photos. Reproduced by permission.*

(1913–1997), Bob Hope (1903–2003), Jack Benny (1894–1974), and Bud Abbott (1895–1974) and Lou Costello (1906–1959). Arthur Godfrey (1903–1983) and Kate Smith (1907–1986) were popular radio hosts.

News journalism

The government exerted control over news reporters and photographers primarily through the U.S. Office of Censorship. Byron Price (1891–1981), an Associated Press news editor,

War correspondent Ernie Pyle, seated front-center, with U.S. soldiers on the battle front in Italy. *© Corbis. Reproduced by permission.*

headed the office. Like the OWI, this office controlled information in order to sustain home front support for the war. War reporters were urged to emphasize traditional American values, such as the importance of family, strong patriotism, and emphasis on the institution of marriage, in their reporting. News accounts of combat were edited to avoid descriptions of death or maiming, mental breakdowns by soldiers, and strife among soldiers under stress. Combat soldiers did not care for these sanitized reports going back to the home front. They believed such reports distorted what was really going on overseas and hid the horrors of warfare from the general public. However, the government thought it was best to keep the home front perspective on the war positive; this was essential because victory would likely hinge on strong home front support.

The Office of Censorship also reviewed the work of news photographers. Photographs of dead U.S. soldiers could not be published until 1943, when the Allied forces began gaining the upper hand in combat.

By then government officials were less worried about hurting home front morale and more concerned that America might become overconfident and decrease its support for the war effort. It was not until 1945 that *Life* magazine, a key news photography publication, chose to show American casualties. Photographs that showed mental breakdowns among soldiers or outbreaks of violence among the troops were not allowed in any publication.

Reporting back home

Ernie Pyle (1900–1945) was the most famous U.S. war correspondent. He covered combat involving U.S. troops in North Africa, Sicily, Italy, France, and the Pacific, sending first-hand accounts back to the home front. Almost four hundred daily newspapers and three hundred weeklies in the United States carried his articles. Pyle won a Pulitzer Prize in 1944. He gained unusual respect among the troops because he depicted the war realistically, even under the reporting restrictions. Pyle was killed by Japanese gunfire on a small Pacific island near Okinawa on April 18, 1945. A highly acclaimed Hollywood movie, *The Story of G.I. Joe* (1945), is based on Pyle's life.

Cartoonist Bill Mauldin (1921–2003) was another Pulitzer Prize winner. Mauldin drew the cartoon *Willie and Joe* from the war front. He used the characters of Willie and Joe, two combat infantrymen, to tell the humorous side of military life abroad. Mauldin started as a regular soldier but was soon recognized for his special talent. The army

Photojournalist Margaret Bourke-White.
AP/Wide World Photos. Reproduced by permission.

reassigned him to its daily newspaper, *Stars and Stripes,* which was distributed to the troops. Through an article written by Ernie Pyle, Mauldin became well known on the home front.

For the first time, women also found opportunities as war correspondents. Noted female reporters during World War II included Helen Kirkpatrick (1909–), the London correspondent for the *Chicago Daily News,* and Sonia Tomara (1897–1982) of the *New York Herald Tribune,* who covered action in China, Burma, and India. Margaret Bourke-White (1906–1971), a

Five Women Journalists

Stationed in Germany in the early 1930s for the *New York Evening Post,* Dorothy Thompson (1894–1961) was the first woman in charge of a news bureau in Europe. When she interviewed Nazi leader Adolf Hitler in 1934 and exposed him for the tyrant he was, Hitler ordered her to leave Germany. In the United States she began writing a column for the *New York Herald Tribune.* The column, called "On the Record," was printed in more than two hundred papers. Through her writing Thompson warned Americans about the dangers of Hitler and the Nazi Party in Germany and their plans for expansion and persecution of Jews and minorities.

Clare Boothe Luce (1903–1987) played many different roles in her lifetime. She was a U.S. representative (1943–47), a playwright, an ambassador, and the wife of Henry R. Luce (1898–1967), the owner of popular magazines *Time, Life,* and *Fortune.* She was also a wartime correspondent. World War II broke out in Europe in September 1939, and in early 1940 she spent four months in Europe simply to witness

Clare Boothe Luce. *AP/Wide World Photos. Reproduced by permission.*

firsthand the developing events. Returning to the United States, she reported her findings in *Europe in the Spring* (1940), a

well-known photojournalist of the 1930s, covered battlefield action for *Life* magazine. Her photographs helped maintain strong home front support for the war effort. These women and others blazed the trail for future female journalists.

Popular music

Popular music promoted optimism and confidence on the home front. Like movies and radio, songs were a vehicle for delivering government messages during the war. The OWI and the Songwriters War Committee book that helped persuade Americans that isolationism (opposition to foreign commitments and involvement in foreign disputes) was a dangerous policy. During 1941 and 1942 Luce spent time in the Far East, Burma, the Philippines, and the South Pacific, writing about what she learned, photographing what she encountered, and sending her observations back to the U.S. home front. During the same period she also spent time in North Africa, reporting on the military preparedness of the Allies.

Hailing from the South, May Craig (1889–1975) was an early feminist who campaigned for women's voting rights. She traveled north and found employment as a journalist in Washington, D.C., where she worked for the Gannett newspaper chain. Her daily column, "Inside Washington," ran for almost fifty years. Craig was an original member of the women's press circle, established by Eleanor Roosevelt, the First Lady, in 1933. Craig constantly championed women news correspondents; she believed they should be allowed to go everywhere male correspondents went to get their stories. During World War II Craig often traveled to Europe to send back firsthand accounts of the war.

Toni Frissell (1907–1988) was a talented wartime photojournalist. Because she was a woman, her early career was full of assignments on clothes and society, topics that were deemed appropriate for women. Frissell was eager to move from fashion reporting to news reporting, so in 1941 she volunteered to document the wartime activities of the American Red Cross. She would also photograph soldiers on the front lines, members of the Women's Army Corps (WACs), black American fighter pilots of the 332nd Fighter Group, and European children orphaned by the war. Frissell used her skills with a camera to influence American attitudes on the home front.

Like Dorothy Thompson, Sonia Tomara wrote for the *New York Herald Tribune*. With sheer persistence she acquired credentials that allowed her to travel to Asia in August 1942 to cover the war in China. She flew on bombing missions and sent vivid accounts of her experiences back to the U.S. home front.

produced informational songs to promote home front participation in scrap drives, victory gardens (private gardens planted by individual families to add to the nation's wartime food supply), and air raid drills. Other government-produced songs provided encouragement to war industry workers.

In the commercial music industry, songwriters began rolling out numerous patriotic songs immediately after the attack on Pearl Harbor, hoping for a big hit. However, none of these proved memorable, and most were considered rather juvenile. ("Goodbye, Momma, I'm Off to Yokohama" and

Couples swing dance the night away to the music of the Jerry Wald Orchestra, circa 1941.
Getty Images. Reproduced by permission.

"Praise the Lord and Pass the Ammunition" are two examples.) Swing, the most popular music of the time, did not translate well into war songs. One of the better-selling records in 1942 and 1943 was "There's a Star Spangled Banner Waving Somewhere." In general, such standards as "God Bless America" (written by Irving Berlin in 1938), "Battle Hymn of the Republic" (from the late nineteenth century), and "Anchors Aweigh" (1906) had to suffice.

Sentimental songs, including songs of loneliness, would become much more popular as the war dragged on. The favorite of the war was "White Christmas," first sung by Bing Crosby (1903–1977) in the movie *Holiday Inn* (1942). Other popular sentimental songs were "I'll Be Home for Christmas" (1943) sung by Crosby and "I'll Be Seeing You," which was the most popular song in 1944 and also sung by Crosby.

Big bands dominated popular music during the war. Big band leaders included Glenn Miller (1904–1944), Tommy Dorsey (1905–1956), Duke Ellington (1899–1974), and Benny

Goodman (1909–1986). The energetic jitterbug dance became popular on the home front, danced to both swing and boogie-woogie music. Servicemen carried the dance style overseas to other countries. Some singers with the bands struck out on their own to gain fame. Frank Sinatra (1915–1998) and Bing Crosby got their start with the big bands. Young teenage girls packed music theaters to attend Sinatra's performances. Other popular singers included Dinah Shore (1917–1994), Kate Smith (1907–1986), and Perry Como (1912–2001).

Books and magazines

Despite a shortage of paper, the popularity of books increased dramatically during the war. Publishers decreased the size of type, thereby reducing the number of pages and decreasing the cost of publication, and published fewer titles so they could focus on printing the more popular titles. Book clubs became numerous. Membership in the Book-of-the-Month Club doubled during the war years. The availability of inexpensive paperback books, first introduced in 1939 by Pocket Books, fueled this increase. Ten million paperbacks were sold in 1941, twenty million in 1942, and forty million in 1943. The most popular books were murder mysteries; self-help and health books were next on the popularity list. About 150,000 copies of murder mysteries were sold each week. For servicemen overseas, publishers established the Armed Service Edition program, which made popular paperbacks available in compact copies, designed to fit in soldiers' pockets. Both best-sellers and classics were printed in this series, and publishers released up to forty titles a month. Some one hundred million copies were printed and provided free to troops. The favorite books among troops were Westerns.

Most books about the war did not make it into print until after the war was over. However, the home front got glimpses of the war through some firsthand accounts that were written and published in short succession. One such book was *Guadalcanal Diary* (1942) by Richard Tregaskis. Based on Tregaskis's own observations of the battle that raged on the island of Guadalcanal, the book was quickly made into a popular Hollywood movie. The government heavily censored combat books published during the war, but the public was eager to obtain whatever was available.

The most popular combat book was by award-winning frontline journalist Ernie Pyle. *Here Is Your War* (1943) sold almost two million copies. He followed it with *Brave Men*, published in 1944. Cartoonist Bill Mauldin published another wartime favorite, *Up Front* (1944), a book that featured narratives between the cartoons. Comedian Bob Hope, who regularly entertained troops overseas, published *I Never Left Home* (1944), which sold more than one million copies.

The best-selling book overall during the war was written by the former Republican presidential nominee of 1940, Wendell Wilkie (1892–1944). The book, titled *One World,* was published in 1943, after Wilkie's journey to the Soviet Union, China, and the Middle East. In the book Wilkie made a plea for harmony in the postwar world—and he found a large audience: *One World* became the fastest-selling book in U.S. history, selling a million copies in two months. The publisher, Simon and Schuster, had to scramble to make enough copies available. Another notable release was *The Lottery* by Shirley Jackson, which examines the support Nazi leader Adolf Hitler (1889–1945) received from common German citizens.

Like books, magazines and comic books flourished in wartime. Among the most popular magazines were *Life, Reader's Digest, Ladies' Home Journal, Saturday Evening Post, Fortune, Time,* and *National Geographic Magazine. Seventeen,* a magazine aimed at teenagers, got its start during the war, in 1944. Designed for even younger readers, comic books became a thriving industry. Twenty million were sold in 1942 and up to sixty million in 1946. An estimated 80 percent of America's youth between ages six and seventeen read comic books during the war. Comic strips in the newspapers were also popular. Seventy million readers followed the comic strips. A special version of the comic book *Superman* was sent overseas to servicemen. Cartoon characters such as Joe Palooka and Dick Tracey joined the military to help the war effort. Other comic strips, such as *Blondie* and *Bringing Up Father,* took amusing looks at life on the home front. Comic books and comic strips, through their scripted dialogue, also encouraged the purchase of war bonds, and participation in scrap drives and other home front activities.

Entertainers on the home front and abroad

Members of the entertainment industry joined the war effort in various ways. Some donated their yachts to the Coast Guard Auxiliary for harbor patrols. Many employed in the movie industry joined the armed services; several of them—Clark Gable (1901–1960), Jimmy Stewart (1908–1997), and Henry Fonda (1905–1982), for example—were big-screen stars.

Other entertainers performed for troops and war industry workers, participated in war bond sales drives, or produced radio announcements encouraging citizens to contribute to the war effort. Actress Bette Davis (1908–1989) served as president of the Hollywood Canteen, a place where servicemen could get free food and drink, dance with starlets, and chat with celebrities who volunteered their time. The Hollywood Victory Committee sent thousands of celebrities to military camps on the home front and abroad. Together these celebrities traveled more than 5 million miles in their mission to boost morale among the troops.

Hollywood stars used their charm and influence to help sell war bonds (government certificates sold to individuals and corporations to raise money to finance the war) to the general public. Actress Dorothy Lamour (1914–1996) was a major contributor to the war bond campaign; she is credited with selling $350 million in bonds. Actress Carole Lombard (1908–1942), wife of actor Clark Gable, was killed in a plane crash in January 1942 while coming back from one of the first bond drives. The first big drive occurred in September 1942. More than 330 actors and actresses participated, and they sold over $838 million in bonds. The war bond campaign included seven tours, covering three hundred cities and towns. Movie theaters pitched in by offering free movie days; people who attended were asked to purchase a war bond instead of a ticket.

Advertising

Despite a wartime shortage of consumer goods on the home front, spending on advertising significantly increased during the war. Companies spent $2.2 billion to advertise their products in 1942; in 1945 they spent $2.9 billion on advertising, an increase of over 30 percent. This big spending was strategic: Even before the United States entered the war, American industries had converted from producing consumer goods to producing war materials for the Allies. The war industry was profitable, but companies knew the war would end sooner or later. Therefore, they spent large amounts on advertising to keep the public familiar with the consumer goods they produced before the war; they wanted to keep their brand names strong so that sales and profits would continue after the war.

Bob Hope and other stars appear in this ad, sponsored by RC Cola, to encourage the purchase of war bonds. *The Library of Congress.*

The government was eager to advertise, too. Shortly after the United States entered World War II, the War Advertising Council was established; its job was to make sure that advertising inspired U.S. citizens to do whatever was needed to help win the war. Government leaders found that advertisers were quite willing to incorporate the war theme in their messages to demonstrate their patriotism to the consuming public and keeping a positive image. Advertisers promoted everything from war bond sales to military recruiting to scrap metal drives. To gain tax deductions businesses also donated advertising space and radio airtime to the government. This also helped the manufacturers keep their names before the public, so that when they resumed manufacturing consumer goods, buyers would still think of them as they had before the war.

Advertisers' portrayal of the war was even further from reality than Hollywood's. They continually showed the strong, individualistic soldier and ideal American family with the wife dealing with war industry work, taking care of children, cleaning house, and supporting her husband abroad while still appearing beautiful and unflustered. Ads were melodramatic and sentimental while encouraging home front sacrifice and contributions. Advertisers steadily portrayed the home front as a place of hard work and unity.

For More Information

Books

Bernstein, Mark, and Alex Lubertozzi. *World War II on the Air: Edward R. Murrow and the Voices That Carried the War Home.* Naperville, IL: Sourcebooks, 2003.

Frederich, Otto. *City of Nets: A Portrait of Hollywood in the 1940s.* New York: Harper & Row, 1986.

Gilbert, Bill. *They Also Served: Baseball and the Home Front, 1941–1945.* New York: Crown Publishers, 1992.

Heide, Robert. *Home Front America: Popular Culture of the World War II Era.* San Francisco: Chronicle Books, 1995.

Lingeman, Richard R. *Don't You Know There's a War On?* New York: G. P. Putnam's Sons, 1970.

New York Times. *Page One: The Front Page History of World War II as Presented in the New York Times.* New York: Galahad Books, 1996.

Schickel, Richard. *Good Morning, Mr. Zip Zip Zip: Movies, Memory, and World War II.* Chicago: Ivan R. Dee, 2003.

Zeinert, Karen. *Those Incredible Women of World War II.* Brookfield, CT: Millbrook Press, 1994.

Web Sites

"Women Come to the Front: Journalists, Photographers, and Broadcasters during World War II." *Library of Congress.* www.loc.gov/exhibits/wcf.html (accessed on July 14, 2004).

Transition to Peacetime and Home Front Legacies

13

The transition to peacetime was under way on the home front by 1944, though World War II (1939–45) was still raging abroad. In 1943 full industrial and agricultural war production had been achieved; that is, the capability to meet the ongoing Allied needs for war materials and food had been reached. While war production did not slow down or cease, special emphasis on war mobilization was no longer needed. It was up to the armed forces on the battlefield to achieve victory, and the chances of victory looked better as time went by. Although some of the largest and bloodiest battles were yet to come, planners in government and industry began to prepare for peacetime. When the war finally ended, the United States was poised to become one of the world's superpowers: The economy was strong, the population was growing, and U.S. military strength was greater than ever before. Having given their all for the war effort, Americans were ready to enjoy prosperity and peace. The legacies of the home front events of World War II would propel the nation as a world power through the remainder of the twentieth century.

A reconversion debate

The beginning of America's peacetime transition was no less controversial than the beginning of its war mobilization. Officials in President Franklin D. Roosevelt's administration wanted a well-planned and gradual reconversion to a peacetime economy. They were concerned that unemployment would skyrocket if war production suddenly ceased. They were also worried about the many small businesses that survived on defense subcontracts during the war; they feared these businesses might not survive in peacetime without some assistance. No one wanted a return of the troubled economic times that had preceded the war, so to guard against that possibility, President Roosevelt (1882–1945; served 1933–45) proposed an "Economic Bill of Rights" in early 1944. He claimed it would provide economic security for everyone and guarantee national prosperity after the war. The bill would ensure jobs, food, medical care, housing, and social security (a government program providing economic assistance for citizens, including the aged, retired, unemployed, and disabled) for all Americans. Responding to Roosevelt's promises of security, Americans reelected him in November 1944, giving him an unprecedented fourth term in office.

Leaders in big business were not enthusiastic about Roosevelt's economic plans. They had controlled much of the defense work during the war, and they wanted to retain control in the peacetime economy. They preferred a rapid reconversion to the production of consumer goods, with a minimum of government supervision. However, the military did not want reconversion to begin until Germany had formally surrendered; therefore, big businesses that had converted to war production were expected to keep producing war materials. Meanwhile, shoppers were ready for new cars, tires, nylon hose, steaks, whiskey, and many other things that had been in short supply during the war. Big business worried that smaller businesses, which were not as involved in war production, would get a jump on producing the consumer goods the public wanted. Holding $140 billion in savings and war bonds, the public had a lot of buying power. With their profits from war materials production, businesses had also accumulated giant sums—$20 billion in cash reserves. They were eager to use that money to reconvert their factories for consumer goods production.

In an effort to get reconversion under way in a manner acceptable to all, President Roosevelt revamped the Office of War Mobilization (OWM), an agency that had coordinated industry's conversion to war production. Recognizing the continued political power of big business, Roosevelt appointed representatives from business and the military to guide the new Office of War Mobilization and Reconversion (OWMR). The agency tackled key issues such as how to terminate long-standing government contracts for the production of war materials and how to dispose of war production plants that would soon be out of service.

Thousands pack Times Square on May 8, 1945, celebrating Victory in Europe Day (V-E Day).
AP/Wide World Photos. Reproduced by permission.

Victory under a new leader

As the nation traveled an uncertain path toward reconversion and peacetime economics, it was faced with a sudden loss: President Roosevelt died of a cerebral hemorrhage (bleeding in the brain) on April 12, 1945, while visiting his retreat in Warm Springs, Georgia. A period of national mourning

A Victory over Japan Day (V-J Day) celebration, August 15, 1945. *National Archives.*

began. As a train carried the president's body to Washington, D.C., thousands crowded the route. Ten thousand watched the train pass in Charlotte, North Carolina. The popular leader who offered hope and security was gone. His vice president, Harry S. Truman (1884–1972), took over as president during the war's last months.

Victory came soon after the president's death. Germany surrendered on May 7, 1945. Large celebrations erupted the following day, which is known as V-E Day (Victory in Europe). Japan surrendered three months later, on August 14, after the United States dropped two atomic bombs on the cities of Hiroshima and Nagasaki; the bombs killed more than one hundred thousand people. After the Japanese surrender, celebrations broke out again and spread from coast to coast. Two million people spontaneously gathered in Times Square in New York City at 7 P.M. on August 15, the date that became known as V-J Day (Victory over Japan). Five thousand tons of paper, including confetti and streamers, poured out of office windows in celebration.

State of the nation

The United States came out of World War II in relatively good shape for the peacetime transition. Worldwide the human toll of the war was massive. Between fifteen million and twenty million military personnel were dead or missing; forty million to sixty million civilians were also dead or missing.

Millions more were injured. In contrast, the United States had 292,000 combat deaths and another 114,000 military deaths from other causes. Though the individual deaths were devastating to the soldiers' families and friends, these figures had a relatively small impact on the country. Other nations were decimated by their human losses. For example, the Soviet Union suffered more than twenty million deaths. In addition, bombing raids had destroyed large parts of the European landscape—farmland and city buildings. Except for the damage inflicted by the Pearl Harbor attack in Hawaii, the American home front was spared from such destruction.

From an economic standpoint, World War II provided some advantages. Despite increased taxes, wage and price controls, and rationing of essential goods, the U.S. economy expanded during wartime, fueled by war production jobs. No other country had a similar home front experience during World War II. At the end of the war Americans had greater purchasing power and a higher standard of living (the level of comfort maintained in everyday life) than before the war. In 1944, while some of the bloodiest battles raged overseas, good times abounded in the United States. Buyers mobbed department stores. The New York department store R. H. Macy and Company had its best day ever in sales on December 7, 1944. Restaurants were busy, as were movie houses and stage theaters. Hotels were often full. It seemed as though the wartime economy had restored the good times

Postwar anxieties

After enduring a decade of economic hardship during the Great Depression and then almost four years of war, Americans on the home front were eager to return to a normal way of life. However, as home front victory celebrations ended, economic concerns returned. Temporary government wartime agencies were quickly dismantled, throwing many government employees out of work. War industries had already begun reconversion, and many war workers were laid off. For example, by the spring of 1945 the giant Willow Run bomber plant outside Detroit, Michigan, started cutting back its workforce, and the temporary government housing built for Willow Run workers began to empty out. Thirteen thousand families had lived in the housing at the height of the war, but by late 1945, only six hundred families remained. The plant became the home of a new automobile manufacturer building Kaiser automobiles, owned by Henry J. Kaiser (1882–1967) and Joseph Frazer. Industry workers who were lucky enough to keep their jobs still lost the overtime pay they had become accustomed to during wartime. To make matters worse, wartime price controls on consumer goods ended, so prices went up just as workers' pay was going down.

Besides laid-off war industry workers, the nation had twelve million war veterans who would need jobs when they returned from overseas. Before thinking about employment, many of those soldiers needed time to heal from physical and psychological

Thousands of World War II veterans reclaimed their civilian jobs upon their return, forcing many temporary war industry workers out of their jobs. © *The Mariners' Museum/Corbis. Reproduced by permission.*

stolen by the Great Depression, the severe economic crisis of the 1930s.

GI Bill

The GI Bill (more formally known as the Servicemen's Readjustment Act) contributed greatly to the postwar economic boom in the United States. The bill passed in 1944 with the strong support of President Franklin Roosevelt and Congress. This notable piece of legislation offered a well-deserved reward for veterans returning to the home front from the battlefield: money for education and low-interest loans for home purchases, new businesses, and fledgling farms. The bill pumped millions of dollars of government funds into the home front economy as the war came to a close. The sixteen million returning veterans and their families made up one-third of the U.S. population; as they spent this government money, it helped millions of nonveterans by creating jobs in construction, manufacturing, and retail sales.

The GI Bill also created social change in the United States. More than half of the veterans, almost eight million, took advantage of the bill's education or training benefits. They enrolled in high schools, trade schools, and colleges. In 1947 half of all college students were veterans. In 1949 three times as many college degrees were awarded as in 1940. The bill had put the cost of a college education within reach of many more people. With more education, veterans were able to find higher-paying jobs and could better afford to start a family. This trend led to a great postwar baby boom and a period of widespread prosperity in the nation.

wounds left by the war. Some veterans suffered from posttraumatic stress syndrome (a psychological reaction to highly stressful events, such as warfare, including anxiety, depression, and frequent nightmares) or alcoholism; others faced family troubles, or economic hardships. The Veterans Administration would play a key role in attending to these physical and mental health problems. Most veterans adjusted satisfactorily to life on the home front. Americans welcomed and honored the returning veterans as heroes, easing their transition back to civilian life.

A postwar lull

Employment concerns continued into 1946. Seeking to maintain jobs and wartime pay levels, organized labor (a collective effort by workers to seek better working conditions) supported a series of strikes that year. The strikes (work stoppages to force an employer to meet worker demands) involved perhaps 10 percent of the workforce, and raised further concerns about the nation's postwar productivity. During the war employers and workers had set aside their differences and worked together to achieve victory; however, that unity was quickly disintegrating.

President Harry Truman (1884–1972; served 1945–53), a Democrat, presided uneasily over the declining economy. Unhappy with the decline, voters gave the Republicans a solid victory in the midterm elections of November 1946. For the first time since 1932, Republicans held majorities in both houses of Congress. The new conservative majority soon pushed through the Taft-Hartley Act of 1947, legislation that labor unions vigorously opposed because it weakened their ability to call strikes by requiring cooling periods and gave courts the authority to block strikes if national interests were at stake. Republicans were in favor of this legislation because they opposed labor's ability to influence management's decisions concerning pay and work decisions.

Prosperity arrives

To the nation's relief, the economic downturn at war's end proved short-lived. Boom times came as industry very quickly reconverted to the production of much-needed consumer goods. The purchase of those goods spurred employment by creating more manufacturing jobs and an overall expansion of the economy. By early 1947 peacetime prosperity was on track, and concerns about the economy receded.

Political consistencies

Despite Republican gains in the 1946 congressional elections, no immediate major political transformation had occurred. Democrat Harry Truman, seeking reelection as president in 1948, won an upset victory in a campaign focused on domestic issues. The Democrats held onto the White House for four more years.

The Democratic coalition of diverse voters—white Southerners, lower-income workers, black Americans, urban working class, Catholic immigrants, and Jews—forged in 1936 under Roosevelt and influential during the political campaigns of World War II remained intact for the postwar. However Republicans and conservatives had steadily gained more power, greatly influencing domestic programs.

An international giant

Ending the war with decisive victories and a strong economy gave Americans a sense of international superiority. They considered their country the world leader in freedom, justice, and economic well-being. The war fed the growth of modern American capitalism (an economic system in which private business and markets, largely free of government intervention, determine the prices, distribution, and production of goods). Big government, big business, big labor, big farming, and a strong military were the building blocks of the new economy. By war's end large organizations had established control over every sector of U.S. society.

Big business thrived during the war. A mere 6 percent of private industrial contractors received 90 percent of all the defense contract dollars. These few corporations gained huge profits from their war production efforts. Certain industries, such as petroleum, electronics, chemicals, metals, and transportation, developed great corporate power and prestige through the large government war contracts they received. After the war, U.S. industry continued to be the most productive in the world. In meeting the demand for new products and technologies through well-paying jobs, working-class Americans achieved a new social status, moving to the newly expanding suburbs, possessing much increased purchasing power and leisure time, and enjoying financial stability that workers in other countries had never known.

The wartime success of big business generally did not "trickle down" to smaller businesses. Some small businesses profited as subcontractors to big corporations, but half a million small companies in the United States failed between 1940 and 1945. The war industries had top-priority access to raw materials, limiting the availability of materials for other manufacturers. In addition many small-business owners left for military service or took better-paying war industry jobs in the larger corporations. As smaller businesses dwindled, big business took over their share of the marketplace and grew even bigger.

The war also brought profits to U.S. farms, both large and small. Money spent on food, mainly from foreign countries, rose from $14 billion in 1940 to $24 billion in 1944. U.S. farmers supplied food to countries around the world, including China, the Soviet Union, and Great Britain. Farm prices and farmers' incomes doubled during the war. Big farmers prospered most, but the small farmers who survived did fine as well. Those that did not survive could not compete with the increasing mass production of big farms. Farm productivity increased, thanks to improved technology and mechanization, increased availability and use of fertilizers, and the development of pest- and disease-control products. Greater productivity meant lower prices for consumers, which, in turn, helped farmers because they sold greater volumes of product.

The U.S. military grew dramatically during World War II, and though it decreased at war's end through mass discharges, it remained a major force in the world. The U.S. government expressed its postwar foreign policy in the National Security Act of 1947. The act created the National Security Council (NSC) within the executive branch to advise the president on national security policy. It also created the Central Intelligence Agency (CIA) to gather information on foreign activities and interpret its meaning. A 1949 amendment to the act created the Department of Defense, which united all the armed services into a single federal department. The emphasis on the prominent international role of the United States was made through this new policy. The military continued to spend large amounts in the postwar period as the so-called Cold War (1945–91) came into existence. The Cold War was an intense political and economic rivalry between the United

Keynesian Economics and Federal Budgets

During the Great Depression of the 1930s British economist John Maynard Keynes (1883–1946) proposed that massive deficit spending (government spending more than it receives in revenues) could successfully end an economic downturn and produce prosperity. Under this plan, increased government spending would replace decreased consumer spending and private investment. Though President Franklin D. Roosevelt had greatly increased federal spending on various relief programs to ease the suffering of the American people, he was unwilling to pursue the amount of spending Keynes suggested. Roosevelt feared Keynes could be wrong and that economic problems could be worsened by large government debts.

World War II provided an occasion to test Keynes's ideas on the home front; despite his reluctance to increase federal spending, Roosevelt had no choice but to spend huge amounts on the war effort. As government spending rose from $9 billion in 1939 to $98 billion in 1945, unemployment fell sharply from 15 percent in 1940 to just over 1 percent in 1944. Incomes rose, industries boomed, and nearly all Americans enjoyed a higher standard of living. The success of deficit spending during the war made a lasting impression on the country and its leaders. Although some people remained critical of deficit spending, most Americans began to see it as an acceptable method of managing the home front economy.

States and the Soviet Union that fell just short of military conflict. The Soviet Union and the United States had been allies in their fight against Germany, but in the postwar period they became bitter enemies.

In regard to labor, unions increased membership during World War II from nine million to fifteen millions workers, the most in the history of the United States to that time. Labor became organized nationally to a greater degree and played important roles during the war in the War Manpower Commission (WMC) and the National

War Labor Board (NWLB). Organized labor became a more accepted part of American society though anti-union sentiment was still prevalent among the more conservative segments of society.

Despite the emphasis on small, temporary agencies to organize the war effort, government also increased in size and influence over the daily lives of its citizens. A new tax structure was established in 1942 to help pay for the war. More people than ever were paying income taxes. The military services enjoyed the greatest growth as defense spending accounted for a much larger share of the annual federal budget. This trend would continue in the postwar years as the superpower rivalry with the Soviet Union immediately grew. National defense would become a major part of government and sustain a large industry through contracts.

A nation on the move

During World War II, fifteen million Americans were members of the armed forces. They traveled from one military base to another, back and forth across the country, to get their training; then they would head overseas for combat duty or serve on the home front. In addition, some fifteen million civilians moved across county lines to seek work in the war industries; eight million moved across state lines. Altogether, about 20 percent of Americans made a major move to a new state or region of the country. Many of them were in their twenties and thirties; most were moving to urban industrial centers and military bases.

The location of new military bases and war production plants determined future growth patterns in the United States. The population shift from rural to urban areas, a trend that began long before the war, accelerated. Between 1940 and 1945 more than six million people—20 percent of the rural population—left rural America to find better-paying jobs in the war industry or military service. Areas that grew dramatically included the South Atlantic Coast, the Gulf Coast, the West Coast, and the upper Midwest and Northeast.

In the South, cities grew rapidly while the population of rural areas declined. Charleston, South Carolina; Norfolk, Virginia; and Mobile, Alabama, all experienced substantial growth during the war years through shipbuilding. Washington, D.C., also grew dramatically as five thousand new government workers were added every month during the peak of the war. Aircraft production centers drew new residents to Atlanta, Georgia, and to the Dallas-Fort Worth area in Texas. The petroleum industry brought new jobs and people to Texas and Louisiana.

In the West Coast region, large shipbuilding and aircraft manufacturers attracted many new workers. The West Coast population grew more than 30 percent between 1940 and 1945, whereas the national population increased by only 6 percent in that same period. The population in San Diego County grew by over 40 percent, the Portland, Oregon, area by over 30 percent, the Bay Area (around San Francisco) by 25 percent, and the Puget Sound area (around Seattle) by 20 percent. Many young adults moved to the West Coast; black Americans also moved to the West, particularly to the Los Angeles area. After leaving farming areas for wartime factory jobs, Mexican Americans remained in the urban industrial centers, particularly in Los Angeles, San Diego, and San Francisco. The West Coast was also home to many military bases, including air bases, naval bases, army training camps, and testing areas. Various service industries sprang up around the bases, offering more jobs for the ever increasing civilian population.

Populations also grew in midwestern and northeastern industrial centers. Like the South, the Midwest experienced a regional population shift as members of the rural population moved to urban areas, especially to cities in Michigan, Ohio, and Indiana. In the Northeast, war production plants brought large numbers of new residents, particularly in Connecticut, New York, and New Jersey.

Women workers postwar

Millions of American women joined the workforce during World War II. As reconversion of industry accelerated in 1944 and 1945, public surveys indicated that most working women wanted to stay employed. However, both industry and the government encouraged women to leave their jobs so that servicemen returning from overseas could find work. The majority of women followed this advice; they left their jobs and stayed at home to raise their families.

If women did not voluntarily quit their jobs, they were often laid off; neither labor unions nor supervisors chose to protect them from this fate. By the summer of 1945, 75 percent of women in the shipbuilding and aircraft industries were laid off. The percentage of women working in the Detroit auto industry fell from 25 percent to less than 8 percent. Five million women were laid off overall. Those who found work outside industry often had to settle for low-paying jobs as sales clerks, waitresses, and maids. Though these positions were less lucrative (and often less interesting) than their wartime jobs, many women over thirty-five chose to remain in the workforce.

Baby boomers, television, and the nuclear age

The birthrate had increased by more than 20 percent between 1939 and 1943, and immediately following the war, births skyrocketed. Between 1946 and 1964, seventy-six million Americans were born, forming what became known as the baby boom generation. By the 1980s one-third of the nation's population was baby boomers.

Baby boomers became the nation's first television generation. Television was introduced in 1939, but World War II delayed further development until after war mobilization was over. In 1946 only six thousand television sets were owned in the United States. By 1953 that number had risen dramatically to seven million. Television would set the baby boom generation apart from previous generations, giving baby boomers a new medium for information and entertainment. Along with television came frozen dinners, which aided the many working mothers on the home front. After the war they became known as "TV dinners" because families could eat these quick and easy meals while gathered around the television.

Besides television setting the baby boom generation apart from the previous generation, there was also the threat of nuclear war. The nuclear arms race through the 1950s between the United States and the Soviet Union increased fears of nuclear war. The children of the late 1940s through 1960s were the first to grow up knowing the world could be annihilated at any time by a shower of nuclear missiles.

The Cold War and civil defense

Home front mobilization during World War II created a strong alliance between big business and the military services. This alliance is sometimes referred to as the industrial-military complex. The alliance began developing after the American Civil War (1861–65) as large industry became more important in the American economy. The industrial-military complex continued to grow during World War I (1914–18), when, for the first time, machine guns and other mechanized weapons played a crucial role in the war's outcome. During World War II the alliance between industry and the military became a more formal and permanent part of the U.S. economic system. Industrial and military leaders directly shaped the U.S. mobilization strategy for World War II by influencing Congress

O. C. Hanes, a bomber pilot during the war, with his wife, Hazel, and son, Richard, in August 1947. Richard was one of seventy-six million Americans born in the baby boom generation. *Sharon M. and Richard C. Hanes. Reproduced by permission.*

to limit the growth of new federal agencies.

When the war ended and the United States made its transition back to a peacetime economy, the industrial-military complex continued to develop and manufacture weapons, aircraft,

Heightened Cold War fears in the 1950s and 1960s prompted some Americans to build bomb shelters, which would protect them in the event of a nuclear attack.
© Bettmann/Corbis. Reproduced by permission.

U.S. military would shape the nation into a military superpower.

Fears raised by the tensions of the Cold War ensured a continued role for civil defense. In fact, civil defense was more important than ever, because newly developed weapons—atomic bombs, long-range bombers, and intercontinental missiles—were deadlier than the bombers of World War II. In 1948 President Truman created the Office of Civil Defense Planning. When the Soviet Union successfully tested an atomic bomb in 1949, fear of enemy attack gripped the United States, just as it had after the attack on Pearl Harbor. In December 1949 Truman signed an executive order that created the Federal Civil Defense Administration as the principal civil defense agency in the United States. However, Congress provided little funding for civil defense until the late 1950s, when U.S. leaders began to suspect that the Soviet nuclear arsenal was growing. It was renamed the Office of Civil and Defense Mobilization in 1958 as public and funding support started to increase. As Cold War tensions continued to escalate through the next decade, President John F. Kennedy (1917–1963; served 1961–1963) became a big supporter of civil defense. Kennedy renamed the lead civil defense agency once again to the Office of Civil Defense and placed it in the Defense Department. The showdown in October 1962 between the United States and Soviet Union over Soviet nuclear missiles being placed just off the U.S. shores in Cuba, known as the Cuban Missile Crisis, led to a rapid growth of

ships, submarines, and missiles armed with atomic warheads. (By playing on the public fears of the Soviet expansion in Europe, industry and the military services were able to successfully lobby Congress for substantial national defense spending on new weapons development, including a nuclear missile arsenal. Many believed it was the Soviet's intent to take over the world.) The alliance between U.S. industry and the civil defense over the following months. More than 112,000 nuclear fallout shelter sites were selected as possible protection for some sixty million civilians. The 1960s would be a peak in civil defense activity. As Cold War tensions lessened in the 1970s many lost interest and its funding support declined.

In 1979 the concept of civil defense was revived when President Jimmy Carter (1924–; served 1977–81) created the Federal Emergency Management Agency (FEMA). Over two decades later threats of terrorism—marked by the September 11, 2001, attacks in New York City and Washington, D.C., killing some three thousand people—sparked a substantial increase in home front defense. A new department of the federal government was formed in late 2001 called Homeland Security.

Civil rights movement

Black Americans had greatly contributed to the war effort, both on the home front and in the military services. However, despite some gains in job opportunities on the home front during World War II, particularly in the later war years as labor shortages grew, black Americans saw little actual progress in gaining the freedoms enjoyed by most U.S. citizens. Black servicemen returned home to the same segregated society they had left. Jim Crow laws enforcing segregation (separation of blacks and whites in public places) persisted, and blacks still faced some restrictions on voting in public elections. Nevertheless, the opportunities experienced by black Americans during World War II planted the seed for sweeping societal changes that would take place in the 1950s, 1960s, and beyond.

Progress remained limited until 1954 when the U.S. Supreme Court issued its *Brown v. Board of Education* landmark decision striking down segregation in public schools. However, black activism was still necessary to extend social reform to other aspects of life. What is referred to as the civil rights movement was born. The movement represented a "freedom struggle" by black Americans to gain freedom from discrimination, including equal opportunity in employment, education, and housing, the right to vote, and equal access to public facilities.

The high point of the civil rights movement occurred on August 28, 1963, when 250,000 thousand persons participated in the March on Washington. The gathering urged the federal government to support desegregation and protect voting rights. The Reverend Martin Luther King, Jr. (1929–1968) gave his immortal "I Have a Dream" speech promoting nonviolent direct action and voter registration. Congress responded with passage of the Civil Rights Act of 1964. Though sweeping in prohibiting discrimination in places of public accommodation, the act did not address voting rights.

In 1965 King led another march from Selma to Montgomery, Alabama, protesting continued voting restrictions.

The March on Washington, August 28, 1963. *National Archives.*

More than 25,000 people joined the march protected by 3,000 federal troops. Congress again responded, this time with the Voting Rights Act of 1965. The act expanded protections of voting rights of blacks by prohibiting use of literacy tests and other forms of discriminatory qualifications. No other twentieth-century social movement, spurred by gains made during World War II, posed as profound an effect on U.S. political and legal institutions.

A lasting legacy

World War II was one of the key historic events of the twentieth century that shaped modern America socially, politically, economically, militarily, and racially. National unity was at its peak on the home front. Americans had understood and supported a clear goal: to defeat the military aggression of Nazi Germany and Japan. Victory had confirmed to Americans that they were in the right. The war's legacies on the home front would be felt for decades to come, through such developments as increased protection of rights for women and minorities and a large federal budget built around national security issues.

The war brought much-needed economic relief to a nation that had been struggling economically for more than a decade during the Great Depression (1929–41). Through massive government war spending—amounting to $321 billion—the nation had amassed the capability to lead the world. Industries were modernized, important technological innovations were developed, and markets were opened overseas as reconstruction of war-devastated European and Asian regions began. The vast government spending during World War II greatly expanded the U.S. economy and hastened national prosperity. The standard of living improved for most Americans, while women and black Americans experienced new, though not always equal, economic opportunities in the job market. For example, wartime conditions brought women into the industrial workplace en masse, something that might not have happened otherwise.

Though distinct progress occurred, when the war ended the home front still harbored social problems and inequities that would continue to divide the population. Nevertheless, the following decades would see the legacies of World War II take root, and poise the United States as a military and economic giant on the world stage.

For More Information

Books

Bailey, Ronald H. *The Home Front, U.S.A.* Alexandria, VA: Time-Life Books, 1977.

Hartmann, Susan M. *The Home Front and Beyond: American Women in the 1940s.* Boston: Twayne Publishers, 1982.

Jeffries, John W. *Wartime America: The World War II Home Front.* Chicago: Ivan R. Dee, 1996.

Takaki, Ronald T. *Double Victory: A Multicultural History of America in World War II.* Boston: Little, Brown & Co., 2000.

Whitman, Sylvia. *V Is for Victory: The American Home Front during World War II.* Minneapolis, MN: Lerner, 1993.

Winkler, Allan M. *Home Front U.S.A.: America during World War II.* Arlington Heights, IL: Harlan Davidson, 1986.

Where to Learn More

Books

Bailey, Ronald H. *The Home Front, U.S.A.* Alexandria, VA: Time-Life Books, 1977.

Bernstein, Mark, and Alex Lubertozzi. *World War II on the Air: Edward R. Murrow and the Voices That Carried the War Home.* Naperville, IL: Sourcebooks, 2003.

Carl, Ann B. *A Wasp Among Eagles.* Washington, DC: Smithsonian Institution Press, 1999.

Cooper, Michael L. *Remembering Manzanar: Life in a Japanese Relocation Camp.* New York: Clarion Books, 2002.

Cooper, Michael L. *Fighting For Honor: Japanese Americans and World War II.* New York: Clarion Books, 2000.

Daniels, Roger. *Prisoners Without Trial: Japanese Americans in World War II.* New York: Hill and Wang, 1993.

Freidel, Frank. *Franklin D. Roosevelt: A Rendezvous with Destiny.* New York: Little, Brown & Co., 1990.

Fremon, David K. *Japanese-American Internment in American History.* Springfield, NJ: Enslow Publishers, 1996.

Gilbert, Bill. *They Also Served: Baseball and the Home Front, 1941-1945.* New York: Crown Publishers, 1992.

Gluck, Sherna Berger. *Rosie the Riveter Revisited: Women, the War, and Social Change.* Boston: Twayne Publishers, 1987.

Goodwin, Doris Kearns. *No Ordinary Time: Franklin and Eleanor Roosevelt, the Home Front in World War II.* New York: Simon & Schuster, 1994.

Greene, Bob. *Once Upon a Town: The Miracle of the North Platte Canteen.* New York: William Morrow, 1992.

Hartmann, Susan M. *The Home Front and Beyond: American Women in the 1940s.* Boston: Twayne Publishers, 1982.

Heide, Robert. *Home Front America: Popular Culture of the World War II Era.* San Francisco: Chronicle Books, 1995.

Hoopes, Roy. *When The Stars Went To War: Hollywood and World War II.* New York: Random House, 1994.

Lingeman, Richard R. *Don't You Know There's a War On? The American Home Front, 1941-1945.* New York: G. P. Putnam's Sons, 1970.

Nathan, Amy. *Yankee Doodle Gals: Women Pilots of World War II.* Washington, DC: National Geographic Society, 2001.

New York Times. *Page One: The Front Page History of World War II as Presented in the New York Times.* New York: Galahad Books, 1996.

Panchyk, Richard. *World War II For Kids: A History With 21 Activities.* Chicago: Chicago Review Press, 2002.

Schickel, Richard. *Good Morning, Mr. Zip Zip Zip: Movies, Memory, and World War II.* Chicago: Ivan R. Dee, 2003.

Schomp, Virginia. *World War II: Letters From the Homefront.* New York: Benchmark Books, 2002.

Stanley, Jerry. *I Am An American: The True Story of Japanese Interment.* New York: Crown, 1994.

Takaki, Ronald T. *Double Victory: A Multicultural History of America in World War II.* Boston: Little, Brown and Company, 2000.

Terkel, Studs. *The Good War: An Oral History of World War Two.* New York: Pantheon Books, 1984.

Tunnell, Michael O. *The Children of Topaz: The Story of a Japanese-American Internment Camp.* New York: Holiday House, 1996.

Warren, James R. *The War Years: A Chronicle of Washington State in World War II.* Seattle: University of Washington Press, 2000.

Winkler, Allan M. *Home Front U.S.A.: America During World War II.* Arlington Heights, IL: H. Davidson, 1986.

Zeinert, Karen. *Those Incredible Women of World War II.* Brookfield, CT: The Millbrook Press, 1994.

Web Sites

The Army Nurse Corps. http://www.army.mil/cmh-pg/books/wwii/72-14/72-14.htm.

Army Women's Museum, Fort Lee, Virginia. http://www.awm.lee.army.mil.

Civil Air Patrol. http://www.cap.gov/about/history.html.

Coast Guard Auxiliary History. http://www.uscg.mil/hq/g-cp/history/Auxiliary%20History.html.

"Dorothea Lange and the Relocation of the Japanese." *Museum of the City of San Francisco.* http://www.sfmuseum.org/hist/lange.html.

Fly Girls. PBS Online. American Experience. http://www.pbs.org/wgbh/amex/flygirls.htm.

Japanese American National Museum. http://www.janm.org.

Rosie the Riveter Trust. http://www.rosietheriveter.org.

United Services Organization. http://www.uso.org.

The WASP WWII Museum. Avenger Field, Sweetwater, Texas. http://www.waspwwii.org/museum/home.htm.

The Women's Army Corps: A Commemoration of World War II Service. http://www.army.mil/cmh-pg/brochures/wac/wac.htm.

World War II Era WAVES. http://www.history.navy.mil/photos/prs-tpic/females/wave-ww2.htm.

Index

Illustrations are marked
by (ill.)

for Japanese children in detention camps, 97–98

for military personnel, 144, 147, 148, 150, 187–188

for war veterans, 80, 188, 217

for women, 151, 153

in Washington State, 187–188

vocational schools, 101, 176

Eisenhower, Dwight D., 96, 145

Eisenhower, Milton, 96

Elections and voter turnout, 71, 74, 76–77, 80–81, 83–84

Ellington, Duke, 206

Emergency Farm Labor Program, 64, 65, 67

Emergency Plant Facilities program, 24

Emergency Price Control Act (1942), 43

Employment. *See also* Unemployment; Wages

absenteeism, 34

average workweek, 24, 30–31, 113, 178

discriminatory hiring policies, 89, 90, 92, 94, 108, 115

employee turnover, 34–35

in aircraft industry, 22

in early 1940s, 11, 15, 30

in federal government jobs, 30, 93, 104, 116–117, 143 (ill.), 178

migration related to, 14, 30, 53, 87, 118, 174, 178, 181, 221–222

postwar, 83, 212, 216, 218

working conditions and, 32, 33, 34, 64, 102, 115–116, 171

Enemy aliens, 93–94

England. *See* Great Britain

Entertainment

books, 207–208

comic books and comic strips, 203, 208

dancing, 166 (ill.), 206 (ill.), 207

magazines, 203, 204, 208

movies, 192–193, 192 (ill.), 194, 195–200, 203

popular music, 204–207, 206 (ill.)

radio, 200–201

sports, 196

television, 222–223

Espionage. *See* Spies and espionage

Evacuation of Japanese immigrants and Japanese Americans, 95 (ill.), 96

Executive Order 8802, 90, 115

Executive Order 9066, 95

F

Factories, 12, 20 (ill.), 21 (ill.), 24, 108 (ill.), 171, 212; *see also* Assembly line production; Industrial mobilization

Fair Employment Practices Commission (FEPC), 90, 93, 94

Farm bloc, 59–61

Farm Security Administration (FSA), 60, 77

Farmers, U.S., 56 (ill.)

cutbacks of aid for, 77

in dairy industry, 56–57

in organized labor groups, 59–61

income of, 53, 69, 219

migration of, 53

population of, 53, 68

production goals for, 53–55

prosperity of, 68–69, 219

Farming

agribusiness, 59

before World War II, 52–53

demand for U.S. crops, 6, 53, 219

government control over, 55–56, 58, 60–61

labor shortages, 57, 60 (ill.), 61, 64

national farm labor program, 64–65

nontraditional and foreign farmworkers, 61–64, 68

output during World War II, 37, 55–58

wages for farm laborers, 60

Farrow, John, 198

Fascist organizations, 93–94

Fats and oils in U.S. diet, 55

Federal Bureau of Investigation (FBI), 94, 198

Federal Works Agency, 107

Feller, Bob, 196

Fiedler, Arthur, 132

Films. *See* Movies

Fleet, Reuben, 174

Fonda, Henry, 208

Food consumption during World War II, 55, 56, 57, 58

Food processing, 58

Food shortages. *See* Rationing: food

Ford, Henry, 19, 181

Foreign policy, U.S., 5, 70, 72, 74, 193, 219

Frazer, Joseph, 216

Frissell, Toni, 205

FSA. *See* Farm Security Administration

Fujita, Nobuo, 135, 137

G

Gable, Clark, 208, 209

Gangs, 102

Gardens. *See* Victory gardens

Gasoline rationing, 45, 48–50, 58, 121, 182–183, 184